WINGS OF RESILIENCE

THE UPS AND DOWNS OF MY 65 YEARS IN AVIATION

Gord Price

Published by NextGen Story: Custom Publishing
www.nextgenstory.com

To my soulmate, Sandy

Table of Contents

FOREWORD

To embark on a journey through the chapters of my father's life is to navigate the vast expanse of the skies—which he not only conquered, but called home. This book is not just a collection of stories from an aviator's career; it is a montage of experiences that paint a picture of a life lived at full throttle, wings wide open. From his earliest years, filled with dreams of flight, through the rigorous demands of Royal Canadian Air Force (RCAF) training, to the precision and thrill of flying the CF-104 Starfighter, my father's story ascends from the foundational to the extraordinary.

Each chapter transitions seamlessly from the analog days, where intuition and dials guided flights, to the digital era, where screens and systems command the cockpit. Yet, at its core, the "Sanity 1" chapter represents a poignant return to the essence of flying—to the joys and skills that are the heartbeat of a pilot's life.

My father's journey through competitive aerobatics, his ventures into world championship arenas, and his personal tales of the Ultimate Pitts, not only showcase his prowess, but also highlight the camaraderie, challenges, and triumphs of the aviation community. His narrative traverses the skies and lands, and recounts not just the flights but the homes and havens that grounded him, the disasters that tested him, and the moments that left us all breathless.

Even after his adventures, bucket list achievements, graceful Yak-50 aerobatic displays, and eventual transition into retirement, my father's story does not simply conclude. It will continuously find new life and laughter and will be a testament to his enduring spirit and love for life—both in the air and on the ground. Perhaps "watercolour artist" is next on the checklist.

The final comments from nineteen aviation photographers offer unique lenses through which to view my father's air show career; they capture the essence of his journey and the indelible mark he has left on the world of aviation.

As his daughter, I have had the absolute pleasure of witnessing the man behind the pilot and the father beyond the aviator. This book is a humble tribute to his extraordinary journey. It invites you to soar alongside him, and perhaps find your own way back to the basics that once defined your passions and dreams. This is a tale of adventure, resilience, and the unbreakable bond between a father and his daughter—all set against the backdrop of the boundless skies.

Welcome aboard.

Stephanie Price, 2024

AN MHM PUBLISHING MAGAZINE // 2023 PHOTO CONTEST BONUS ISS

SKIESMAG.COM

SKIES

AVIATION IS OUR PASSION

DAM PUB

THE **BEST** OF THE

2023 **SKIES** PHOTO CONTEST

Patrick Cardinal Photo

INTRODUCTION

This is my air show retirement flight at age eighty-one as recorded on the cover of Skies magazine. Patrick Cardinal took the photo and commented, "This is the picture of you at the top of your tail slide, showcasing the precision of your flying. What made this picture extra special for me, was hearing some children behind me enchanted with your performance, as you inspired the next generation."

My cataracts were done, my prescription glasses were available, my hearing aids were plugged in with "telecom mode" selected for enhanced radio reception, my stent was installed which allowed my heart to function normally, and—most important of all— because I had passed the annual stress test, blood tests, and echocardiogram, all the required government permissions were granted. Now I was able to take this final flight.

This book is an attempt to outline a life lived, as seen by me, with all the memories I can still muster. I am going to try to fill in the gaps, from my birth day to my third retirement, eighty-one years later (29,820 days).

It will serve as an outline to strangers of the future of how one life was lived during a period when change happened faster than ever before—sometimes at supersonic speeds. It's also a gift to future family members, to at least explain part of the reason why they are the way they are.

I may not have been famous or particularly courageous, but my life has been spectacular and wonderful—full of tears and joy, love and turmoil, and a mix of highlights and lowlights. I recognize that my readers come from all walks of life, with varying degrees of education and different interests. Some may be familiar with aviation terms, while others may not know them at all. To cater to both groups, I have tried to write my recollections in a way that is simple, yet hopefully detailed enough to satisfy more knowledgeable readers. One thing I can say for sure: it has been an interesting ride!

Gord Price, 2024

THE EARLY YEARS

My dad, Frank James Price.

My mom, Kathlyn Mitchell Evans.

MY PARENTS

I was born at the old Galt General Hospital in Galt, Ontario on a cold day in January of 1942. My parents were both twenty-six years old at the time.

My dad, Frank James Price, was born in Toronto, Ontario on January 2, 1916. He enlisted in the Highland Light Infantry Regiment, 9th Brigade, 3rd Division as lieutenant. He was wounded in Italy during World War II, thanks to hand grenade shrapnel. He returned home in the spring of 1944 where he resumed his career with Loblaws (Loblaw Groceterias Co). He never spoke of the events of the war. Dad had almost reached the age of ninety-four when he died on December 13, 2009. His pension from Loblaws after a lifetime of service was thirty-five dollars per month.

Dad was wounded in Italy in WW2.

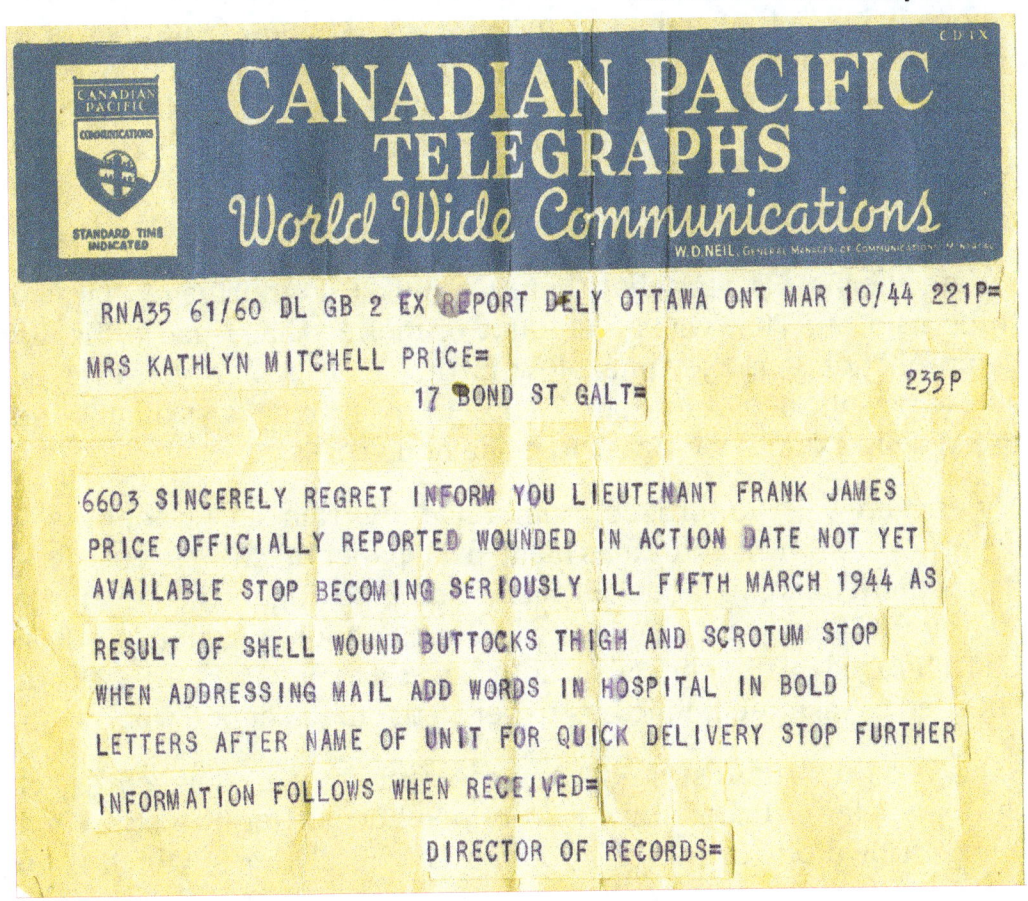

My mom, Kathlyn Mitchell Evans, was born in Galt, Ontario on March 28, 1915. She was a very gifted organist and choir leader throughout her entire life. She also taught piano and voice. I remember her keeping a box of tissues on the piano in case any of her students burst out crying. I also remember that she really detested Elvis Presley. At the age of eighty-four, Mom died on December 7, 1999.

Both of my parents came from large families. Mom had three sisters and a brother and Dad had five brothers and two sisters. I had a sister who was born in 1943 but who died a few hours after birth, so I grew up as an only child, a fact that my lovely wife Sandy frequently uses to explain why I am the way I am. I had wonderful parents, and growing up I had everything I ever wanted.

BOYHOOD AND SCHOOL

As I recall, we lived in three different homes in Galt and one in Simcoe before 1952. At that point we moved to Kitchener, Ontario where we lived in a new house for about a year. From there we moved to Wexford, in Scarborough into a new home that still had coal as a heating source; later it was converted to oil heat. To the east of the house was nothing but open fields. Pharmacy Avenue was the end of the subdivisions in Scarborough in those days.

I remember Dad saying that there was a $5,000 mortgage that had to be paid off. That was an amount of money that I had difficulty comprehending at the time. How in the world would you ever be able to pay off such a large sum? Those were still the days of milk and bread delivery and doctors who made house calls.

My domain was the furnace room. I had my train set wandering all over the room with mountains made from paper mâché. I spent many hours there building model airplanes and listening to the new radio station CHUM. I went to Wexford Public School and then Winston Churchill Collegiate. The public school was a twenty minute walk but I needed to take the public bus to get to the high school.

I was not the brightest student in the room, but I managed to get through school successfully. I do remember getting the strap and being thrown out of the classroom a couple of times, which is an indicator of my character at the time. I was into baseball, hockey, lacrosse, and I took swimming lessons, violin lessons, and oil painting lessons.

TEENS AND EARNING AN INCOME

As a kid I was used to having an income of sorts. In my school days I had a variety of paper routes. I delivered The Globe and Mail for a while and that started every day at 5:00 in the morning. I did it in all sorts of weather before beginning my twenty minute walk to school. The Toronto Star had much better hours as it was delivered after school, but that Saturday paper was a brute to carry as it was so heavy! That was probably the start of my back problems.

I was a good little salesman as a paper boy—so good in fact that at the age of thirteen, I won a trip to New York City along with sixty other paper boys from Toronto. It was all pretty exciting stuff.

Early days as an air cadet.

My first job with Loblaws was as a stock boy. I was responsible for keeping the shelves full of goods for sale. I was paid twenty-five cents per hour. Since Dad was a supervisor for Loblaws, I always had to be on my best behavior which wasn't much fun. So, I moved on to bigger and better jobs such as being an "assembler of things" for Zellers, a department store. That's where I learned that putting things together can be fun or a nightmare. (Now that I've reached the age of eighty-two it's becoming more of a nightmare.)

But the best job I held in those days was setting pins at the five-pin bowling alley at the Golden Mile Plaza. It was a great place to hang out. It became a game for my friends to try to nail me with a bowling ball while I set up the pins. I remember walking home up Victoria Park Avenue from the Golden Mile Plaza on October 15, 1954, during Hurricane Hazel. It was quite a task to just stay upright against the force of that storm. The Golden Mile Plaza was one of the first shopping plazas in Canada. The Queen even visited it during her state visit in 1959.

Mom was a VW lover, and she had several before she got her 1959 VW Beetle. I learned to drive using mom's VW when I was only fourteen—without anyone knowing. This is how I did it! As mentioned, Mom was a wonderful musician and as long as I can remember she was an organist, choir leader, and piano and voice teacher. She used to teach from her studio in the basement at the back of the house. The VW was parked in the garage in the front of the house. I discovered that if I opened the door very quietly, and gently pushed the VW out of the garage, the driveway, having a slight slope, allowed the car to roll, so all I had to do was to jump in, and bump start the VW into life without detection. Then I would creep off for some discreet driving practice.

Of course, a lot of this had to do with impressing my wife to be, Sandy, who I had met in grade seven. I would show up at her house much to the consternation of her mother, Blanche, who loved me dearly. Although she told me that I shouldn't be driving, she would not turn me in. Before the lesson that Mom was giving was over, I would have the VW back in the garage and she would be oblivious to any wrong doings.

631 SENTINEL RCAC SQUADRON

On November 5, 1956, about fifty boys between the ages of fourteen and nineteen met for the first time. The gathering took place in an old General Engineering Company of Ontario (GECO) building, a former munitions plant on the south side of Eglinton Avenue, about a kilometer east of Pharmacy Avenue in Scarborough. Tom Turner, Doug Walton, and another gentleman, whose name escapes me, formed 631 Royal Canadian Air Cadet (RCAC) squadron. I was fourteen at the time.

We were issued RCAF battle dress uniforms along with black boots. The boots were to be polished to a very high gloss finish using paste shoe polish and lots of rubbing in with a soft cloth and spit. The final gloss was obtained thanks to rapid buffing with a nylon stocking. They were to be polished to a mirror-like finish. We had classes on aviation subjects and sports activities, and we did lots of marching and drilling. I learned how to use a rifle and regularly shot at the

Fairchild C-119 "Packet." Photo © Larry Milberry.

65 HP Aeronca 7AC Champ. Photo © Eric Dumigan.

range on Jarvis Street in Toronto using .22 caliber rifles.

In 1959 the RCAF celebrated its thirty-fifth year anniversary with a model building contest. Being an avid model builder, I entered my scale model of the Curtiss HS-2L flying boat. I took second place with a great prize, an all-expenses paid trip to the Pacific National Exposition (PNE) in Vancouver! I was thrilled and thoroughly enjoyed the trip to Vancouver and back in an RCAF Fairchild C-119 "Packet" military transport aircraft.

RCAC 631 Squadron was one of the first squadrons to invite girls to join and of course my wife, Sandy, was one of the joiners. She was also into rifle shooting and to this day says that she is a better shot than I am—a point I never argue.

Over the years in the RCAC, I advanced to the rank of warrant officer class 2 and I took command of some of the parades. It was a wonderful experience and had quite an effect on my life—in a good way. Those were exciting days; life seemed to be much simpler then.

I was very fortunate to be selected as one of four candidates for the Air Cadet Flying Scholarship in 1959. Bob Hill, Peter Dzulinsky, John Fielding, and I travelled daily from Scarborough to Oshawa for flight training. We trained on 65 horsepower Aeronca 7 AC Champs.

My first instructional flight was on July 6, 1959 and my first solo was eleven days later on July 17, after 9½ hours of instruction. Fourteen days later, on July 31, I passed the flight test for my private pilot's license. My total flying time including the flight test was thirty hours and fifty minutes. It took a total of twenty-five days from the first instructional flight to me getting my private pilot's license.

The significance of those numbers becomes clear if you look at today's (2024) Transport Canada requirements of a minimum of 45 hours, with a country-standard of approximately 90 flight hours to meet the required standard.[1]

All four cadets passed with flying colours. The success of the Air Cadet Flying Scholarship program is very apparent. Besides my aviation career, which has been colourful, exciting, and rewarding, the other cadets also did very well in theirs. Peter Dzulinsky was with Air Canada and was the first Chief Pilot on the Airbus A320. This was an extremely demanding position that oversaw the introduction of a new technology into the fleet. A sad note here is that Peter Dzulinsky left us at the early age of forty-eight when he suffered a massive heart attack. This was before Air Canada had officially introduced the A320 into its fleet.

Bob Hill, who was also with Air Canada, was the chief pilot of the Douglas DC-8-70 freighter program (another very demanding position) and later was a Boeing 747-400 check pilot. Bob also occasionally flew the Avro Lancaster heavy bomber for the Canadian Warplane Heritage Museum in his spare time. I lost track of John Fielding; however, I understand that he pursued a successful career as a meteorologist.

In 1960 I turned eighteen and finished high school. At that point in time, jobs were scarce. I convinced a local dry cleaner that he should let me use his truck (it was sitting idly out behind his store) to drum

[1] "Private Pilot License (PPL)," Brampton Flight Center Website, Brampton Flight Center, Accessed January 2024, https://www.bramptonflightcentre.com/recreation/pilot-licenses-endorsements-ratings/private-pilot-licence/.

up some business for him. Again, as a good salesman, I brought him lots of business and made some good money in the process. It was a win for him and a win for me—the best kind of deal.

On several occasions back then I had hitchhiked to Malton Airport (now Toronto's Pearson International Airport) just to climb the fence so that I could catch a glimpse of the CF-105 Avro Arrow. I was planning on being one of the pilots flying it. Unfortunately, and sadly, the program was cancelled so that dream never came true. I thought it was a stupid decision then—and I still think it was a stupid decision. Little did I know that I would fly its replacement only four years later—as a nuclear strike pilot.

CF-105 Avro Arrow. Photo © Larry Milberry.

I had accumulated a grand total of sixty-one hours of flying time so far. My master plan was to be a fighter pilot and I wanted it immediately! I had no time for university; only the RCAF flying training program would do—if I could get accepted!

A flash forward .... to 60 years later!

My Russian Yak-50, serial number 01, built in Moscow. A CF-105 Arrow replica is in the background. Edenvale, Ontario 2019. Photo © Kevin Prentice.

Read on, dear reader. This story captures the unique twists and turns of a family adventure that spans two centuries. It offers a glimpse into a journey unlike any other.

EARLY RCAF

The bed had to be made perfectly.

Bob Hill and Gord (foreground) scraping old wax off the floor during basic training.

In the summer of 1960, I presented myself to an RCAF selection board for tests, exams, and physicals. There were two hundred candidates going through this process during the summer of 1960. They were being selected to become officers, gentlemen, and leaders. A board of officers and doctors asked all sorts of strange questions that had little or nothing to do with flying.

Eventually the RCAF called back and said that I had made it. I was ecstatic! Obviously I had given the selection board the right answers as I was one of the twenty candidates still standing after the smoke cleared. Those twenty made up RCAF Training Course 6016. Both pilot and navigator positions were in the group, and thankfully, I had secured a pilot position.

BASIC TRAINING

We assembled at RCAF Station Centralia, near the village of Centralia, Ontario, for basic training. This was raw recruit stuff. Drill instructors, bunk house inspections, gleaming boots, and brass.

Officers would check under the radiators and beds with white gloves for dust. As cadets, we crawled all over our barracks to try and make them spotless. Most of us were dedicated because we knew it would be worth all the crap to hang on and to get to the flying. But it was tough during the six weeks of basic when we saw those who were ahead of us in the other courses. They were already flying, and we could only watch the airplanes because we were not allowed to get near them. It was especially tough for those of us who already had civilian pilot licenses—like me with my whopping sixty-one hours of flying time!

Nobody seemed to care that I, and a couple of other guys already had our pilot's licenses. It meant nothing—in fact—it was worse than nothing. Really, it was a disadvantage, because it meant that they would have to break you of your bad civilian flying habits and teach you all over again the right way—the RCAF way!

It was demoralizing for a while. Six cadets dropped out during the six weeks of basic training. The rest graduated to Primary Flying School, which included a total of 24 hours on the beautiful de Havilland

De Havilland Chipmunk. Photo © De Havilland Aircraft of Canada Limited.

Chipmunk training aircraft. This was a reward worth all the initial hassle! There wasn't much tomfoolery at this stage either. Most of the cadets were still afraid of washing out.

Ground school was thorough and intense: navigation, meteorology, aerodynamics, engines. It was probably the best aviation training in the world. It was so good that there were usually foreign students sent over by their respective governments to take part. For example, on my course there were several Danish air force trainees.

Everybody toed the line at Centralia. When they said, "Jump" we asked, "How high?" We weren't very secure in our primary training. They would immediately toss you out if you were not up to standard. One of the fellows was subject to airsickness and frequently upchucked in the air, but he still made it through. However, if you stepped over the line in discipline, or flunked an important exam—you were gone. It was tough, but we learned what we had to learn.

The group I was in came together through our shared experiences of basic training. After making it through Primary Flight Training, we were even more closely knit. We had become comrades. We had a party to be remembered for "graduation"! The legal drinking age

Harvards on the flight line at RCAF Station Penhold, near Penhold, Alberta.

was twenty-one at the time but "would-be fighter pilots" apparently were exempt. There wasn't much time to recuperate from the party. We were to immediately report to our next training base, which was Penhold, Alberta, in my case, and Moose Jaw, Saskatchewan, for some of the others. We were off to learn how to fly the legendary North American Harvard trainers.

My good friend, Bob Hill, and I headed west in a car that I had just bought from my mother—it was the same 1959 Volkswagen Beetle that I had learned to drive on. (Mom went on to buy a VW Karmann Ghia to replace it.)

It was a long trip to Penhold. The Bug fought the westerly winds, but at times it was impossible to get it over 45 miles per hour (mph) unless we caught the draft of a transport truck by tucking in closely.

LANDING A HARVARD AT THE OFFICERS' MESS

While I was in Penhold, a good friend of mine, Bjarne Prendal—he was one of the Danish cadets—brought his fiancé from Denmark so that they could be married in Moose Jaw. A bunch of us from Penhold drove the 738 kilometers to Moose Jaw for the wedding. It was quite a lively event and there was a great party afterwards. I cannot remember who came up with the idea and who did the planning, but we decided that we would steal a Harvard and put it in the officers' mess patio compound. This was carried out with great military precision.

It was quite an ingenious plan. We had to "liberate" a crane first. We needed the crane to lift the airplane over the fence. Lloyd Rain and I "liberated" the crane the day before, but we had to hide it! We just parked it in front of the officers' mess in the parking lot. Everyone drove past it assuming that there was some good reason for the crane to be there.

After the wedding and celebrations, we sent one of the Danish cadets into the weather office. It was now about three in the morning. The office was in the same hangar as our target airplane. The cadet had a bunch of Playboy magazines and a radio with the volume turned way up; the idea was to distract the weather guy who happened to be the only person close enough to hear us. The Danish officer in charge of the Danish cadets had forbidden them from participating in moving the airplane. However, they were allowed to be look-outs and distractors.

The rest of us went to the hangar, shoved the doors open and pushed out the airplane. We then closed the doors and pushed the big yellow beast across the base and up to the front of the officers' mess. At one point a car approached as we were pushing the airplane along. We all dove off the side and left the airplane sitting by itself in the middle of the road. Fortunately, the car went down another street. We were saved. We resumed the task of pushing the airplane to the officers' mess and into position for the hoist over the fence.

We started up the crane, moved it into position, hooked it to the airplane with ropes, hoisted the plane over a six-foot fence and gently set it down on the patio. We put all the tables and chairs back around the Harvard and made everything look as normal as possible. Then we took the crane back and went back to the barracks. We packed up, jumped into my Volkswagen, and drove back to Penhold.

As we drove away, I noticed a few concerning (or at least unusual) things. There was a flurry of activity at the officers' mess including lots of flashing lights, trucks, and the big crane (we had used the little crane). I also saw some high-tension wires that we had narrowly missed when placing the airplane on the patio. Luck had been on our side.

The operation had been carried out in plain view of the base entry guardhouse. However, the guards had miraculously failed to see us. The following article appeared soon after in the Moose Jaw Times-Herald:

Unorthodox Landing?

A Harvard! trainer fully mounted, sits proudly on the sunny patio outside the officer's mess at RCAF Station Moose Jaw this morning, a mystery to all who pass by. It being an official holiday at the camp, public relations officials are not present to give an accounting for the aircraft's unorthodox abode, and the orderly officer refuses to comment.

The patio is surrounded by a high board fence and is situated on one side of the officers' mess, the last building to the west of the station. Due to the cramped quarters the aircraft must have been dismounted and reassembled at the new location. But when and by whom has not been released for public information.

Under some serious duress, the Moose Jaw contingent of Course 6016 finally fessed up to the prank. The commanding officer assembled them and announced that the base needed a new swimming pool, and, in view of the Harvard prank, Course 6016 would be digging it—by hand. How far that went I really don't know, but it sure makes for a good story.

It wasn't all beer and pranks though. We learned more navigation techniques, aerobatics, and formation flying until we could do it in our sleep. When the course was over, I had 163 hours and 40 minutes

Removal of Harvard from Officer's Mess Patio.

on the Harvard. With the Chipmunk time added in, the total was 187 hours.

PORTAGE LA PRAIRIE

After Penhold, it was off to Portage la Prairie, Manitoba, to fly the Canadian version of the Lockheed T-33 Shooting Star trainer—the Canadair CT-133 Silver Star—and to continue on to more advanced jet aircraft training.

Our course in Portage la Prairie included some new ejection seat training. The idea was to give you a feel for the ejection seat and to practice the ejection sequence. The kicker (so to speak) was that you would be fired on rails up a tower. The seat utilized an explosive charge. We measured our height before and after the ejection. In my case, I was one inch shorter after the blast up the tower. It is no wonder that I have chronic back problems! The ejection training program was soon abandoned. I suppose that someone realized that the liabilities exceeded the value of the training. The seat in the Lockheed CF-104 Starfighter, a plane that I got to fly later, provided a softer launch since it was rocket powered.

As RCAF flight cadets, we had been used to having our own mess hall with the officers having a separate mess hall. Since in Portage la Prairie we were in our final stage of becoming officers, we were allowed to dine in the officers' mess—but the decorum didn't seem to be any different.

Bizarre happenings were quite common in the officers' mess. For instance, for some reason one cadet ordered a raw egg in a glass and then promptly downed it. Another cadet said that he was "not impressed" by the action and he ordered a raw egg in the shell and proceeded to eat it shell and all! That's when Archie Tichkowsky exclaimed that he certainly was not impressed with either stunt. To prove it, he took a standard beer glass, bit off a good chunk, proceeded to grind down the glass with his teeth, and then swallowed. I was aghast! So was everyone else. I vividly remember Archie's passion for eating glass on two other occasions.

Sandy had come out to Portage to see me get my wings. We had

T-33 ejection seat training.

Gord and the Canadair CT-133
Silver Star (T-33).

a room in a hotel nearby. Archie came by to visit after making a purchase at the liquor store. He had bought a bottle of vodka but he accidentally dropped it on our floor. Vodka and broken glass were everywhere. He was so upset that he picked up a thick chunk and ate it!

The last time I saw Archie was in Clinton, Ontario, on some special occasion. I went to say goodbye to him. He was sound asleep in bed with a rum and coke half-finished on his bedside table—a chunk taken out of the glass.

Advanced training at Portage La Prairie was completed on April 18, 1962, and I was presented with my RCAF wings. To date I had flown a total of 311 hours in the Air Force.

The pilots on the course were assigned to various aircraft. Most of the course was assigned back to Training Command to continue flying the Harvard. However, two of us, Dave Huddleston and I, were assigned to fly the CF-104.

I had made my dream of being a fighter pilot come true. As a side note, Dave had quite a career as well, ending up as a lieutenant general and commander of Air Command from 1991 to 1993.

Only experienced pilots had been flying the CF-104, but it had been inevitable that pilots right out of training would eventually be assigned to it. I was in the right place at the right time with the right requirements. I was about to become part of the experiment—part of the first CF-104 course with pipeline pilots. There was only one problem: the CF-104 program was backed up.

CENTRALIA AND TYING THE KNOT

In the meantime, they had to keep me busy. I was assigned to Centralia as the maintenance test pilot flying the Chipmunk. My job was to test fly Chipmunks that had just had maintenance checks performed on them. I accumulated another eighty-two hours of Chipmunk time during this four-month assignment in Centralia. It got so that I could do the required checks in about five minutes; I would then go and practice low level flying in the low-level flying area, or I'd fly an aerobatic routine where Sandy could see me from the window of our apartment in Exeter. She'd watch to see if my loops were round, and my lines were straight.

Sandy and I were married on July 14, 1962, at St. Jude's Anglican Church, in Wexford, Scarborough, Ontario. We both recited our vows and I distinctly remember that Sandy's vows included "to honour and obey"—however, it seems that that part of it has never been put into practice!

The reception was held at the officers' mess in Downsview, in North York, and it was quite a party. We left for Niagara Falls in the VW with fish oil having been put in the heater and tins dragging from the bumper. We eventually ended up on Anna Maria Island in Florida for our honeymoon. We lived in an apartment in Exeter, Ontario, until the end of September.

CHATHAM, NEW BRUNSWICK

On the first of October I was assigned as operations officer for 416 Squadron to RCAF Station Chatham. The base was located just south of the town of Chatham, New Brunswick. It was a job I never understood since the squadron of McDonnell CF-101 Voodoos was based in Bagotville, Quebec. There was little for me to do even though the Cuban Missile Crisis was in full swing from October 16 to October 28 of 1962. I maintained my flying currency by flying the T-33 on various missions.

There was no room for us on the base, so we rented a studio apartment in Chatham from the Duffy family. Mr. Duffy was a local fishing inspector with the government. He had connections, so we were often treated to fresh salmon from the Miramichi River.

FINALLY, I began flying the Canadair CL-13 Mark 5 Sabre. This was an F-86 Sabre built in Canada by Canadair under license from North American Aviation. My first flight was on June 7, 1963. I was on the Sabre Transition Unit (STU) course which was the lead-in course to the CF-104. Once the initial training was completed in the F-86, we practiced low level navigation and bombing in preparation for moving on to the CF-104.

Gord and the Canadair CL-13 Mark 5 Sabre.

The F-86 was a single engine, single seat fighter of Korean War vintage. But you shouldn't let its age fool you—it was a real hotrod. The first flight was solo since it only had one seat. The checkout was straight forward as it was a relatively easy aircraft to fly. This was another dream come true for a twenty-one-year-old.

The instructions were as follows: "OK son, take this F-86 Sabre jet and fly it low and fast all through New Brunswick and then we will learn how to drop bombs!" What could go wrong? Lots could go wrong but, in my case, everything went right—including my first flight through the sound barrier.

The F-86 Sabre was classified as a transonic aircraft which meant that it was a high-speed aircraft that was able to exceed the speed of sound. However, it did not operate very well beyond Mach 1.0.[2] In

[2] In simple terms, the Mach number for an object is the speed of the object divided by the speed of sound. For example, if an object is moving at twice the speed of sound, it is moving at Mach 2.0. If the object is moving at half the speed of sound, it is moving at Mach 0.5.

fact, to exceed the speed of sound, massive preparation was involved. First, you had to be at a high altitude—say 35,000 feet. Second, you had to roll the airplane on the longitudinal access, to the inverted position. Third, you had to pull down into a vertical dive under full power. Fourth—hang on!

I remember that the aircraft shook quite a bit as it passed through Mach 0.96. Then the shaking continued as it slowly approached Mach 0.99. It continued to shake as it passed through Mach 1.0, and finally it reached Mach 1.02 at which point I had to start pulling out from the dive. Thanks to the swept wing on the F-86 there was no control reversal when passing through the sound barrier.[3] Basically, it was a struggle to break the sound barrier in the F-86. I would soon find out that the opposite was true when flying the CF-104.

CF-104 TRAINING IN COLD LAKE

We left for Cold Lake, Alberta, after I had successfully completed the Chatham STU course. We were in our 1959 Volkswagen Beetle with all of our possessions. Sandy was expecting our first child, Stephanie, at the time, so I dropped her off in Scarborough with her family.

I arrived at Cold Lake in northern Alberta on October 1, 1963. I was immediately given six weeks of intensive CF-104 ground school training.

Stephanie was born at about 1:00 a.m. on October 25, 1963. I received the news right away. When I heard of her arrival, I was pretty excited. Arrangements were made for me to do a cross-country practice flight from Cold Lake to Toronto with Wing Commander Arnie Bauer. I showed up at the general hospital in East York in my orange flying suit having just arrived at Downsview in the T-33 with minimum baggage. I managed to get to the hospital by 10:00 p.m. to meet her the day she was born. I returned to Cold Lake with Arnie

---

[3] Control reversal near the sound barrier, also known as Mach tuck or compressibility effects, occurs due to several aerodynamic phenomena that affect aircraft stability and control. Design features such as swept wings, all-moving tailplanes, and advanced flight control systems help mitigate these effects and maintain control near and beyond the sound barrier.

on the twenty-seventh and flew my first trip in the CF-104 simulator on October 28.

Sandy and Stephanie stayed until Christmas with the family, and then flew Air Canada out west to join me in Cold Lake.

CF-104 Course 9 official picture; as of 2024 Dave Huddleston, Gord Price, Brian Smith, and Eric Mold are still alive.

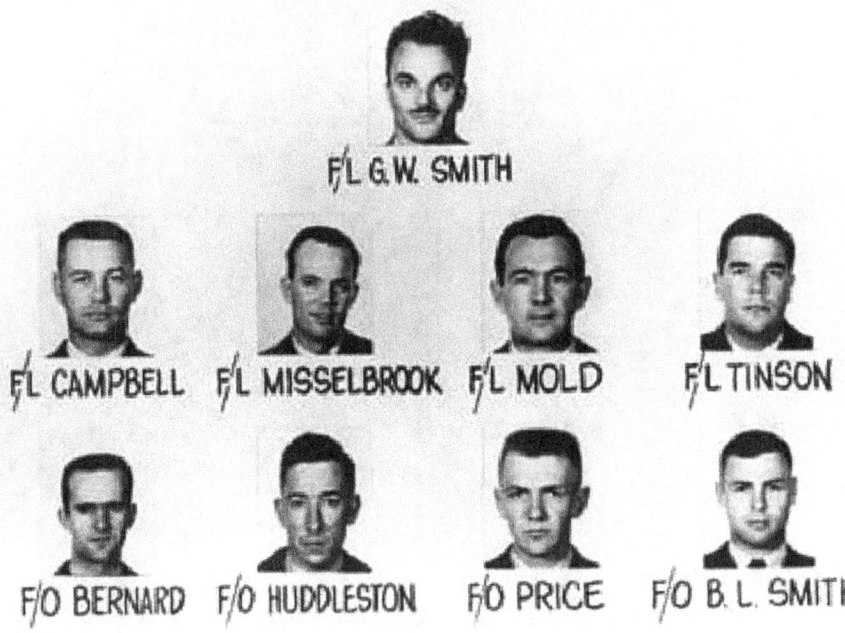

6 ST/R Operational Training Unit
COURSE 9

F/L G.W. SMITH

F/L CAMPBELL F/L MISSELBROOK F/L MOLD F/L TINSON

F/O BERNARD F/O HUDDLESTON F/O PRICE F/O B.L. SMITH

FLYING THE CF-104 STARFIGHTER

CF-104 at Cold Lake Alberta. RCAF photo.

THE FIRST FLIGHT

This is it, I thought as I strapped into the front seat. I was in a supersonic jet fighter—the CF-104D Starfighter. It was November 4, 1963, in Cold Lake, Alberta. I was twenty-one and I was READY. I was primed for my first flight in the "104." My instructor, Flight Lieutenant Don Williamson, strapped himself into the aircraft's rear seat.

The engine had been started and all the checks had been completed. We taxied onto the runway. Now the engine had to be run up to full power. The roar and power buffeted the sleek, needle-nosed aircraft. Then the power was backed off, before being shoved all the way up again. We were checking the engine nozzle operation. We wanted to make sure that it was opening and closing as it should, and that the temperatures and pressures were normal.

Then I just rapped the throttle wide open and we felt the Orenda J-79-OEL-7 turbojet engine snap to 100 percent power. [4]

The next step, after I had made sure that all instrument indications were normal, was to push the throttle all the way forward again and then slip it into the outboard detent. Then I pushed it forward even more until the afterburner lit up. Once it was lit, I pushed the throttle forward to the very limit to light up the afterburner's second stage. I did all that perfectly, I thought. But the airplane started hopping down the runway like a large jack rabbit!

"GET OFF THE BRAKES!" was the yell I heard from the back seat! I thought I had done everything correctly, which I had, except I had forgotten to release the brakes! I released them. Instantly I found myself slammed into the back of the seat as the machine literally rocketed down the runway.

It was a cold -20°F day, and the engine was loving it. There was only one way to say it: Mega Power! I had never felt acceleration like that! Here we were in an airplane that was roaring with full afterburner on. In a heartbeat we had gone from a bunny hop down the runway to maximum acceleration with me pinned to the back of the seat.

---

[4] This was so unlike the T-33 Silver Star (T-Bird) training aircraft. In that machine there were no automatic features. You had to ease the throttle up or you'd end up blowing the airplane's end off. But in the "104" ... you just rapped it and felt the power.

As we broke ground, I heard my instructor shout: "GET THE GEAR UP! We're going to exceed the gear limit." Dutifully I brought the gear up, but, as he had warned, we had exceeded the limit.

Once we had left the ground, the angle of climb was startling, but under control—sort of. Everything seems to be going quite nicely, I thought. Suddenly, I heard from the back, "You'd better pull back a bit more." I told him that I was holding the airspeed, until he said, "Yeah, but look at the Machmeter—we are going SUPERSONIC!" I had been watching the airspeed decrease while we were climbing, but I hadn't noticed that the Machmeter had been going up like mad. So, I pulled back some more. We were going up at an unbelievable angle! What a beautiful airplane to fly!

The CF-104 was the type of aircraft that didn't really come into its own until it was supersonic. It just sliced through the air. To it, turbulence was just a gentle buzz. No wonder the American pilots referred to their Starfighters as Zippers, as it could zip through the sky like nothing else. It made for a good stable gun platform even at sub-sonic speeds like 540 knots and even when it was at a low level. The aircraft's short, thin wings sliced through turbulence at any speed or altitude. This plane moved like a missile, carried aloft on those tiny knife-like wings. This was the most enjoyable machine that I had ever flown, and I was allowed, nay, encouraged to fly it to its limits.

NUCLEAR STRIKE PILOT TRAINING

The main purpose for all this activity in northern Alberta was to teach pilots how to deliver a nuclear bomb in one of the most difficult and dangerous ways—at high speed and at low level. We were essentially the forerunners of the present-day cruise missile. However, our missiles were manned. In a real shooting war, our targets would have been located somewhere within the Warsaw Pact countries; for the time being, though, we practiced on the forests and lakes of northern Saskatchewan.

There were two kinds of CF-104 missions: photo reconnaissance and nuclear strike. I was training as a nuclear strike pilot. We were the pilots who would have to take a nuclear bomb and put it where the

On the way to Primrose Lake Bombing Range.　Photo F/O Andrew Henwood 422 Sqn.

planners thought it would do "the most good" if you could call that good. We got to the point where we could put our practice bombs within three hundred feet and three seconds of the target. Primary navigation was carried out using a stopwatch and a strip map that was attached to a kneeboard.

That means that the time and place of the target were assigned; the pilot would deliver the bomb there within three seconds of the time and within three hundred feet of ground zero. As I reflect now on the mission profile and what it was that we were being trained to do ... it is just terrible. When I finally got to Europe and saw that there would be nothing left of most of it, absolutely nothing if we ever had to fly those missions—I was chilled.

But we were highly trained and we were very good at what we had to do. In the meantime, at Cold Lake we trained and flew hard. Life was lived to the fullest. When one was young and engaged in such a challenge one had no difficulty accepting one's perceived immortality. When you are strapped into the cockpit of a supersonic fighter and encouraged to roar low and fast across the landscape dropping bombs, it becomes virtually impossible to recognize anything more important. Excitement and danger were day-to-day experiences for us, and we gloried in it.

Let me tell you about one particularly memorable flight out of Cold Lake. It was January 10, 1964—two days before my twenty second birthday. We were a four-plane formation on a visual bombing mission at the Primrose Lake Bombing Range. There were three students and one instructor. We had completed the bombing mission and were coming back to the airfield in an echelon left formation, which means each airplane holds a position slightly to the left and to the rear of the aircraft in front.

The formation was at fifteen hundred feet and coming in for the pitch out to land. [5] We were slightly off the runway heading and the lead aircraft had to turn a bit to the left to get us lined up. Generally, it is a rule that you, as leader, are not supposed to turn into the echelon. But, there's another rule that says that the formation is supposed to fly on the leader. So, he should be able to turn whichever way he has to.

Anyway, he turned slightly into us. I think because of the 104 having anhedral (slightly downward angled) wings that it is difficult to see a slight turn. Pilot number 2 must have missed the slight turn toward him because the two airplanes started drifting together. Right there in the sky the two fuselages suddenly slammed together. It was a very strange thing to see!

These two airplanes just started beating the hell out of each other! Number 2 couldn't pull up and away or he would have broken the leader's horizontal stabilizer off. He couldn't pull out to the left or he would have slammed into the number 3 aircraft. He couldn't descend, or he would have pulled the nose off his own airplane. He was in a real fix and the only way out was to go back. He throttled back and started sliding down the side of the leader's fuselage with the two sleek aluminum bodies sliding against each other as he slipped backward. Both airplanes were violently slamming together.

[5] A 4-plane pitchout to land is a coordinated maneuver used by a formation of four aircraft to break from their formation and set up individually for landing. This maneuver, which requires precise timing and coordination, allows the planes to sequence themselves efficiently for landing while maintaining safety and order.

Somehow, they were still intact. At about this time, number 3 pulled out towards me. I had anticipated something like that would happen because I was already moving out to avoid being hit.

It was surreal as I watched the events unfold just a few yards away. I watched number 2's airplane sliding and banging against number 1's as number 2's drifted rearward. Everything seemed okay until number 2's fiberglass nosecone slammed against number 1's exhaust nozzle—that's when number 2's radar set, which is housed in the nose, blew up with a flash!

There was no sound audible to me in my cockpit other than the whine from all the surrounding J-79s. There was only the sight of the explosion. That added to the unreality of it all. No sound. A weird chaotic pantomime of carnage in the cold sky of northern Alberta— and there I was right in the middle of it.

The entire nose cone of that airplane came off. I was now staring at a 104 with a very blunt nose. It rolled over and started to go in. I yelled on the radio for him to bail out. He probably didn't hear me, but he lost little time in figuring it out for himself anyway; it was with great relief that I saw the rocket-powered ejection seat come out.

There was one small problem with the ejection, though. By the time he punched out, the airplane had already rolled about 120°. He had been fired out of his stricken machine strapped to that ejection rocket while aimed downward and all of this drama was taking place only about fifteen hundred feet above the ground.

The airplane went straight into a frozen-over lake and blew up with a rising fireball. Number 2's chute opened just in time for about half a swing and he landed on the shore of the small lake right beside the crater in the ice made by his Starfighter as it had punched through the surface.

Meanwhile, number 1 managed to limp home. He was accompanied by number 3 who assessed the damage. They both got down okay. I flew around Number 2 and guided the helicopter in for his rescue. This is when I realized that the 104 was not a good airplane for low and slow circles. I had to drop full flaps just to keep it in the air, as going slow was the last thing its designers planned for it to be doing. I could have found myself down there on the ice next to number 2 if

I hadn't been careful. Without doubt my airplane was just not happy limping along at those slow speeds.

The rescue helicopter came along soon after and picked number 2 up. In the end everything turned out fine. The chopper took him to the hospital but there wasn't anything seriously wrong with him. He certainly had an interesting story to tell for the rest of his career. Number 1 made it in with his damaged aircraft without anything else going wrong, and as you can imagine there was a lot of beer consumed in the mess that night.

The thing that is most striking to me now about that entire episode was the eeriness of it all. It probably took less time to happen than it takes to talk about it. It all happened in slow motion and in an eerie silence. Lots of violent things were happening—the two airplanes were crashing together, there were two explosions, and an ejection—but it seemed a very visual, separate thing to me like I was somehow removed from it. It was like I was in the audience watching it happen.

PUSHING IT TO THE LIMIT: BEYOND MACH 2

In the midst of our Starfighter training, I embarked on a Mach run. The goal was to push the aircraft to Mach 2.35 (1,550 mph or 2,494 kmh) if possible. Surpassing the speed of sound by more than double was a rare feat; it ignited a surge of excitement within me. I was cruising at 0.95 Mach while nestled comfortably at 35,000 ft. Now I eagerly advanced the throttle. This unleashed the full force of both sectors of the afterburner.

The acceleration was intoxicating as the Mach needle steadily climbed: 1.2, 1.5, 1.7, 1.9. Finally it hit Mach 2.1. The SLOW light started flashing. This signaled the critical moment when the engine's compressor inlet temperature limit of +121 degrees Celsius had been reached. It was time to slow down. However, lost momentarily in the thrill, my gaze drifted downward so that I could actually see my speed across the ground. While doing this, I unwittingly pulled back a little bit on the stick. This triggered an unprecedented ascent.

Before I could fully comprehend the situation, I found myself hurtling past 47,000 feet. This was alarmingly high. I swiftly realized the danger and executed a roll to inverted, while instinctively pulling back to regain control and descend to a safer altitude. Notably, I wasn't clad in a pressure suit.

Thus, while a Mach run promises unparalleled excitement, a slight misstep—a mere tug on the stick—can swiftly escalate the experience into uncharted realms of adrenaline-fueled intensity.

LIFE IN BADEN-BADEN WEST GERMANY

Upon completion of the Starfighter course, Flying Officer Gord Price is posted to R.C.A.F. Squadron 422, Number 4 Wing, Baden-Baden West Germany.

That's what the official orders said. At twenty-two years of age, with seven hundred and ninety hours of flying time (ninety-four of it in the CF-104), I had become a key player in NATO's defense forces. Holy crap!

I distinctly remember the looks Sandy and I got from the other squadron pilots and wives when we arrived. It was sort of like they were saying: "My God! They are sending children over now!" 1964 was a significant year for us. We went through an awful lot of growing up in a very short time. It is hard to believe the responsibility that I was given when I was only twenty-two years old.

When I was stationed in West Germany I didn't have the seniority to be housed in the Permanent Married Quarters (PMQs) so we didn't live on the base. Instead, the Squadron had found us an apartment on the upper floor of a new house in the Village of Lichtenau. They had also found a car for us, a 1959 Mercedes-Benz 220S. It was a four-door that was right at home doing 100 mph on the Autobahn.

Initially there were three of us: Sandy, me, and Stephanie, who was just six months old. My son Glen didn't come along until a year later.

The family who owned the newly built house took on quite a role in setting the direction our life would take—especially Frau Mehlhorn.

We used to sit on the floor and drink great local beer. They would tell us stories and we'd get into the odd argument like the value

The new kid on 422 Squadron, May 1964.

Frau Mehlhorn's Hummel Music box.

of the German mark compared to the dollar. It took close to four German marks to buy a Canadian dollar. No wonder there was a book published, *Europe on $5 a Day.*

We frequently went out for dinner (with lots of beer and wine) for under fifteen dollars. Wolfgang and Manfred, Frau Mehlhorn's sons, were adamant that the German mark should be valued one for one with the dollar. I, of course, disagreed. It took over forty years for that to happen, but they were ultimately right.

Frau Mehlhorn's husband had been a test pilot in his early days and the family had come from East Germany. Their aircraft parts factory that had been built up over the years had been confiscated by the East German government. Things were so bad in East Germany that they planned an escape to West Germany on a train. They carried only one suitcase. It was a fascinating story for a young Canadian couple to hear.

When they arrived, they had absolutely nothing. They started all over again and somehow scraped together enough to build a house with the aid of a bank loan. That was something that we would experience later in life. The Mehlhorns had even created a factory in their basement! I'd never heard of that concept before. I grew up knowing that factories were one thing, and houses were another. However, we learned from them that factories did not have to be big.

Their new "factory" was in their basement where they fabricated Hummel music boxes. They were made of circular cherry wood frames and little Hummel pictures. They were varnished, put together, and then sold to both retail and wholesale customers.

Frau Mehlhorn would sell the Hummel music boxes at the Post Exchange duty-free stores (PXs) on the nearby American bases and at German trade shows. She did not have a car. She travelled by train with several suitcases. Despite it all they made a very good living using ingenuity, perseverance, and hard work. We learned an awful lot from the Mehlhorn family. Both the RCAF and our experiences living "on the economy" in Germany (instead of on the base) would serve us well later in life.

During the Cold War, military security within NATO was extremely tight due to the high level of espionage activity and the constant threat posed by the Soviet Union and its allies. Pilots were under strict orders to be very cautious about discussing their duties, missions, and any sensitive information. We had to be mindful of who we spoke to, both within and outside the military, to prevent any inadvertent leakage of classified information.

The presence of espionage was a constant concern. Soviet intelligence agencies like the KGB were highly active. They were constantly attempting to gather intelligence from NATO forces. Consequently, we were trained to be wary of potential spies and informants, and to report any suspicious activities or approaches.

Taking pictures, especially in or around our sensitive military installations, aircraft, or operations, was heavily discouraged and often prohibited. Unauthorized photography could have

compromised security by revealing details about capabilities, locations, and operations to potential adversaries.

The tight security measures in place reflected the high-stakes nature of the Cold War; any lapse could have had significant consequences for national and alliance security.

MEETING "THE SHAPE"

When I joined 422 Squadron there was some minor training to be done—but for all intents and purposes, I was ready, willing, and able

A CF-104 and the BDU-10/E 'shape'. (A dummy B28RE thermonuclear bomb). Photo RCAF.

to deliver a nuclear bomb within 300 feet and three seconds if I was ever instructed to do so. That's if everything went right! One training mission to the bombing range in Vlieland in the Netherlands made me wonder about that.

It was a low angle drogue delivery (LADD) of a 2,140 pound bomb commonly referred to as a "shape." Normal practice bombs were quite small and relatively inexpensive. The "shape" was not dropped very often due to its much higher cost. The bomb was to be delivered after a "2.5 g within three seconds" pull-up to 45° from one hundred feet while going 540 knots. I came in fast and low, pulled up to the required 45° angle, and the shape released as planned.

There was a parachute on the bomb which would deploy and slow the bomb down allowing it to gently descend to a pre-programed detonation altitude. The plan was to roll inverted after the bomb departed the aircraft, pull down, and go like hell at low level to get away from the descending bomb. This would put distance between me and the soon to occur blast. Once I was flying upright again and had a good visual on where the ground was, I was to pull an aluminum blast shield over my head to protect me from the nuclear blast which was expected to catch up to the airplane. On this mission, the bomb released on schedule (when a 2,140 pound weight suddenly lets go it's quite noticeable!) and I rolled inverted. I was upside down now and I was about to pull down when I looked up and saw that the bomb was right there—flying in formation with me!

The parachute had failed to open and the bomb hadn't slowed down! (It takes a while for a 2,140 pound bomb doing 540 knots to slow down.) I stared at it for a few seconds. Slowly it began to drop away. I missed the target by about a mile!

As a thermonuclear weapon the B28RE utilized both fission and fusion reactions to achieve a significantly higher yield when compared to pure fission bombs. The B28RE was available in 4 different yields; 70 kilotonnes (Kt.) of TNT, 350 Kt. of TNT, 1.1 Megatonnes (Mt.) of TNT, or 1.45 Mt. **To put these yields into perspective, the Hiroshima bomb was only 15 Kt.** The fuze mechanism could be set for an air burst or ground detonation. A total of 4,500 B28s were produced.

FRIDAY THE THIRTEENTH AND THE SARDINIAN FISHERMEN

The other bombing range that we used often was Decimomannau in Sardinia. To get there, we would fly around Switzerland since it was a neutral country and not a part of NATO. In August of 1965, I happened to be in Sardinia on vacation with Sandy and the kids. I went out to the base to see how my fellow squadron members were doing. Al Seitz was just preparing to leave for Baden, and I jokingly said to him, "Hey Al! You're not going today, are you? It's Friday the thirteenth."

He laughed and replied, "Yes of course. I don't believe in that stuff, Gordy." At 35,000 feet, just north of Sardinia, Al's engine blew up. The 104 flight controls are hydraulically powered so due to the severing of hydraulic lines and a subsequent lack of hydraulic pressure they ceased operation. Al deployed the emergency ram air turbine (RAT) to get the controls working again. [6] The RAT failed to operate, and the airplane was now diving out of control. Al's only option was to bail out—regardless of his excessive air speed.

After he pulled the handle between his legs, the cables attached to his boot spurs pulled his legs in tight so that he wouldn't lose them on the way out. Then two machined aluminum arms —one on each side of the seat—rotated forward. This extended a nylon strap mesh that kept his arms in tight. Finally, the canopy was blown off the airplane with an explosive charge and the rocket that he was sitting on launched him into the freezing air at about 25,000 feet. Al rode the rocket seat out with the plane going faster than 0.90 Mach! Ouch!

It was violent and Al was badly bruised. When it all settled down (so to speak) there was a fully blossomed parachute above him to which he was securely attached. Below him was the emergency pack and a fully inflated dinghy. With time to think, Al came up with what he hoped would prove to be an ingenious plan!

The wind was blowing at about twenty-five knots and carrying him in the direction of a small island. Al re-rigged the straps and attached

---

[6] The RAT is a sort of windmill that you can extend into the air to generate electricity during emergencies.

the dingy to the parachute. He was hoping that this would allow him to land in the dinghy and maybe not even get wet. He would then hang on to the chute straps and ride the wind into the island.

The dinghy hit the water. The waves were about six feet tall. Al missed the dinghy and went underwater only to surface in time to see the dinghy hurdling towards the island at about twenty-five knots—thanks to the parachute. All he had now was the Mae West inflatable life jacket he was wearing to help keep him afloat.

Al was taking on water in the six-foot seas; he was nearly drowning. What he didn't know was that the crew of a small Sardinian fishing boat had seen him hit the water. They were doing their best to get to him before he slipped down to Davy Jones's locker. Fortunately, they were successful.

Al was in bad shape. He had swallowed a lot of water and he ended up in the Cagliari Hospital where I visited him. He said that he was sure it was the smell of dead fish that had caused him to throw up violently—but it might have been all the salt water he had swallowed.

Wanting to express the squadron's deep gratitude to the fishermen for saving one of our pilots—and wanting them to do it again if the occasion arose—Wing Commander Bill Bliss decided that we would have a special mess dinner in honour of the fishermen. It would be held in the Italian officers' mess in Decimomannau on January 20, 1966. We used a bunch of 104s and several T-Birds to get there. The mess hall was all set up for a formal dinner. The dozen or so fishermen arrived by bus. They were greeted by W/C Bliss and the festivities began—mainly drinking!

I never realized until then that the Sardinians were quite a bit shorter on average than we were. They were very enthusiastic and boisterous and they spoke a mile a minute in Italian. There was plenty of nodding of heads and waving of arms, but the incredible thing was their ability to drink! They were downing straight rye whisky in beer glasses! We were all impressed.

It wasn't long before we discovered that their tolerance for alcohol was really the same as ours. They started dropping like flies. You would be having an animated conversation with them when they would suddenly slow down, their eyes would roll up and back, and they would pass out—crumpled to the floor in a heap of sodden Sardinian.

About half of them were already out cold on the floor when W/C Bliss suddenly announced that the dinner was about to start and that there was something we needed to do. "First of all, boys, get this place cleaned up. Just pile the bodies under the tables." It was quite a party.

The next day we returned to Baden—while avoiding Switzerland of course. Baden was shrouded in fog with the temperature hovering at the freezing point. There had been recent freezing rain and the runway was slipperier than an oil-soaked eel.

Canadair CT-133 Silver Star
(T-33) Photo RCAF.

I was paired up with Squadron Leader Don Enman in a T-33. Don was in the front seat, and I was in the back. He briefed me on his intentions. "OK, I'm gonna put it on the runway and try the brakes. If there's no braking, I'm going to go around, and we'll go to 3 Wing." I agreed with the plan. "Sounds good to me," I said.

There was a line up to land since the ceiling was 200 feet with only a half mile of visibility in fog. This meant that we all had to do a ground-controlled approach (GCA). The GCA operator would watch you on his radar scope and keep you on the approach centerline. He would correct your glidepath angle by constantly giving you heading corrections, rate of descent changes, and other vital information.

In this type of situation, there is constant radio chatter. Conversation on the aircraft intercom between Don and I was blocked out by the GCA controller's transmissions to another aircraft on approach. Don

RCAF 422 Squadron, Baden-Soellingen 1964. Gord is standing 5th from the right.

flew the approach, and we broke out at 200 feet in the right position for landing. The controller said goodbye and started talking to the next aircraft behind us. However—his transmissions were blocking further conversation between Don and me. We touched down with the throttle in idle. Suddenly, Don slammed the throttle from idle to full power!

I instinctively glanced at the jet pipe temperature (JPT) gauge. It was just going through 1,000°F. This meant that the engine was probably going to blow up. I immediately grabbed the throttle and pulled it back to bring the temperature under control. I was just in the process of advancing it slowly when the throttle left my hand. Don had gone to full power again!

I glanced at the JPT gauge. It was again heading past 1,000°F so I retarded the throttle a second time. Suddenly, Don pulled the throttle back to idle and announced, "We're going in!" All through this there had been constant GCA transmissions to the aircraft behind us which had blocked out our attempts to communicate with one another.

The T-33 did a leisurely one hundred-and-eighty degree about-face on the ice while slowly decelerating. It continued backwards, slid off the runway, and ended up just under the tower. The only damage that occurred was one bent landing gear door. My silent prayers went out to Lockheed for designing such a sturdy aircraft.

Don was used to flying the CF-104. On the CF-104 it was ok to slam the throttle because the fuel control unit metered out the fuel automatically. The T-33, as an older aircraft, did not have an automatic fuel control unit, so you had to be careful when advancing the throttle to not exceed the JPT limits. Also, the T-33's ejection seats were not capable of a successful ejection below 200 feet. If the engine had blown up, the ejection would have been fatal.

Note that Flying Officer Price had just caused Squadron Leader Enman to damage a T-33. I was ready to accept the consequences of my (out of rank) intervention since we were both still alive. We would not have been, I still earnestly believe, if I had not intervened. As it turned out there were no repercussions from the incident. Whew!

SPECIAL TRAINING IN ESCAPE AND EVASION

Europe wasn't all fun and games in the air, however. There was lots to do on the ground. There were special courses to take. For example, the Forward Air Controller (FAC) course was where one went off with the ground troops and learned how to call down air attacks on enemy positions in support of the army. There were other courses too: a ski course in the French Alps and bombing courses in the sunny Mediterranean. All exciting and valuable stuff.

Being the junior man on the squadron, I realized that I was being passed over for these courses. Being the dedicated professional that I was, I marched smartly into the boss's office and insisted that I be allotted my fair share of the workload. Wing Commander Bill Bliss looked at me for a moment, no doubt impressed by my desire to do my share. "You are absolutely right my boy. The next course that comes across this desk is yours!"

I left the office quite satisfied. I was looking forward to the next adventure. A week later, the wing commander called me into the office. "I just got your course, Gord, and it is Escape and Evasion."

"Uh, Escape and Evasion sir? What is that all about?"

"Well," he said. "You go out in the countryside and pretend you've been shot down, and the populace, police, and well-trained US Army troops are all trying to capture you. You'll be in ditches and swamps and barns, stuff like that!"

"Well, uh, how about I pass on that one, if you don't mind sir, maybe wait for a ski course or something else."

"Sorry Gord, we made a deal. The next course was promised to be yours. Off you go."

I suddenly recalled something that had happened back in Cold Lake. It was one very cold winter's day, and a bunch of pilots—who were just walking away from their jets after a mission—were grabbed and told that they were going to go out in the bush and that they had to survive for the night. They were allowed to take anything that they had had with them in their plane. Nothing else.

It was -30°F. They had just come from a heated cockpit and a heated hangar and were not dressed for the cold. The boss had apparently noticed the casual way in which his pilots dressed for the climate. He saw a potential catastrophe. There they were, roaring off nearly to the Arctic Circle at low level, and would have found themselves in considerable danger of death by exposure if they had ever had to bail out on a flight. They were not wearing the proper clothing and a good lesson in survival was in order. Well, they nearly froze that night, but the point was made—everyone now wore the proper arctic clothing when on a mission.

So, escape and evasion it was! Yikes! When I went off to the NATO Escape and Evasion course in Ramstein, West Germany, I weighed 145 pounds. On my return, less than two weeks later, I weighed 118 pounds!

Classroom instruction included training in survival, orientation, evasion, and how to conduct yourself during interrogation. Just name rank and serial number stuff. That was it. No more. We had an Australian instructor who taught us all about it.

"There you are, you've been caught. Now you all know that you are required to give only your name, rank, and serial number. But the enemy no doubt will want to know more—right?" he explained.

"Well, it is at this point you will have to assess the effectiveness of your interrogator. You've given him all you are required to give him and he's not happy. He's slamming you in the back of the neck with a rifle butt, kicking, slapping you around, and well, now you know you've got him because it is obvious—he's not a very good interrogator!"

I was glad to hear this, because I had been thinking the guy sounded like a pretty good interrogator. The instructor went on, "The good interrogators make friends with you. Try to get you to talk freely. They use psychology on you. It is more effective."

I, of course, thought that the other guy would be just as effective. I figured that kicking and slugging would have worked out just as well as pleasant conversation—maybe even better! It was something that always stuck in my mind: how would I handle being shot down and captured for real?

After the classroom lessons were over, we were told that we were going on a day long orientation hike. An all-day hike! We loaded up forty-pound back packs and marched out into the drizzly northern European April weather. We slogged up and down hills behind the instructor who was obviously tireless.

By about 3 p.m. we aviators were tired. The instructor allowed us to stop for a rest and a smoke break. We all flopped to the ground and shrugged off our packs. I tried one of the C-rations from my backpack. It was so awful that I decided to throw them all away rather than to carry them through the woods.

After a short breather, the instructor gathered all of us around in a circle. He began giving us a short briefing. He picked up a stick and with it began to draw a crude map in the dirt. "Ok boys, here is the situation," he said. "We are on this hill, here. Down there,"—he was pointing—"is a road. It forks and goes around the hill like this."

He stopped for a moment, smiled, and looked around at us, his students. "Can you hear that noise?" We became aware of a kind of pervasive rumbling noise in the valley. "That's right, that rumbling is motor noise. Those are the troop trucks. They're bringing the 400 American troops needed to surround this hill. Your job is to evade those troops and to get to the safe house in that village we talked about, remember? Here are the details," he said as he handed out detailed maps.

"Have a good time and best of luck!" he said as he trotted off down the hill. And it didn't take long for him to disappear! "Hey, wait a minute, aren't we supposed to do this tomorrow?" everyone asked. "How come we have to do it now?" But it was too late—he was gone!

The evaders scattered. We were only to travel at night. We were allowed to be caught three times. We each had a ticket that had a piece torn off at each capture. The third time we would be incarcerated and subjected to interrogation which was guaranteed to be very unpleasant. It was time to practice what we had learned.

I was caught once, out of impatience. I had been hiding with some others in a dismal hole in the rocks that I would be hard pressed to call a cave. It was quite cramped and uncomfortable in there. Two of our group of about thirty, still picturing all of this as a game, decided that we could break the rule about only travelling at night. We very carefully crept out of our hidey-hole. We were caught almost immediately. A soldier had appeared out of nowhere. He pointed his rifle at us and demanded our tickets. He grabbed a piece of my ticket and immediately took off. He went straight up the side of a hill like a mountain goat and disappeared! After that, my friend and I decided that it might work out better if we travelled alone, so we went off in separate directions.

After my initial capture, I played by the rules. I stayed hidden and motionless during the day and I waited for nightfall to travel. I was able to observe some of the goings on while in hiding. The physical abilities of the American troops were amazing. They must have been special mountain troops. They were just like goats running all over the place. It didn't seem to make any difference if they were going uphill or down; I never saw one out of breath. It tired me out just watching them!

Darkness came. It was time to venture out and head for the safe house. We had been told in the classroom how to use a pole by poking it around in front of us. I had by this point found a long pole, and I was creeping quietly through the forest while using the pole to help me find my way. I was alert to every sound and movement. In the near distance I heard a strange sound. It was somebody yelling, "Aaaahhhh!" Then there was a "whump" followed by silence.

I heard this combination of sounds three or four times, but I couldn't figure out what it was. It sounded like it was coming closer each time it happened. I just kept moving cautiously along. I was using the pole when suddenly I stepped into nothingness. I did a flip and landed at the bottom of a six-foot embankment—all while uttering the same sounds that everyone else had. I had found out what the noise was. Fortunately, I did not break any bones.

A bit later I stumbled on to another of our team and we decided to join up. We crept along in silence for a while, but then we heard a squad of troops approaching. We dove for cover and laid low. The troops came closer until they were only a few feet away. They stopped right beside us and prepared for a coffee break. It was pitch black and nobody moved. But the troops had a diabolical plan to secure the area before settling down. They all stood there and hollered, "Okay, get up there, we can see you. Yes, you, over there!" It worked; all over the place guys started getting up out of the bushes—even my buddy!

I couldn't believe it. Guys got up that I never knew were even there! But I wasn't about to move. They'd have to step on me to get me up!! After a while things calmed down, the newly captured fugitives were led away, and the troops brewed up their coffee and started to talk. I listened.

"Hey, did you see that guy up there behind the tree? I had him picked up at 300 feet." They all laughed. They talked more while passing some piece of equipment between them. I noticed a kind of red light on it. Suddenly it twigged—it was a pair of infra-red night glasses!

Here I was, stumbling around in the dark with a stick and falling over cliffs. There they were with the latest equipment. What the hell was I up against?

What was there to lose? I decided to go for the road. I made great time on it as there was nobody there. They must have all been in the

CF-104s in Bavaria. Painting by F/O Andrew Henwood, 422 Sqn.

bushes with their "night scopes," picking guys off at 300 hundred feet. Here I was—running down the road past it all!

Suddenly I heard something a ways up in front of me. I dove off the road and landed on a small embankment that sloped upward and away from the road. It was at a very steep angle, and I had to lay on my back; in fact, I was almost standing straight up. Down below me I could see the lights of the town. That was my objective. I knew I was getting close to that nice, warm safe house. It was cold and raining and I was tired, especially as it was my second night in the woods. More than anything I wanted to be inside and to sleep in a bed.

The silhouette of a soldier with a rifle passed in front of the town lights. I held my breath and stiffened. The soldier stopped; he came back. He stopped again—this time right in front of me! His every move was backlit by the town's lights. The soldier stooped down and picked up the pole that I had been using. He looked at it, and then started poking it into the bushes around me. I tensed up.

I was lying there, inches away from this guy, with my legs apart to stop myself from falling. I knew I would scream if he poked me, and I had no idea what his reaction would be. But the pole missed as it passed between my legs. Shortly after, the soldier put the pole down. Then he put his rifle down and sat down on the embankment and lit a smoke. I was tempted to reach out and touch him, just for the wonderful effect it would have on the man. But I didn't.

I began to really feel the cold. My teeth were about to begin chattering so I slowly put my finger in my mouth to stop them. I couldn't stop the shivering and expected that the soldier would notice me at any moment. But the guy just finished his smoke, slid down the embankment to the road, picked up his rifle, and trotted off down the road. I remained motionless for a few minutes. He didn't return. I got up stiffly and set off down the hill towards the town.

I had been on my way to a rendezvous with a contact who would have taken me to the safe house, but I missed the meeting time because of my encounter with the soldier. There was another, secondary rendezvous I thought I just might make if I was lucky.

On the way down the hill, I heard something ahead and crept up on the sound. It turned out to be a jeep on the road, and it was running! I really wanted to steal the thing, but it seemed too much like something out of a movie. I really didn't need to, and I was too close to the safe house to risk it. But it would have been fun.

I crept on in the darkness toward the town below. I made the second rendezvous time and was guided by a local underground contact to an attic in the safe house. It was already crowded with a dozen escapees who had arrived there before me. As I remember, we dined on potato soup and blood sausage for several days, and we slept on the floor.

SHENANIGANS, SKITS, AND LIVING LIFE TO THE FULLEST

I suppose it was our having to deal with the fact that we had a very nasty job to carry out—if we were ever launched for real—that created an atmosphere of: Live to the fullest today because tomorrow—who

CF-104 model that I built, 422 Squadron installed it in the Officer's Mess.

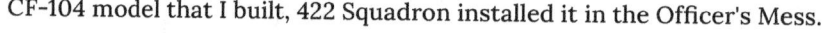

knows? We partied quite a bit. Friday nights' beer calls were almost compulsory.

Prior to 1964, the official 422 Squadron drink was a Nikolaschka, which was 2 oz of brandy with a teaspoon of instant coffee and sugar on a slice of lemon on the top. You chewed the lemon, sugar, and coffee; then smashed back the 2 oz brandy and spit out the rind. It was outlawed after one too many boozy incidents, and then they came up with the Afterburner (the recipe for which is included at the end of this chapter).

The shenanigans in the mess were endless. Once seated for the mess dinner, most pilots would put their bun in the water glass. Soaking up the water gave the bun more mass for better accuracy when the bun throwing inevitably started.

Also, there was "night landings." This consisted of someone being launched off a table in the dark onto carefully placed cushions which served as the runway. Candles in beer bottles simulated the runway lights. Then there was DEAD ANTS. In this game, whenever someone shouted, "DEAD ANTS," the last person to hit the floor had to buy the next round. However, the most popular game in Baden-Soellingen was full body check CRUD.

CRUD is a game that was invented in the RCAF at the end of WW II. The two teams can have any manageable number of players. The more players, the more chaotic the game. In order to play the game, you need a snooker or billiard table, one red ball, and one white ball. The red ball stays on the table and the white ball (the shooter ball) is rolled on the table by hand.

The red ball is placed on the centre dot at the far end of the table. The first player (who must stand at the opposite end—not the side) rolls the white ball at the red ball. They try to sink the red ball into a pocket or at least move the white ball the minimum required six inches while at the same time keeping the white ball away from the next player. Player one has three tries to hit the red ball or they lose a life. Each player has three lives. Once you lose three lives you are out of the game and that team loses a player. The second player grabs the white ball once there has been contact with the red ball. They run to the most advantageous end of the table. (It must be noted here that we used to have the "balls around the corner" rule to ensure that the

PRESENTED TO THE 4WG
WEATHER GUESSERS BY THE
OFFICERS OF 422 ST/A SQN
IN RECOGNITION OF
THEIR ETERNAL OPTIMISM

The Horse's Ass Award.

shot was indeed taken from the end of the table. I suppose that rule has been changed to "crotch around the corner" given the fact that we now have quite a few lady fighter pilots.)

The second player must hit the red ball before it stops moving and of course they are also trying to sink it into any pocket while trying to keep the white ball away from the third player. If the red ball stops before the second player hits it, that player loses a "life." As more and more players lose all three of their lives, one or both of the teams eventually become quite small. This is where it gets interesting.

Suppose each team starts with six players. As players lose lives and are dropped from their teams, the person that you are following changes. It requires great concentration to keep track of who is still in the game, and who you are following. You quite often end up with two or three players on one team and only one left on the other team. That one player will be run off their feet going from end to end. If the teams choose to allow the "full body checking" rule, the game

422 Squadron float that I built for the festival in Bühl, 1965.

can be a bit rough.

I was assigned to be "Squadron Skit-Master" and I had to come up with ideas for skits to entertain my squadron mates. One Friday night we presented the Meteorological Section with the "Horse's Ass" award after a week of bad weather. I made the horse's ass with plaster of Paris as part of my Skit-Master job. It was hung up on Met Section's wall. If you wanted to know who was on duty you simply lifted the tail and the duty forecaster's picture was right there, hung on a hook.

One other such assignment was to ensure that a certain visiting army general would remember his visit to 4 Wing. During the mess dinner I was seated close to the head table where the general was seated. I had been quite rowdy and had been under the table a couple of times. I had occasionally caught his eye and he was obviously perturbed.

After dinner we all assembled in the bar area where everyone stood around talking and drinking. I bumped into the general several times. He was not pleased.

The skit was on.

Bob Marion got on the PA and started talking about the upcoming winter carnival; we now had everyone looking one way. I had gotten ready before the dinner. I was wearing a hot water bottle under my uniform which had been filled with soup and stew. I had taken the top off the bottle and had the spout coming out of my shirt. We were ready.

I stumbled out in front of the general, did a quick 540° turn, and leaned over. I was now facing him. I bent down while at the same time squeezing the hot water bottle. Out came the soup and stew in a disgusting torrent right in front of him and all over his shoes.

There was complete silence.

Bob yelled over the PA, "HOT FOOD!" He proceeded to pull out a soup spoon from his tunic and he and Rocky Paquette got down on their knees and pretended to lap up the soup and stew. I quickly disappeared to the washroom to clean up where I was surprised to be joined by several others who had weak stomachs—they were throwing up for real.

Yes. We were bad!

DON CALDWELL'S CLOSE CALL

On June 11, 1965, 421 Squadron Pilot, F/O Don H. Caldwell, was forced to eject from his CF-104 near Wernersberg, Germany, when the aircraft experienced an engine compressor stall shortly after takeoff.

As I remember the day, I was flying a landing circuit at Baden-Soellingen when I heard the bail-out tone on the radio. [7] The tower gave me the magnetic bearing for the tone and asked me to fly out on that bearing to see if I could find the airplane or a parachute.

I set up to fly low level at about 1,000 feet at a reduced speed and I headed northerly up the Rhine. It wasn't long before I came up on the Vosges, a mountain range in France near the border with Germany,

---

[7] A landing circuit, also known as a traffic pattern or circuit pattern, is a standard path that aircraft follow when landing at an airport. It helps ensure safe and orderly flow of air traffic in the vicinity of the airport.

and had to start contour flying. I skimmed over the tops and slid down the sides of a few hills. I went up one hill that was about 2,000 feet high, and just skimming the tops of the trees. As I went down the far side, I caught a glimpse of something white in the trees.

I circled back to the right, but I needed to climb up the side of the hill with full power. I was in a box canyon[8] at lower-than-normal speed and this really got my attention. Having got out of there I set up for another look following the same initial approach. I went up the 2,000-foot hill, over the top, and down the hill. Looking right I caught a glimpse of the parachute hung up in the trees, but I had to get the power on to get out of the box canyon.

I notified the tower that I had found the parachute, and a helicopter was dispatched from Kaiserslautern. I hung around at a higher altitude while I waited for the helicopter. It arrived in good time, and I directed it to the spot where Don was hung up. I saw them hovering over top of him. The downwash from the helicopter blades was playing havoc with the branches. It must have been terrifying.

They quickly realized that that method of extraction was not going to work, so they went down the hill to an open area where they landed. At that point I returned to Baden. Here is the event in Don's words.

> I was scheduled for a low-level flight on 11 June 1965 with a bomb drop at the Vliehors bombing range in northwest Holland. This was a long trip with a 2,000-pound simulated cement nuclear weapon on the centerline and a full fuel load including tip and pylon tanks. A very heavy aircraft.
>
> I signed out CF-104 tail number 12871, and after takeoff I headed west to commence my route. Six minutes after takeoff at 450 KTS [knots] and about 500 to 1,000 feet AGL [above ground level], I heard a rapid banging noise, saw a fire warning light and the EGT [exhaust gas temperature] was "off the clock." This was not good. I did not know what was wrong except that I had indications of an engine on fire. I immediately throttled back and the EGT dropped back, and the fire warning light went out, so I increased the throttle, but the fire warning light came back

---

[8]A box canyon has only one entrance/exit point. Other than that, it is completely enclosed by steep walls.

PRESENTED TO
F/O D.M. CALDWELL
BY
SAFETY SYSTEMS SECTION
4(F) WING
EJECTED FROM CF-104 12871
11 JUNE 1965

Ejection D ring pulled by Don Caldwell.

Route to Don Caldwell's parachute was 25 nautical miles from Baden Soellingen.

on.

I declared a Mayday and checked the area I was over which was all bush. I heard someone saying to throttle off, however at that same moment the VSI (vertical speed indicator] rapidly dropped out of sight. Starfighter number 12871 had stopped being a sleek fighter/bomber aircraft and became a hunk of metal and cement that was falling toward a very unpleasant meeting with the ground!

I pulled the "D" ring!

I recall seeing the canopy lift off and my knee pad fly off and that I was instantly in my parachute. I looked down and saw that I was drifting into a pine tree, so I crossed my arms over my face and slammed into the tree. I estimate that the entire sequence from my first indication of a problem until I was stuck

Rescuing F/O Don Caldwell who hung in a tree for 20 minutes after ejecting from a CF-104.

escuing F/O Caldwell who hung in a tree
r 20 minutes after ejecting from a CF104

Choloy War Cemetery near Nancy, France. Photo © Canadian War Graves Commission.

in the tree was less than a minute!

I did not see where the aircraft had dropped; however, it must not have been too far from where I was. I looked down and saw that I was still a long way from the ground and the chute was caught up in the top of a very tall pine tree. I touched myself all over and said to myself "self—I think we are alive." I was very relieved as I thought for a moment about my wife and kids.

As I hung in the tree, I tried to reach for a branch to pull myself into the trunk of the tree. Anything that I could grab onto was too far away! My seat pack which had provided good protection when I hit the tree was still attached. I released it and attempted to swing the contents toward the trunk of the tree; however, I was too far away. It was then that the American helicopter arrived, and, while hovering above the tree, loosened the chute and I dropped about twenty feet further before the chute caught again. I was now close enough to a branch that I grabbed and pulled myself to the trunk of the tree. I released my chute harness *and shimmied down the remaining fifteen feet or so until I was happily on the ground.*

Don was returned safely to base. It was Friday and there was a big celebration at beer call.

Don lost two of his 421 Squadron buddies a few years later. Twenty-five-year-old Captain Wally Brason died in a CF-104 accident and Captain Larry Mealing, twenty-four years old, was killed in a car accident just outside of Baden-Baden.

Both pilots are buried in the Choloy War Cemetery which is the last resting place of casualties from the First and Second World Wars. It is managed by the Commonwealth War Graves Commission. It is also the final resting place for many Royal Canadian Air Force members and their families who died while serving in Europe as part of 1 Air Division between 1953 and 1967 and other service members serving with NATO in Germany following Canada's departure from France. It was not policy to bring the remains back home to Canada ... much to the dismay of most families.

A STRING OF BAD LUCK

In West Germany we often flew in low visibility conditions. This was normally below 1,000 feet and at 450 knots, so it was not uncommon to have near midair collisions with birds, and yes—even other aircraft. I was very lucky. Unfortunately, the other pilots managed to get my share of the bad luck. The RCAF lost thirty-seven pilots and 110 of our 238 CF-104s over a period of twenty-five years from 1961 to 1986. That was a loss rate of 46 percent! It is hard to believe that that was peacetime. Their sacrifice, in the name of our freedom, is just as noble as if they had been killed by a sniper's bullet or a roadside bomb.

Sometimes, things happened so fast! On one occasion I experienced a barrage of potential bad luck—yet I managed to emerge unscathed.

The mission called for a high speed, low level (450 knots, 1,000 feet or lower) cruise to the target. This was to be followed by "the dash," where the pilot dropped down to less than five hundred feet and cranked up the speed to 540 knots! I was in the initial part of the mission; I was doing 450 knots at about 1,000 feet when suddenly a British Hawker Hunter aircraft flashed by so close that I was able to catch a glimpse of the pilot's helmet.

I have no idea how we missed each other. Instinctively, I pulled up. I was looking back over my shoulder and climbing rapidly when I flew right through a formation of Belgian F-84 Thunderjet fighter-bombers that were taking part in a low-level mission. It was a gaggle of jets coming at me head on. I rolled inverted, pulled down, and headed for 200 feet where there were no aircraft except the odd Brit—I thought. It seemed that the only safe place was on the treetops.

Throughout all this excitement I had been distracted from navigating; I was getting awfully close to the 540 knot dash to my target. I bumped the speed up to 540 knots and flashed across the treetops. I was

From L-R: Gord Price, Ed Krahn, Ron Potter, George McKay, ready to go in QRA.

looking very intensely for familiar landmarks. I wasn't too worried about my position—just very alert.

However, as no familiar landmarks were visible, I began to suspect that I may have been a little bit east of where I should have been.

Just as this thought settled into my mind, a formation of helicopters suddenly rose up out of the forest below me—right into my path! I had little time to think; I streaked directly under a couple of them. This last episode took away whatever concentration I had had left. My fuel was being slurped at an alarming rate at low altitude and I now suspected that I was thundering into East Germany at 540 knots. This was somewhere I absolutely didn't want to be. I might have unwittingly penetrated their air defense identification zone (ADIZ). If that was the case, I was already being tracked by some very unfriendly sorts.

I did the only thing I could do; I pulled up and did a quick 180° to get myself out of Dodge as fast as I could. On the radar scopes of NATO, it must have looked spectacular: a target suddenly appears from out of nowhere at 0.99 Mach—it is coming from the east and clawing for altitude. Being less than anxious to start a World War, I called my position and intentions to a German radar station post haste. This was the proper thing to do, and fine as far as it went. However, it seems that the Germans were not speaking to the Americans that day for some reason, and the Americans launched an intercept.

Three American Convair F-102 interceptors out of Hahn were scrambled after me. I was happily cruising at 0.94 Mach and at 30,000 feet on the way to Baden; I flew directly over top of them. Once in the Baden area, I flew a standard penetration let-down procedure in order to enter the landing pattern.[9] Pitching out over the airfield, I was suddenly surrounded by three F-102's. It was quite a surprise! In the end, there were no repercussions from the incident since I had done nothing wrong. Someone had simply dropped the communication ball.

---

[9] A standard military penetration let-down is a procedure used by military aircraft to descend from cruising altitude to a lower altitude in preparation for landing, often in controlled airspace or in poor visibility conditions. This maneuver ensures a safe and orderly descent while maintaining separation between aircraft.

QRA DUTY AND THE NO-LONE ZONE

Our main job during this time of the Cold War era was to be ready to launch on a moment's notice, should the decision ever be made. If they blew that whistle, we had to be out the door pronto.

We sat Quick Reaction Alert (QRA) one or two times per week.[10] It was a twenty-four-hour session. Civilians sometimes wondered how we prepared for this. One asked in jest, "Did you sleep in your uniform?" Actually—yes! I wore my flying suit and boots with spurs; I kept this on the whole time I was on QRA duty. My colleagues did the same. That was how we were always ready to go. We also used to play bridge a lot. Sometimes, we didn't even go to sleep because we were expected to be alert for twenty-four hours. So, nobody was in pajamas.

When the session started, you would accept the aircraft and put the proper settings on the nuclear bomb according to the target requirements—these changed from mission to mission.

The aircraft was parked in what was called the no-lone-zone. There was a yellow line denoting the restricted area around the loaded aircraft. The no-lone-zone could only be entered by three designated people and all three had to "skip across the line together. The three people were the designated pilot and mechanic, and the assigned American guard. The guard had orders to shoot anyone else who entered the no-lone zone or anyone found in the no-lone zone by themselves.

The QRA area was very secure. There were two barbed wire fences surrounding it, an armed guard was stationed with every airplane, the area was patrolled by guards with German Shepherds, and machine guns were available nearby.

One day, an airman rushed over, "There's a bomb under your airplane. We need you to get over there right away."

---

[10] Quick Reaction Alert (QRA) is a state of readiness and operational capability in which military forces, particularly nuclear strike forces, are prepared to respond rapidly to potential threats. This typically involves having fighter/bomber aircraft and crews on standby, ready to scramble The goal of Nuclear Strike QRA is to ensure a swift and effective launch.

Being the way I am, I said, "Yeah, is it six feet long, white, and weighing about 2,000 pounds?"

They said, "No. It's another bomb!" I got out the binoculars to have a look at this bomb, and there it was— a package with a whole bunch of wires wrapped around it, and it was sitting underneath my airplane! I was the only one that was allowed to get in the airplane, and we had to move it out. We had no idea what the package might be, and we were taking no chances.

I carefully got in the cockpit of the airplane and we towed the airplane out. The bomb squad came up to dismantle the bomb and discovered that it was just a bunch of rags joined together. A false alarm—to the relief of all concerned. The guard made a ball out of it and he was amusing himself by kicking the ball around, when he accidentally kicked it under the airplane. He couldn't go in and get it, because it was a restricted area.

Another rather scary event took place while I was on QRA duty. I had dropped the nose of the bomb and was putting in the required

French Air Force F-100 Super Sabre. Photo © Mat Herben.

settings for my target, when I noticed an American guard right behind me. He was watching carefully as I set up the bomb.

These settings were classified as COSMIC Top Secret, and the guard did not have "a need to know." I asked him to back away. He became confused, drew his gun, and said, "Up against the wall!" My mechanic and I complied. We then gently talked him into calling for the American duty officer to defuse the situation. He finally did so much to our relief. The guard was suspended, and he was removed from the base the same day. This was not a singular occurrence. In the previous two months, two Belgian pilots had been shot by American guards.

STRASBOURG SONIC BOOM

All of this Cold War military activity was exciting for us, but it didn't always amuse the local civilians. During one low-level training mission, I was part of a supersonic group that accidentally broke a lot of windows in Strasbourg, France. After the completion of the mission, I climbed to 30,000 feet or so to produce a good contrail on my way back to base. (With the mirrors in my cockpit set up to watch my six o'clock position (behind me) and a good developing contrail, I would sometimes do this to bait someone for a mock dogfight. It was sort of like fishing. You just never knew what you were going to catch.) Well, I hooked four French F-100 Super Sabres who took the bait. They were setting up for an attack.

Before they got too close, I popped in the burner and leapt up to 35,000 feet. This left them in my vapour. I looked down, and there they were, all out of position. I went back down to 30,000 feet. They formed up for another try. As they approached a good attack position, I zoomed up again to 35,000 feet. With a little maneuvering I dropped back down to 30,000 feet, but this time I was directly behind them. I was now in the perfect position for the kill!

They accelerated while in a slight diving turn to get away from me, but I accelerated with them.

Enough was enough; the fun was over. I accelerated and gave them a wave as I passed by. Having been so intent on my positioning, I had neglected to glance at my Machmeter. It was too late. I was already supersonic and was doing Mach 1.4 as I went by. They must have been doing about Mach 1.2 themselves, which was almost as fast as that airplane could go. So, there we were with five descending sonic booms hitting Strasbourg all at the same time.

Hmmm, that wasn't good. I quickly descended to a very low altitude on the west side of the Vosges Mountains heading north. I crossed the Rhine valley, got to the east side of the Black Forest mountains, and then turned south to join the Baden-Soellingen traffic pattern from the east. This was a very circuitous route, and a long way from Strasbourg.

It took a few years, but my boss, Wing Commander Bill Bliss, finally learned what had happened that day. I explained it to him some fifty years later in 2015 when I visited him in Dallas, Texas. Bill Bliss was my hero. He was a Spitfire pilot during D-Day in World War II and he flew the F-86 Sabre jet in combat during the Korean War. He was a pilot's pilot. It's sad to report that Wing Commander Bill Bliss died in May of 2016. They don't make them like him anymore, and that's for sure.

TRANSITIONING OUT OF THE RCAF

When I had enlisted in the RCAF, I had done so under the Short Service Commission contract. This meant that after obtaining my wings and commission, I was under contract to stay on for five years. If my performance met with my superior's approval, it was possible to obtain a permanent commission and stay on for twenty years plus. The permanent commission was my target and I put forward my best effort to attain this. However, by late 1965, time was running out.

There was no guarantee that I would be offered a permanent commission and it seemed unlikely since they had, in the previous year, force released 500 pilots who had been considered surplus to requirement. We were a family of four and there was the possibility we'd be facing unemployment in only eight months. The only responsible thing to do was to see what other employment was available. I flew back to Canada and set up some interviews with various airlines.

I was in Canada for a week of interviews. I ended up being offered employment by three different airlines: Trans World Airlines (TWA), Canadian Pacific, and Air Canada. I returned to our home in West Germany satisfied, confused, and wondering what I should do with all these possibilities.

I went into Wing Commander Bill Bliss's office and explained the situation to him in detail. He listened intently. When I was finished, he paused for a moment. Then he handed me an envelope and said, "Here is your permanent commission. Congratulations, Gord!"

I was shocked. I had just been handed what I had worked so hard to attain over the past five years. I did not expect this at all. I thought their wheels turned slowly, and that my time with the RCAF would soon be coming to a close. But, now what?

The next day I asked the wing commander if I could have a meeting with the base commander as I had some questions for him. At that meeting, the base commander told me the simple truth. "You will be flying a Hercules in Transport Command in the not-too-distant future Mr. Price, and then no doubt, you will be flying a desk at some point after that."

This was a cold-water shock! Inside, I knew the truth of the situation, but somehow it didn't seem real that I'd have to give up my beloved Starfighter and end up flying transports. It was the wakeup call that I needed. So, the crystal ball told me that my future was to be flying transport aircraft—either military or civilian—take your pick. It was the most difficult decision we have ever had to make.

We opted for the path to a higher salary, freedom of choice of domiciles, and what turned out to be an unbelievably exciting and rewarding life. My boyhood dream had been attained. I was one of the very fortunate pilots who had experienced the CF-104 Starfighter as a combat-ready pilot.

It was a fact that besides being a fighter jock, I was also a family man, and my family was (and is) very important to me. I had had an immense amount of fun in my fighter-pilot days—but now it was time to change direction. Sandy and I loved the air force life, but we thought that we might find more opportunities outside it and since I was going to have to fly transport aircraft anyway, I might as well get paid better money for it. We decided to accept the offer of employment from Air Canada.

THE 1970 CHATEAU ROOM REOPENING

In May 1970, four years after I had retired from the RCAF, I found myself lucky enough to be part of a unique slice of RCAF history. The story begins in 1964. Amidst a geopolitical chess game, Canada had decided to relocate its CF-104s from France to Germany. This move had been necessitated by France's insistence on having sole control over nuclear weapons within its borders. It was a situation that put the entire NATO concept into jeopardy.

Amid this strategic shuffle, a piece of history was carefully preserved:

Entrance to the Chateau Room. Officers' Mess, RCAF Station Moose Jaw. Photo © Edward Soye.

the Chateau Room from the officers' mess from Marville, France was dismantled, shipped across the Atlantic, and reassembled at RCAF Station Moose Jaw. The reopening of this room was to be marked by a grand celebration, drawing guests from across Canada for what was then billed as an historic occasion.

The journey to this celebration was an adventure all on its own. It took place aboard an RCAF Hercules transport—an aircraft that crossed the country to collect us: a group of select ex-RCAF officers. I joined the flight in RCAF Station Downsview in Toronto. The trip was an informal affair. There were sandwiches and lots of beer and wine which helped to generate a jovial atmosphere among all the old comrades who were busy telling war stories. Upon landing at Moose Jaw we disembarked—only to find ourselves marooned way out on the ramp. This was a puzzling choice that soon revealed its thrilling purpose.

Chateau Room bar made from the oak stairs of a French Castle on which medieval knights have trodden. Photo © Edward Soye.

As we trudged towards the welcome tent, the quiet of anticipation was shattered by the thunderous roar of four CF-104 Starfighters that split the air in a loose "line astern" formation as they made a low pass that quite nearly flattened us. This wasn't just an arrival; it was an initiation by jet wash into what would spiral into the most legendary party of my life.

In the grand tradition of RCAF officers' mess shenanigans, my story unfolds in the heart of Moose Jaw's finest room, the Chateau Room, where the walls echoed with the ghosts of past exploits, not least of which involved a Harvard aircraft mysteriously finding its way onto a patio. I found myself stepping into a scene that managed to seamlessly blend the familiar with the utterly chaotic.

As I navigated the threshold of the officers' mess, the sense of déjà vu was palpable. The stairs, the smell, the sounds: all were as I remembered—a comforting reminder of days filled with camaraderie and occasional overindulgence.

My nostalgia, however, was abruptly shattered by the sight of the bartender. This was a man known for his unflappable demeanor, but in that moment he was a living portrait of terror. His eyes darted around the room like a cornered animal, and his hands shook as if he were trying to juggle invisible grenades—ones that had had the pins

Chateau Room, RCAF Station Moose Jaw. Photo © Edward Soye.

pulled! Then, as if on cue, the room was rocked by an explosion. The bartender dove for cover, narrowly escaping the chaos that had been unleashed from the far side of the room.

Amidst the leather upholstery of an unsuspecting chesterfield was the infamous makeshift bazooka crew. Unperturbed by their initial missed shot, this trio of mischief-makers was a sight to behold. At the helm was the officer in charge, a man whose strategic acumen was now dedicated to the art of indoor bazooka warfare. Beside him was the bazooka grunt, a position that demanded both strength and an unwavering ability to follow the most ludicrous of orders. Finally, there was the live-fire specialist who was armed with nothing more than a BIC lighter, a penchant for pyrotechnics, and a fearless demeanor. Their weapon of choice? A cardboard calendar tube that had been ingeniously modified with a metal end which had a hole punched in it, a generous dousing of lighter fluid, and a tennis ball jammed in for good measure that served as the destructive round.

The process was simple, yet fraught with anticipation—and just a hint of mystery. The officer with a practiced eye would calculate the trajectory and issue commands with the gravity of a general in the heat of battle. "Left, right, adjust the azimuth"—a ballet of instructions that would end with the decisive command: "FIRE!" At that moment, the live-fire specialist would flick his BIC; this would ignite the lighter fluid, sending the tennis ball streaking towards their target. Often the result was a spectacular miss, a collective tumble, and a room filled with both laughter and the smell of lighter fluid. It was the stench of battle in the Chateau Room.

Dear reader, this was the officers' mess as I truly remembered it—a place where the absurd became commonplace, and where a night could turn from mundane to explosive in the flick of a BIC. The bazooka crew, in their misguided glory, reminded us that the spirit (and joy) of serving in the RCAF wasn't just found in the skies, but in the brotherhood that could turn a simple evening into the stuff of legend.

A formal mess dinner marked the ceremonial opening of this important event. Attendees enjoyed the evening's traditions with a light-hearted spirit. The setting was elegant, with meticulously arranged tables that created an atmosphere of refined celebration.

As the evening's entertainment unfolded (which of course included the playful and time-honoured, traditional throwing of the soaked buns), the mood was one of joyous camaraderie. However, it was a memorable mishap by a well-meaning doctor that became the highlight of the night. For the sake of this retelling, the doctor's name remains unrecalled—a detail forever lost to the collective memory of those who witnessed the event.

The incident occurred during a moment of reflection, as the gathering observed the saying of grace. With everyone's attention held by the solemnity of the tradition, the doctor, unfortunately, found himself losing his balance. In a frantic attempt to steady himself, his hand caught the edge of the tablecloth.

What followed was a moment of pure slapstick comedy. As the

Chateau Room, RCAF Station Moose Jaw. Photo © Edward Soye.

doctor fell, he pulled the tablecloth with him. This led to a premature clearing of the head table. Utensils, glasses, and decorations were swept away in an instant. They flew wildly in every direction, leaving the table bare and the attendees in a mixture of both shock and disbelief.

Despite the unexpected turn of events, the situation was met with good humour. The initial surprise soon gave way to laughter, which turned the incident into a memorable story for all present. The doctor's act, though maybe not planned, added a unique touch to the evening, elevating it to mythic status.

It also served as a reminder to everyone: it's often the unforeseen moments that make for the best stories.

The hosts had thoughtfully prepared small brown bags of hangover remedies and medications for each of us, and we could pick them up before we made our way back to the barracks for a nap. For three days we partied in shifts, ensuring that the festivities continued around the clock.

With a unique blend of humour and nostalgia, I look back on it as not just one of the wildest parties that I've ever attended, but as my last great bash—a fitting finale to my time with the RCAF. Sic itur ad astra is Latin for "Such is the pathway to the stars." It is the motto of the Royal Canadian Air Force and it is a sentiment that I have honoured throughout my life spent scudding through the clouds.

Thank you RCAF, those were the best years of my life!

THE AFTERBURNER

Ah, the legendary Afterburner—a concoction as daring and flamboyant as the 422 Squadron itself. A drink not for the faint of heart, or for those with any sense of self-preservation when it comes to their morning-after well-being.

The ritual begins with the pouring of white crème de menthe, as pure and as chilling as the squadron's flying acumen. This layer sits at the bottom, a foundation as solid as the squadron's reputation, and twice as likely to knock your socks off.

Remembering the RCAF 422 Squadron drink – the Afterburner. Photo © Stephanie Price.

CF-104 climbing. Photo RCAF.

Next comes the apricot brandy, as orange as a pilot's flight suit after a particularly spirited sortie. This layer floats atop the minty base with the grace of a well-executed barrel roll, adding a touch of sweetness and a hint of danger.

But wait, there's more. The pièce de resistance: a 50/50 blend of sloe gin and rye, carefully layered on top. This represents the squadron's balance of precision and recklessness, a combination as potent and unpredictable as their notorious flybys.

The creation of this drink is not complete without the sacred chant, "Four two two, four two two, Everybody loves us, Four two two," sung to the tune of the Campbell's soup song. This is not just a chant; it's a war cry, a declaration of unity and slightly-inebriated affection for one's squadron mates.

And then, the moment of truth. The Afterburner is not merely sipped or savoured. No. That would be far too civilized for the likes of 422 Squadron. Instead, it is "ceremoniously smashed back," a gesture as bold and fearless as the pilots themselves. It's a test of will, a challenge to the laws of physics and common sense.

To engage with an Afterburner is to dance with destiny, to flirt with the morning's regret, and to momentarily possess the invincibility of youth. It's a tribute to those who live by the motto, "Fly low, fly fast, and leave a smoky streak in your wake."

So, here's to RCAF 422 Squadron and our Afterburner—a drink that captures the essence of our spirit. Just remember, like the most daring aerial maneuvers, it's best approached with caution ... and perhaps a pre-arranged sick day for the morning after.

THE ANALOG AIRLINE PILOT

I'm often described as a type A personality. I take charge, and I'm naturally inclined to lead. This can either inspire or irk others. Some have labeled me a maverick for my unconventional choices in life, but there's an inherent contradiction between my personality and my career choice. Being part of the RCAF, a strict government agency, clashed with my desire for autonomy and creative problem-solving.

You might wonder how I managed to reconcile these two. Truthfully, I adapted. In the cockpit, especially when I was piloting the Starfighter, adherence to protocol was non-negotiable; deviating meant risking my life. Despite my youthful energy in my early twenties—I wasn't reckless. Training allowed for some levity such as off-duty antics and fun skits, but in the air it was all professionalism and discipline. This strict adherence to rules wasn't just about personal safety; it was crucial for survival.

I left the RCAF at twenty-four, and transitioned to commercial aviation where the same principles applied. Flying a commercial airliner demands the same rigor and respect for rules as flying a fighter jet does. I've always been comfortable with this; obeying the rules in the air just makes sense.

April 11, 1966. That was my last trip in a CF-104. It was fin number 757 and it lasted for one hour and fifteen minutes. I had logged 505 hours in the CF-104, 375 in the T-33, 85 in the F-86, 185 in the Harvard, 138 in the Chipmunk, and 18 hours in an Expeditor. That gave me a total of 1,306 hours.

While I had had suspicions that there would be fewer and fewer opportunities to strap on the Starfighter, I hadn't known that that would be my last trip. The next entry in my logbook would be in faraway Vancouver—in an Air Canada Link trainer.

AIR CANADA TRAINING

It was July the fourth: the day I completed initial training on the Link and started on the Vickers Viscount (a turboprop powered British airliner) for fifteen hours of flight training. I came out of all of that with a Class I instrument ticket and a job as first officer with Air Canada.

Back then they'd give you an airplane just to train on. Imagine having a Viscount to go flying in!

Nowadays they give you simulator time up to your first flight, and then you go on a regularly scheduled flight with an instructor. Back then, they put two of us and an instructor in a Viscount; one would sit in the jump seat and observe the other guy, then we would switch. We flew lots of different approaches in the Viscount, and wouldn't you know, I kind of enjoyed it. It was quite a challenge. Flying the aircraft with precision was not easy.

I remember one time, not in the airplane but in the simulator, when the "Captain" in the left seat neglected to turn on the engine de-ice. So, the instructor thought it would be a good idea to give us an extra challenge. There we were, droning along quite happily when all four engines quit at the same time! Being a keen young first officer with great reflexes and rapid hands, I managed to get them all going again in record time, much to the amazement of the simulator's "Captain" who had hardly even realized that they had quit.

It was nice to be young and to be able to react so quickly. But now that

Vickers Viscount. Photo used with permission.

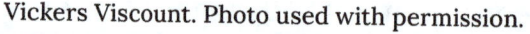

I'm an old, retired captain, I can understand why he hadn't reacted as fast as I had! It is a good thing to have the age mix in the cockpit, I think: keen young first officers and older experienced captains make for the perfect combination.

I began to realize that going from the Starfighter to the Viscount wasn't all that bad. The Viscount (affectionally known as the $50,000 dog whistle) was quite a handful to fly. It was something of a task to take that "big old piece of metal" and fly it through the sky competently. There was a lot more happening, even though it was happening at a slower rate than it would have in a fighter.

Besides, when we were flying at lower levels and lower speeds (about 220 knots and 15,000 to 20,000 feet), turbulence and weather were bigger factors than when I had been strapped into a Starfighter. In the 104, a "go fast" machine, turbulence had just been a vibration—in the Viscount it was sometimes very interesting!

McDonnell Douglas DC-9's were new airplanes in 1966, and I went on to the "Nine" with a smile on my face having only been on the Viscount for nine months. It always puzzled me in those days about

Douglas DC-9-14. Photo used with permission.

the instructors. They were good pilots, but they seldom knew much about teaching, about having to instruct pilots in the things that they needed to know.

All they had was a lot of practical experience on the airplane itself. They had not taken the RCAF School of Higher Instructional Technics course affectionally known as the "SHIT" course. The airline eventually realized the difference between someone who was a great teacher and someone who had lots of experience, but back in the day things were different.

My DC-9 instructor was like that. He was an old timer, a wartime pilot with all kinds of experience. But—he didn't know how to tell someone else how to fly.

My first instructional trip with him in a DC-9 was out of Halifax at night. (Again yes, in those days we still had an airplane to play with, but we had to take them whenever they were available.) We were up about 20,000 feet and I was quite enjoying myself. I liked the feel of the airplane, how it flew, and how it handled.

I was doing turns and thought I'd like to try increasingly steeper

Douglas DC-9-32. Photo used with permission.

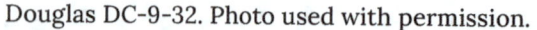

ones to feel out the airplane. I turned to the instructor and said, "Do you mind if I do a couple of 45° bank turns?"

It was as if I had poked him with a pencil. The old guy sat up straight and looked at me wide eyed. "At night??"

"Well, yes why not?" I replied because that hadn't seemed the appropriate response to such a question.

"Well, no, not at night," I was told. "Not a 45° bank turn!"

Another little episode took place shortly thereafter. One was not supposed to use the speed brakes while the flaps were extended in the DC-9. Being the curious sort of aviator that I was, I suggested that we drop 15° of flap and pull the speed brakes out to see what happened. This was because I was a firm believer in finding out the reasons for things whenever possible. I was hoping to understand from personal experience the reason for the flap/speed brake rule. This would, I thought, give me a little more mastery over the airplane.

The instructor looked at me as though I was some sort of madman to even suggest such a thing. With wide eyes he said, "It crashes!" Just like that, from 20,000 feet, it crashes! Wow! I realized then that there was not going to be a lot of learning taking place in this environment. I became silent and did as I was told.

The instructor said that he would demonstrate the landing. I sat back to observe. At that time, we were flying a brand-new stretched model DC-9-32. The instructor had logged all his time on the older, smaller DC-9-14. He had never landed a -32. Basically, a -14 had what is known as a "hard wing" (there were no leading-edge slats) and a -32 had slats which were extended for takeoff and landing. Because of this, the -14 landed with the nose down (level position) and the -32 landed with the nose up about 5°.

So, our instructor came in like he was landing a -14 and he demonstrated it quite well actually. However, he put us onto the ground so violently that I suddenly gained a lot more confidence in the structure of the airplane. The impact was incredible. I thought the wheels were coming up through the wings. But when he turned around and said, "Well boys—that's how you do it!"—that's what absolutely shocked me.

I was now terrified of the airplane and that I would have to subject passengers to these "carrier deck" type landings. But I soon learned that that was not actually the way to do it. The airplane could be put down smoothly and the passengers' dentures would be quite safe.

IMAGINATIVE EXTRA EARNINGS

One of the facets of our new life that had nothing to do with airplanes being flown around the sky was the sudden drop in income. It went from about $10,000 per year to $200 per month ($2,400/year) when I was training. Out of that we had to keep an apartment in Montreal in addition to the place in Toronto during initial training. It was a lean time for quite a while.

We had to economize, cash in insurance policies, dip into savings, and more. But being somewhat imaginative, we found some innovative ways to cope. For example, one of the beneficial perks was that as employees we could travel on standby for little cost. Sandy and I would take short trips to Europe from time to time, and in addition to having a small holiday, we'd buy a variety of inexpensive paintings that caught our fancy.

You could buy art by the yard in some places—Hungary for example. We just bought art that we liked, and usually others liked it too. They were primarily decorative paintings, nothing exotic. Then we'd have an art show back home when we returned. We'd advertise in the local paper and sometimes on the radio. When I was asked, "What do you know about art?" I would reply, "Not much, but you don't have to in order to sell it. People make up their own minds as to what it all means, and then you just agree with them."

This little endeavor helped us to keep our sanity. It got us out of the house and allowed us to do things (like stay in hotels and travel) that we wouldn't have been able to do if we had simply tried to live within my salary alone. Of course, it did make us a little bit more money as well.

THE CANADIAN AIR LINE PILOTS ASSOCIATION

As it seemed that during these early times at Air Canada most of our energy was going to be spent simply trying to afford our new lifestyle, then one area I wanted to explore to help alleviate this was the Canadian Air Line Pilots Association (CALPA) that I was now a member of. I went to their meetings and expressed my opinion that the wages for the new hire group were far too low and that they should be raised. I was told that the pay rates were set in a contract that would not be changed for several years.

There had been quite a hiring spree so there were a lot of very junior pilots that wanted a pay raise anyway. I contacted as many as possible and asked them to attend the next CALPA meeting. Quite a few showed up, and there were enough of us to get a motion passed for creating a wage study committee. The three-person committee would put together a report on new hire wages, and I was appointed its chairman.

The report was assembled. At the next meeting, a motion was passed that we be allowed to present the report directly to Air Canada's Director of Flight Operations, Captain Lindy Rood. Lindy was a legend and ruled with an iron fist. Before entering his office to give him the presentation I was warned that he would interrupt me and be generally very difficult to get along with, particularly because CALPA had a signed agreement with Air Canada that had been previously negotiated.

We entered his office. Lindy was most cordial and seemed very interested in what I had to say. I presented the report with a myriad of colourful charts and graphs. I explained how we were having to sell our insurance policies to make ends meet and that young families were having a very difficult time surviving. He listened intently. When it was over, he said genuinely, "I had no idea the situation was so bad!"

On the way out I asked him when his birthday was: not the year, but the day and the month. He told me, and I then pulled out a newspaper clipping with his horoscope and mine. I compared the two of them, noting that it looked like he was going to change the Pilot's Agreement and that I was one of the people that would benefit from the change. We both laughed.

Less than a month later, the new hire pilots received a significant pay raise. It turned out that those who had obtained their airline transport pilot's licenses would be making $750 per month. I had just negotiated a 300% pay raise for myself!

At the next CALPA meeting, I was surprised to hear that many pilots were upset that I had negotiated a pay raise for the junior pilots. After all, they reasoned, there was only so much money in the pot and it wouldn't have been long before we were more senior. Therefore, the money should have gone to the more senior pilots.

FLYING DC-9s FOR AIR CANADA

The airline pilot system in Air Canada is governed by the seniority system. The sooner you hire on, the lower your seniority number is and the better your life is. Seniority governs your choice of equipment, vacations, flying destinations, and your days off.

In 1966, with the introduction of the DC-9, it became impossible for the company to operate by a strict seniority agreement. So, CALPA and the company came to an agreement that pilots could be trained on the DC-9 without considering seniority. The agreement was for two years. When the two years were up, the seniority system had to be followed.

In those days, the top salary of DC-8 captains approached $30,000 per year. With this agreement in place, pilots senior to me were stuck flying sideways on the DC-8 as second officers while for two years I flew the DC-9 as a first officer.

Again, I was one of the lucky guys!

Airplane hijack threats were prevalent at the time and on one occasion, Air Canada received a call that their flight to New York was going to be hijacked. It turned out for that flight that I was the first officer and Doug Moore was the captain. We showed up for flight planning and it was noted that we would probably receive special treatment since air traffic control had been advised of the threat. That was the first time I ever experienced the security checks before we got on the airplane. They were set up at the departure gate.

Enroute to New York we received preferential treatment, and the air traffic controllers were obviously aware of the hijack threat. We landed, taxied in, and just before we arrived at the gate, the ground controller said, "How is everything tonight?" Doug said to me, "I got it Gord!" He picked up the mic and answered, "Everything is OK. I guess I am going to have to smoke these cheap cigars after all."

That did it! The FBI and other security services were sure that Doug's last transmission was code for "We need help!" They stormed the airplane as we arrived at the gate with guns drawn. We were surrounded.

Another Air Canada rule was that a legal layover must provide eight hours of prone rest and duty days could be up to fourteen hours long. I used to bid on what are called "illegal layovers"—which provided me with lots of time to do other things.

Typically, these trips were the last flight of the day to New York and the first flight of the day from New York, so they fell within the fourteen-hour duty day—however, they did not provide the required eight-hour prone rest rule. I was not senior enough to get Christmas off, so I ended up having to fly to New York on Christmas Eve and then return home on Christmas morning. The family was quite disappointed, so I said. "Why not come with me? The flights only have a few passengers, so we can use our passes to fly."

Sandy, Stephanie (who was six), and Glen, (who was four), came with me. On the way to New York, I made an announcement noting that Santa had been sighted on radar and that he was behind us and to our right. The kids were glued to the windows! We checked into the hotel near the airport where we would get about four hours sleep. When the kids woke up, low and behold, Santa had been in our room and their stockings had been stuffed with all sorts of goodies! We were back in Toronto by 9:00 a.m. I rushed home and got all the presents out and put them under the tree before Sandy arrived with the kids. They were impressed that Santa had been in both places.

Vickers Vanguard Type 952. Photo used with permission.

THE VICKERS VANGUARD AND MARITIME ROUTES

After two years on the DC-9, I transitioned to the Vickers Vanguard—a four-engine turboprop aircraft. The Vickers Vanguard Type 952 (built by Vickers-Armstrongs, a British shipbuilder) was an ideal aircraft for flying the maritime routes and for going through the winter storms that often ravage Canada's east coast. In the late 60s and early 70s, Air Canada offered its pilots a certain pairing of flights (set of flights with appropriate rest periods) that, although tortuous, was much sought after for the consecutive days off.

Working three days and having four days off seemed like the thing to do, but during those three days you could get to feeling bleary and drained; or as we sometimes say, that you felt that you "had been to war." It had a lot to do with the weather systems in Canada and the luck of the draw. At least there were four days to recuperate before doing it again!

Starting from Toronto, the first day consisted of six landings: Sault Ste. Marie, Thunder Bay, Winnipeg, Thunder Bay, Sault Ste. Marie, and Toronto. Now, if you timed it right, there would be a weather system with a warm front and a cold front between Toronto and Winnipeg along with the associated thunderstorms.

So, you would fight your way through on the way west to Winnipeg and then turn around an hour later and fight your way through it again back to Toronto, no doubt catching the worst of the weather on three or four of your landings.

This would be followed by a drive home through heavy traffic to have a short night's rest, then back to the airport for Day Two. Oh, and while you were sleeping, the weather system would pass over top on its way to the East Coast.

Again starting in Toronto, Day Two consisted of seven stops: Montreal, Moncton, Halifax, Sydney, Stephenville, Gander, and St. John's, Newfoundland. Since the system had passed over you the night before, it was normally in the right position to cause you trouble a couple of more times as you worked your way to the Crow's Nest (the naval officers club in St. John's).

While laying over in St. John's in those days, we stayed in the old CN Newfoundland Hotel. I recall that the rooms had two temperatures depending on which way the wind was blowing—hot or cold. The upwind room was always cold, and the downwind room was hot, so the window was opened in the downwind room. Doing this freed up the pressure on the upwind side and this allowed the cold air to blow through any place it could find. This made the place a challenge at any time of year.

Day Three of the marathon included eight stops from St. Johns: Gander, Stephenville, Sydney, Halifax, Moncton, Montreal, Ottawa, and finally Toronto—and yes, the same troubling weather system was probably going to affect at least five of those landings. All in all, it was a good workout for budding airline pilots as it made life very interesting.

OF CAPTAINS AND CO-PILOTS

The Vanguard was developed as a three-pilot airplane and flown as such by British European Airways and other carriers. Air Canada, however, crewed it solely as a two-pilot airplane. The infamous Vice President of Flight Operations Lindy Rood insisted it be a two-pilot airplane and he had the engineer's overhead instrument cluster covered up with a metal panel.

There were some valuable instruments and warning lights behind that panel, and it would take an incident to ultimately have parts of the panel uncovered, by way of a directive, so that we could see what was going on. I remember on one trip that we had to troubleshoot a problem; I was trying to remove the panel to get a glimpse of exactly what warning light was on—but I didn't have my tools with me.

Lindy was right, though. We never had a problem operating with two pilots and if we convinced him that we needed visual access to something behind the panel, he would have a small visual access hole cut out of it.

Being a co-pilot during this period, and flying with a variety of captains, I discovered that the job was akin to taking an entry-level psychiatric course. It was probably even better than that, as no course designer could have imagined some of the interesting human interactions that I and others had the pleasure of experiencing.

It was this sort of experience that was extremely valuable as you worked your way towards your captaincy. You learned how to act, and how NOT to act.

Some of it was just quirky. Like this one fellow who thought it would be fun to bring his dog along, at least in his mind. I was first introduced to the concept of the "phantom pooch" when I heard him say: "Down boy! Get down! We're taking off now, just sit down!" Then he would bark a few times before he poured on the coal to the 22,000 horsepower (hp) that was put out by the Vanguard's Rolls-Royce Tyne turboprops. Then off we went, presumably with the invisible dog there in the cockpit with us.

It took a few legs of the journey to get used to this, but it wasn't long before I was talking to Fido, too. Not all co-pilots were as tolerant as I was, though. On one flight, this same captain was chatting with his dog just before takeoff. He was letting out a few barks when his co-pilot finally decided that he had had enough. He pulled out his right hand shaped like a pistol. "BWAM, BWAM, BWAM!" He blew the smoke off his finger and holstered it.

The captain was aghast! "What did you do?" he asked.

The co-pilot said, "I just shot your damn dog!" The only conversation in the cockpit from then on was strictly business.

Having an interesting captain made our flying together more enjoyable or at least more interesting. The case of another captain comes to mind. The cockpit door would open and a bubbly young flight attendant would prance in and cheerfully say, "Good morning fellows and what would you like to drink this fine day?" I would look over at the captain, who was visibly not pleased at being interrupted halfway through his cockpit check. He would glare at me while giving me a "T" sign using both his index fingers. I would say, "And good morning to you dear. The captain would like a tea, and I will have a coffee with cream please." Smartly, the flight attendant would pivot and head cheerily for the galley.

The captain would then begin speaking again. "Damn! She interrupted my cockpit check and now I have to start all over again." Which is just what he would do—go right back to the beginning. He would touch, almost caress, every damn switch, knob, toggle, and light with his deft fingers, until he had touched everything. As a rule, we wouldn't see much of the cheerful flight attendant for the rest of the trip.

ONE DARK AND STORMY NIGHT

The Vanguard was a big airplane. It was close to 123 feet long and it had a wingspan of 118 feet. It weighed up to 141,000 lb. For a turboprop it was fast. It was even faster than DC-9's and DC-8's on the descent—something that kept us amused whenever we found ourselves in a position to race. We operated with a mix of economy and first class seats which held 106 people. The first class cabin was at the rear, where it was quieter.

The one thing that pleased us pilots the most was the tremendous fuel load that we could carry. This gave us the capability of carrying on to alternate airports that were removed from the weather that we were flying in. So, we had the opportunity to try to get in during very bad weather, but still have the option to miss the approach a few times and then fly to a safer alternate airport a long way off.

There we were one dark and stormy night. We had bypassed Sydney because of moderate turbulence on the approach. (I note that after moderate turbulence comes severe turbulence, which basically means that the aircraft is sometimes out of control.) In this case it was very difficult to fly the aircraft on a procedure turn at about 1,500 feet above the airport, since the airspeed fluctuations were plus or minus twenty knots, and we were getting thrown around quite a bit. When Sydney radio reported the surface wind as fifteen knots gusting to sixty knots, the captain said we might as well pass and head on to Stephenville. Good idea!

The weather was different at Stephenville, and it looked like we would be able to break out visual and see the ground by getting down to the minimum enroute altitude early. This was good because the instrument landing system (ILS) for runway 28, which had a 4.5° glide path to guide your descent between the mountains on either side of the approach, was unserviceable.

The preferred runway in this case was runway 28, as the wind was out of the northwest at five to ten knots. However, we elected to use the opposite runway, Runway 10, because that was the only way we could get down low enough to see the airport. The fly in the ointment was that there had been some freezing rain and the runway had not been treated. This was not a good situation. However, the runway was 12,000 feet long; this gave us plenty of time (and space) to get seventy tons stopped.

After surveying the situation, I suggested to the captain that he should make the landing since it could prove to be a bit tricky. He said, "No, no, Gord, you go ahead. It will be fine." Reluctantly, I proceeded.

The approach was normal, without any of that annoying turbulence. This allowed us to keep the speed as low as possible so that I could plunk it down on the runway very close to the end at about 150 mph. The Vanguard had a couple of different prop settings: flight fine and ground fine. Ground fine reduced the pitch of the propellers and offered more drag to slow the airplane down.

I retarded the throttles to flight fine pitch on touchdown. To bring in the ground fine pitch at that point, which was normally done, would not have been a wise thing to do as it would probably have upset our somewhat minimal directional control. I had decided to wait until I tested the brakes before using that setting—this was a good move! There was zero braking on that slick, wet, ice-covered runway. It was going to take a long time to decelerate.

Unfortunately, that quartering tailwind was now a factor and it was doing two nasty things to the airplane. Number one, it was gradually pushing the airplane off the runway to the right, and number two, it was gently pushing on that nice big tail, twisting the nose to the left. The bottom line was this: we were going to be off the right side of the runway before the airplane stopped. Something had to be done to change the equilibrium.

In times like these, although time is short, your mind seems to go into a slow-mo mode, which gives you the capacity to slow things down, so that everything occurring seems to take an eternity. So, there we were, the airplane was skidding right and turning left, with a brief timeline that would put us off the runway and into a real mess.

I had an instant epiphany: What if the turn rate to the left was increased? What if the airplane was turned around so that we were going backwards? What if I did this before we went off the runway?— the thoughts flooded my mind.

I had the brilliant idea to use normal forward thrust as our brake, as by that point we would be going backwards. It just might work. Instinctively, I gently pulled the number one engine[11] into full reverse. This was to increase the rate of turn to the left. It was working—I could see that the aircraft's rate of turn to the left had increased, and I wanted it to keep increasing until I saw the north side of the runway come into view. As soon as that was the case, I moved the number one engine out of reverse and back into flight idle to maintain a constant rate of turn. Just before we were lined up with the runway again,

---

[11] Engines are numbered starting from the far left from the point of view of the pilots sitting in the cockpit.

(but now going backwards), I took all four throttles and rammed on full power (22,000 hp). This helped to slow the 141,000 pounds of careening aluminum.

The aircraft stopped in the middle of the runway. I pulled the engines back into ground fine pitch and set the parking brake. "You have control," I said to the captain—in several octaves higher than my normal voice. This confirmed to me that I had just blown every bit of adrenaline that a twenty-seven-year-old could possibly produce. It was another thirty minutes before we shut down the engines on the ramp; the captain had had a terrible time taxiing on a virtual skating rink without slipping off the side.

Once we had shut down the engines, I went back to get a coffee from the forward galley. While I was standing in the galley, a passenger approached me quite excitedly and told me what he thought of that landing. "I just love flying and the excitement of it all, especially the takeoffs and landings—but that last landing was the very best one yet!" I almost spit out a mouthful of coffee.

He continued, "I am flying to St. John's from Victoria and could have substantially shortened the trip by taking nonstop flights from Vancouver and Toronto, but I prefer to experience lots of takeoffs and landings."

On the way home I noticed that one family had packed a lunch. They hadn't realized that we had a full meal service on board. I thought it was amusing at the time, but as it turns out they were just fifty years ahead of their time.

DOUGLAS DC-8 AND LOCKHEED L-1011

After several years of flying the Vanguard, I moved over to the right seat in the DC-8.

When moving from one type of aircraft to another, you must forget everything you learned about one airplane so that you can then "relearn" it on the new one. That skill has sort of become part of my psyche now. I may not be able to remember much, but I have the unique ability to absolutely blank out everything that I have learned

Douglas DC-8-43 powered by Rolls Royce engines. Photo used with permission.

Douglas DC-8-63 powered by Pratt and Whitney engines. Photo used with permission.

Lockheed L-1011. Photo © Gary Vincent.

previously. This is especially useful when switching airplanes.

Air Canada had six different types of DC-8 at the same time, and you never knew which type you were going to be flying; it was a job keeping up with the different procedures for each type of aircraft. The -41 and -43 were powered by Rolls-Royce Conway engines and the -53, -54, -61, and -63 were powered by Pratt & Whitney engines. The maximum takeoff weights varied from 300,000 to 350,000 lb. The most senior captains flew these aircraft, so I learned quite a bit as a first officer flying throughout Europe, North America, and the Caribbean.

After several years of flying the DC-8, I had the chance to bid on the First Officer position for the Lockheed L-1011 TriStar, a jumbo airliner. It was a dream to fly.

FOURTH STRIPE: DC-9 CAPTAIN

After eight years as a first officer, I bid for the DC-9 captain's position and secured it. The transition went well, and the instruction and guidance were very good. I did several scheduled "passenger trips" with other captains that had been designated to fly in the right seat. I flew in the left seat to gain experience and to get the muscle memory going. The training captains ensured that all the correct procedures were followed, and these checks were carried out on regularly scheduled flights.

During one of those trips—into Halifax as I remember—I solved the mystery of the "What happens if you extend the speed brakes when the flaps are at 15°?" question that I had asked my instructor on my first trip in the DC-9, and where he had replied "it crashes!" Fortunately, in our case it didn't "crash."

On the downwind leg to land, I said to the captain who was in the right seat, "It seems to be taking a lot of power to maintain the altitude!" A quick check revealed that the speed brake lever was fully extended and that there was 15° of flap. How that had happened I do not know. I gently retracted the speed brakes, and everything went back to normal. That was it, we didn't crash, the mistake was never made again, and the mystery had finally been solved.

I officially received my "fourth stripe" as captain, and it wasn't long before I was called to fly a trip from Toronto to Sudbury and back.

I showed up at the airport and met my first officer; I was very happy to see that he was a familiar face. Also, I knew that he was very experienced. I flew the first leg to Sudbury. They had great cheeseburgers there so I grabbed a quick one and ate it onboard to make sure that we would be on time for the trip back.

The first officer flew the trip back to Toronto. The weather had deteriorated in Toronto to a 400-foot ceiling, and given that the wind was from the east, we were assigned to land on runway 06 left. The best landing approach available in those days was a "back-course ILS" which provided lateral guidance but no vertical glide path guidance for the approach to land. The rate of descent was estimated with consideration given to the reported wind and then translated to elapsed time and rate of descent. So, you used a stopwatch and flew the rate of descent using the vertical speed instrument.

Once we got to 400 feet, we either landed or did a go-around. In this case, the ceiling was right on the limit. For some reason the approach controller kept us quite high until the last minute when he finally cleared us for the back course approach to runway 06 left. I was uncomfortable, since stabilized approaches were the norm, and this approach was not stabilized at all.[12] I expressed my opinion to the experienced first officer, and he replied, "No problem, we will be ok."

---

[12] Approaches where the airspeed and rate of descent were both steady.

I watched as the descent rate through 4,000 feet go to 2,000 feet per minute down as he desperately attempted get to the proper altitude at the outer marker. We were high and fast by the marker. This was not good! I quickly ordered, "Go around!" He immediately applied full power and we went around. He then flew a successful, stabilized approach and landed. And that dear reader, was my welcome to the world of command decisions! I had just made my first critical decision as a captain.

I loved the DC-9 and flew it for a total of sixteen years. It was a great airplane with some fun flying. I flew throughout Canada, the US, and the Caribbean with most of my flights in the Maritimes. They were long days and sometimes quite exhausting. So much so, that I developed the ability to nap in the cockpit in between turnarounds.

As soon as we had the engines shut down, I would recline the seat back, put my feet up, and totally relax, going into a light sleep mode. I would be totally oblivious to the banging and crashing of the loading of the galley and all the conversations going on. There was a distinctive snapping sound when they unlocked the front door to close it. At that point, I'd immediately wake up, straighten the seat back, and call for the engine start checklist. It is a skill I developed that I still use today!

INTUITION AND A CLOSE CALL

On September 17, 1979, Flight 680 from Boston to Yarmouth, Nova Scotia had an explosive depressurization while climbing through 20,000 feet. The fuselage aft pressure bulkhead failed. In the cockpit, the captain and first officer struggled for control. Miraculously they got the airplane back on the ground in Boston.

I flew a flight to Boston just after the incident and persuaded the station personnel to drive me over to the hangar which housed the damaged DC-9. The damage was much more serious than I had envisaged. The tail-cone was missing but so was the aft pressure bulkhead and most of the rear washrooms. They had all been sucked out. In fact, a flight attendant had been almost sucked out as well before she was grabbed by passengers to keep her in the airplane. Passenger oxygen masks were all deployed, ceiling panels were missing, and insulation was lying everywhere. The cockpit door was blown off its hinges and there was raw insulation all through the cockpit. Basically, it looked like a bomb had gone off.

I flew back to Halifax for a layover and then woke up early in the morning for a flight to Toronto. It was still early morning when we arrived at the airport. We went over the flight plan and boarded the aircraft. I reviewed the logbook and checked for discrepancies. The three red stamps and inspection signatures were there which certified that the aft pressure bulkhead had been checked and that it was free of cracks as per the critical maintenance directive.

But the picture in my mind of that aircraft was still there. I said to the first officer, "I'm going back to check the tail for cracks." I went to the back, removed the aft pressure bulkhead door, stepped into the tail cone area, and turned on the light. I turned around to face forward and started checking for cracks around the doorway using a flashlight.

I couldn't see much because the insulation was glued to the bulkhead. So, with both hands, I ripped it off and there they were. Cracks! They were easily visible because of the nicotine stains from the cigarette smoke that had seeped through them. Who would have ever thought that smoking would provide such a benefit?

I returned to the cockpit and called maintenance. They showed up promptly. Fortunately, an engineer from Douglas, who had investigated the Boston incident was in a hotel close by. He was called to the airport and about an hour later he showed up. I explained the problem to him. He went to the rear of the aircraft on his own and we waited for his return. It took quite a while. When he returned, he was white as a sheet! "This airplane is not going anywhere," he said. We flew the airplane to Montreal for immediate repair. The flight was unpressurized at 10,000 feet and only the crew was onboard.

STILL A FIGHTER PILOT AT HEART

At one point I sort of combined my aerobatic experience with the DC-9 simulator sessions. The simulator to me was a check on whether I was doing ok, so I would never study beforehand. After all, I never studied before I flew a normal passenger flight. All flights were a challenge for me.

One of the exercises was to fly 45° bank turns to headings as specified by the instructor, while maintaining altitude within fifty feet. "Ok Gordy, give me a 45° bank turn to the left and roll out on a heading of 090 degrees," the instructor would say.

"Ok," I would reply, "Would you like that upright or inverted?"

In some cases, they'd respond, "Inverted? All right then!" I would roll the sim upside down and push it around to the required heading. This led to more aerobatics, including loops over runway 06R in Toronto and rolls on takeoff.

"Cleared for takeoff and give me a roll after takeoff," was one clearance I received. I took off, we got the gear up, and I rolled the sim in the climb as requested. Art Lindop, who was older than me, was the fellow in the right seat. He said, "Hey, can I try that?"

The instructor re-set the sim to the takeoff position. Art took control, took off, called for gear up, started the climb, and then started the roll. About halfway through the roll, I hit him in the arm and said, "Art, we're going to die!" The sim went into the ground upside down, a smoldering wreck. The sim was reset to the takeoff position, and I resumed the ride. Rolls after takeoff were not for everyone.

In the 70's and 80's we had some horrendous traffic back-ups getting into John F. Kennedy International Airport (JFK) in New York City. On one occasion while flying in a holding pattern east of Kennedy, I thought it might be a good idea to practice my 45° bank turns. Maybe I was missing my old Starfighter. After all, I reasoned, we were flying in solid cloud, and no-one would know the difference. Besides, I could do them quite smoothly.

I was doing quite well after several turns in the holding pattern when the cockpit door opened.[13] The flight attendant sort of clomped weirdly into the cockpit and said, "Captain there seems to be

---

[13] A holding pattern is a maneuver designed to keep an aircraft within a specified airspace while waiting for further clearance from air traffic control (ATC). It's often used during times of congestion at an airport, poor weather conditions, or other situations that require delaying an aircraft's arrival or departure.

something wrong. I am feeling quite heavy and it's hard to walk!"

It seems that the extra one quarter of applied g-force that my nice smooth turns were affecting the cabin crew's ability to walk about the cabin. I had never thought about that.

So, that was the last time I did that.

THE DIGITAL AIRLINE PILOT

I flew as a DC-9 captain until 1990 at which point I transitioned to being a digital airline pilot. I was one of the first pilots to fly Air Canada's Airbus A320s.

The first Air Canada Airbus A320 course was held April 1990 in Miami, Florida at the Airbus facility, and I was there. It was quite an experience. The Airbus philosophy was much different than the existing conventional flying philosophy. So much so that I remember being told, "Just forget everything you have ever learned about flying and you will do just fine." I was both shocked and apprehensive.

The biggest change was the fly-by-wire system which utilizes a sidestick control instead of the traditional control column. There are two sidesticks. When you move one sidestick. The other one does not move. Normally, when one control column moves so does the other control column—that way you can immediately see control inputs being used by the other pilot. This is valuable information to have.

Bear in mind that I am describing the transition from one time-honoured and established philosophy to another entirely different way of doing things—by people who had very little experience with this new philosophy. It was a case of the blind leading the blind. Today, this philosophy is well accepted and has become normal. In 1990 it was something right out of science fiction. The bottom line is this—I found the transition difficult. And I wasn't the only one to have those sentiments.

Our worries about the Airbus philosophy had already had serious precedence. I remember watching the video of Captain Asseline, chief of Air France's A320 training program, landing an A320 in the middle of a French forest on June 26, 1988. The plane crashed while making a low pass over Mulhouse–Habsheim Airfield as part of the Habsheim Air Show. The crash sequence occurred right in front of several thousand shocked and horrified spectators.

Normally a pilot would not attempt to fly an aircraft so close to stall speed with the engines at flight idle (minimum thrust setting in flight). However—here the pilots flew the aircraft below its normal minimum flying speed because the purpose of the flyover was to demonstrate that the aircraft's computer systems would ensure that safe flight would always be available.

Bad plan it would seem! That tragic decision left three fatalities and fifty injuries in its crumpled wake. Captain Asseline was later sentenced to ten months in prison and ten months' probation for manslaughter. Now, back in Miami, they wanted me to forget everything that I had learned about flying!

My stress meter was off the charts. I was under a lot of pressure to successfully pass the final ride, as I will detail in another chapter. The company I had founded, Ultimate Aircraft Corporation, had just been forced into bankruptcy. Sandy and I had also been forced into personal bankruptcy due to being guarantors for the company. We were in the process of losing our house and all our RSPs when Sandy's mother, Blanche, passed away on Easter Sunday, April 15, 1990. Now I was needed at home for the funeral.

I didn't want to leave the Airbus course, given the problems that I was having with it, so I worked out a solution. I approached the chief pilot, who was scheduled for the first check ride, and I asked him if I could do the first check ride instead because I was needed at home for the funeral. He agreed. To help pull the plan together, the family delayed the funeral by a day.

Airbus A320. Photo used with permission.

Two nights before the scheduled check ride, I awoke at about 3:00 a.m. with severe chest pains; it was utter agony that would not go away. I dressed, went downstairs, got on my bike, and peddled to the hospital several blocks away. I described my symptoms to the doc. They immediately put me in ICU, wired me up, and got the paddles out. There was another fellow in the same room with me who was dying.

They performed a myriad of tests, and I was still lying there at 9:00 a.m. when a doctor finally came by. He announced that I had severe heart problems, probably angina, and that I should immediately see my doctor at home. He prescribed nitroglycerin tablets and said to take them if the pain returned. I returned to the hotel on my mountain bike. I did not pedal very fast.

I flew the final check ride as scheduled, with the nitroglycerin tablets squirreled away in my shirt pocket. Of course I told no one about my little problem. I figured that if I was going to go, then this was as good a time and place as any. Fortunately, I didn't have to use the nitroglycerin tablets. After we finished the simulator ride, I said to my instructor, "Well, I guess it's over. There is no way I passed that ride! It was awful!" Then, to both my shock and delight he said, "You

Air France A320 crash site. Photo courtesy Bureau of Aircraft Accident Archives.

did just fine! If you think your ride was bad, you should have seen the inspector's ride—his was really bad!"

The next day I returned home for Blanche's funeral. There was a small reception at our house and two of my friends who were doctors were there. I explained what had happened in Miami and about the nitroglycerin pills. They had lots of questions. I told them that it was a puzzle because that same day I had put in two hours on my mountain bike with a 150 bpm heart rate. Both docs agreed that it must have been stress that caused the pain, not angina like I had been told.

With training complete, I flew the A320 for five years throughout North America and the Caribbean. I quite enjoyed the flying once I discovered that it was just another airplane. It was possible to turn off all the magic and just fly it as you would any "normal" plane. For a while though, pilots were frequently heard to say, "What's it doing now?"

I am a firm believer in "flying the airplane" which to me means manipulating the controls or "hand flying." Disconnect the autopilot and the auto throttles. Turn off the flight directors. Try to feel the airplane and develop actual flying skills. A visual, hand-flown approach should be simple—not an emergency procedure! I saw some wild visual approaches while flying the A320 in those early days. In fact, I even had a first officer once nervously ask me, "Can you do that?" after I had disconnected the auto-throttles for a hand flown approach.

It did take some getting used to, since, as noted, there is no physical feedback from the controls with the Airbus sidestick. But it really didn't take that much time to fully understand the airplane and to merge the old experience with the new technology.

FROM AIRBUS A320 TO AIRBUS A340

Air Canada took delivery of their first A340 on June 15, 1995. When they decided to start operations with the Airbus A340, they were faced with a tremendous training schedule as pilots bid according to seniority to the various positions available. The obvious choice for a home base for the A340 was Toronto, but the retraining costs would have been horrendous. The decision was made to base the A340 pilots in Winnipeg.

At the time, I was a senior pilot on the A320, so when there were openings in the Winnipeg base, I bid in as a senior captain. Most Winnipeg pilots bidding on the A340 were from the DC-9 or Boeing 727 aircraft. They thus lacked experience flying larger aircraft on overseas routes. The Airbus facility in Miami was again used as the training facility for the A340 conversion course.

Just as I had experienced problems five years previously on my A320 conversion, the Winnipeg group of pilots experienced problems converting to the A340. This became very apparent when the number of failures recorded during the final simulator ride turned out to be quite high. In fact, the course eventually became known as the "Miami Mess." It even required a visit from the director of flight operations to sort the "Mess" out.

Some pilots were throwing up just before the final ride due to fear; the first officer that had been assigned to me was particularly worried. I calmed him down by telling him that we would be just fine

Airbus A-340. Photo © Gary Gentle.

if he ignored all the "chatter" from his friends and just concentrated on the procedures that we were practicing.

Our turn for the final ride came. There was an extra observer in the simulator to monitor exactly what was going on. The ride went beautifully and there were no problems—that is until the final approach which was being flown by the first officer.

As we approached the decision height, I called "100 above" but I did not get the correct response from him. He then mumbled something, and I said immediately, "Go around," which he did! There were gasps from behind us. What happened? Why had the go around occurred?

Once we had the go around in hand and the proper procedures had been carried out, I asked the first officer what the problems had been and what it was that he had been trying to say. He said that he wasn't sure, and it was confusing, but the picture that he had been getting on the flight director had not been right. The ground had seemed to be coming up too soon. We called the tower (the simulator operator) and asked for the altimeter setting. It was correct so we wondered what the problem could be. There was now quite a bit of activity and a discussion between the instructor and the operator of the simulator. Suddenly, there was an exclamation, "Oh Shit!"

Somehow, the simulator airport altitude had been set for Toronto (568 feet) instead of Ottawa (374 feet). If we had continued the approach indicated, we would have crashed inexplicably. No one would have known why we crashed, and we probably would have failed the final check ride.

In the end it was a good lesson. If there is any confusion whatsoever, go around! That sounds like good advice in any aspect of life.

INTERNATIONAL TRAVEL ON THE A340s

Air Canada leased two A340s for flights to Japan for the first year or so. The only route we flew was Vancouver to Osaka, Japan and return. The pilots were based in Winnipeg and they were deadheaded to Vancouver for a layover so that they were in position to take the flight to Osaka the next day. On the return from Osaka, they would layover in Vancouver and deadhead[14] home to Winnipeg the following day. The pairing of those flights lasted four or five days.

Sandy and I were living in Bermuda at the time (as I will detail in another chapter), and I would commute to Vancouver via Toronto from Bermuda, layover in Vancouver, do the flight to Osaka, and then go back to Vancouver before returning to Bermuda through Toronto. That trip would take five or six days, and generally I did it twice per month. I was a senior pilot on the A340, and this allowed me to pick and choose the flights that best fit my schedule.

Due to the length of the flights, we had an additional first officer who served as a relief pilot. This enabled us to rest in an assigned business class seat or in the bunk room equipped with two bunks. However, the bunk room's location left much to be desired. Situated next to the forward galley, it was a hub of noise—from the clanging of galley carts and dishes to the loud conversations of the flight attendants. The final straw was the flight attendants' spring-loaded seat which was attached to the bunk room wall. Every time an attendant rose from the seat, it would snap back against the wall with a loud bang. This was like being inside a drum. The constant anticipation of this disturbance made it difficult to sleep.

There was sufficient layover time in Osaka to do some touring. High on my tour list was to visit Hiroshima. Since I had been in the nuclear delivery business in the RCAF during the 1960s, I wanted to see the actual devastating results of a nuclear bomb.

I travelled there by the Hikari Shinkansen "bullet train" which covered 400 km in about an hour and a half. The city then was like any other modern Japanese city. I spent the day touring the site of the blast and the museum. It was a very moving life experience. I recorded it by painting some watercolours on site. Painting was a hobby that I had taken up about a year earlier.

When in Osaka, I preferred to avoid the Japanese Flight Planning Centre so I often sent the first officer and the relief pilot to retrieve the flight plan. However, on one trip I felt it was necessary, since there were two typhoons swirling around out in the Pacific Ocean. I was

---

[14] When a person is paid to fly so that they can reach another airport, but they aren't technically on active duty.

Hiroshima, watercolour by Gord.

pretty sure that to be a Japanese dispatcher one of the requirements was that you smoked—a lot! We arrived at the Flight Planning Centre to find everyone smoking up a storm. It was difficult to breathe, so I wanted to make this fast.

I was quickly briefed on the route and this was followed by a briefing on the weather which included the locations of the typhoons. I asked, "Where are the typhoons located, in relation to the planned route?" The planner overlaid the route map on the weather map, paused, and then said in a stereotypical accent, "Oh, BAD RUCK!" I changed the route that he was planning, and as a result we had an uneventful flight to Vancouver.

For the first two years we only flew to Osaka but starting in year three there were some great Air Canada routes on the A340. Besides North America and the Caribbean I flew to Tel Aviv, London, Frankfurt, Delhi, and Hong Kong. Hong Kong was particularly interesting since we operated into Kai Tak Airport.

Sleepers on the Bullet Train, watercolour by Gord.

Water was on three sides of Kai Tak. Kowloon City's residential apartment complexes were to the north-west and 2,000-plus foot mountains were to the north-east. We could not fly over the mountains because this would have forced us to lose altitude too quickly for the final approach. What we had to do instead was fly above Victoria Harbour and Kowloon City. En route we would pass north of Mong Kok's Bishop Hill.

Once Bishop Hill was passed, we would fly towards Checkerboard Hill with its large red and white checkerboard. Once the Checkerboard was sighted, we then had to make a 45° right-hand turn—at low altitude. After this came a short final approach and touchdown. If that wasn't difficult enough, it was even more challenging if there was a strong southwest wind blowing.

One very memorable trip was to Delhi through London. Delhi was the most difficult city to get a breath of fresh air in. The thick smoke was from the funeral pyres. My November 28, 1998 watercolour impression of Delhi is on page 121.

On the flight back from London to Toronto, it came about that my lovely wife, Sandy, ended up occupying the first officer's seat for about three hours. We were about 30° west, (middle of the Atlantic) when the cockpit door suddenly opened. The in-charge flight attendant rushed in. "Captain, we have your first officer on the floor in the galley. He passed out. Should we give him oxygen?" I replied, "Yes, please do, and keep me up to date."

It was a full flight plus there were two "cons" (passengers who were employees and/or their families) on the flight deck and one in the bunk. I asked if there were any pilots travelling on the flight, but the answer finally came back "*no*". Well, I knew of one extra pilot on board. Sandy had upwards of one hundred hours experience on an Aeronca Champ and a Clipped-wing Piper Cub. I said to the in-charge flight attendant, "I am drafting my wife Sandy to sit in the right seat for the remainder of the flight. Do you have any objections?"

Airbus A340 and the Checkerboard landing at Kai Tak, Hong Kong.
Photo © Daryl Chapman.

The answer was "No," so we proceeded. In the meantime, my first officer, who was incapacitated, was moved into the bunk. I advised air traffic control of the situation and declared a precautionary "Pan" emergency which gave us priority over other aircraft for landing. Sandy took her seat as the first officer. We went over how she could help monitor the radio and how she could help ensure that communications were clearly understood. I gave her instructions on how to read the computer messages to me if an emergency developed.

It was only when I was beginning the descent for landing that my first officer came back up to the flight deck. We discussed how he felt, and we concluded that he was ok to sit in the right seat again. The landing was uneventful. Sandy never did get a paycheck for her three hours of A340 flying time.

Delhi as seen from the hotel room, watercolour by Gord.

Sandy and I with my First Officer and friend on our way to Delhi.

The Tel Aviv five-day layover was one of my favourites. There was just so much to do and see. On several occasions I rented a van and took my flight and cabin crew all over Israel. We travelled to Caesarea, Bethlehem, and the Sea of Galilee. We swam in the Dead Sea and visited Masada quite a few times. I even brought my golf clubs on several trips.

My daughter, Stephanie, accompanied me on one memorable trip to Tel Aviv. Steph was used to sitting in the jump seat and was very aware that no extraneous conversation was allowed on the flight deck.

So, it was with great hesitation, as we were taxing out for takeoff in Toronto, when she said, "Dad?"

"YES?"

"I smell smoke!"

Immediately, everyone on the flight deck began madly sniffing the air; the consensus was, YES, we could all smell smoke. I taxied back to the departure gate, shut down the engines, and began looking for the source of the smoke. It didn't take long to find it. It was in the forward galley behind one of the ovens. When the passengers had been boarding, one of the flight attendants had been ripping off part of the boarding passes and setting them on top of one of the galley carts. They had somehow been pushed to the back and fallen behind the oven where they had become lodged against a heating element. Then they had started to burn. It wasn't long before we were on our way to Tel Aviv once again.

Once in Tel Aviv, Stephanie couldn't get over the visual remnants of war and how the city was so bustling and alive. It was a series of revelations for her to discover that you couldn't buy a cheeseburger (because eating meat with dairy was not kosher), that the hotel did not have a thirteenth floor, and that the elevators did not work on Saturdays (the Sabbath). I rented a van, loaded up the crew and Stephanie, and we spent several days touring.

One day we explored Jerusalem. Stephanie fondly recalls:

> It was quite an adventure! We walked with an Arab gentleman, who happened to be married to a Jew. He was smooth, confident, and gave us an incredible history lesson while tracing the path of Jesus's crucifixion. We even met the custodian of the Church of the Holy Sepulchre.
>
> The vibrant market with its unique smells and sounds, the fascinating Wailing Wall, and sharing lunch with our new friend added to the richness of the day. We captured moments with soldiers at the entrance, turning a photo into a watercolour memory.
>
> When the day concluded, our "new friend" escorted us to a parking lot, initiating a negotiation for his services. He demanded $250 US cash, but we only had a total of $125. Tensions rose, he called my dad a heathen, and when he revealed he was armed, panic set in. We somehow managed to convince him that was indeed all the cash we had; he had no choice. Take it or shoot us. He took the money, and we were out of there in a flash.

Stephanie remembers the following day:

I rode a camel with the nomads. We were on our way to the Dead Sea, and I asked you to pull over. It was just us and the nomad, the camels, and his leather wares he was selling. A seemingly routine stop turned tense when a family with a son—about four years old—arrived a few minutes after us. They parked on the side of the road, behind our van, and got the child out of the car. Then the husband walks around to [the] passenger side door, reached into [the] glove box, pulled out a handgun and tucked it into the front of his pants. I remember thinking: holy shit!

The Dead Sea swim was an unforgettable experience with its soft, buoyant water. Masada, despite the scorching heat, left us in awe with its clever water management, architecture, and breathtaking views.

Stephanie's last reflection was on leaving Israel:

They separated me from you, and I was directed to go through a separate customs /immigration. I was nervous. You told me don't be surprised if they interview you two or three times, you'll be fine. By then I was terrified! You reassured me and said, everything will be fine, I'm the captain and this flight will not be leaving without you, I promise. As intimidating as it was, all went smoothly, and I was soon headed to the aircraft for our

Wajeeh Y. Nuseibeh
**Custodian and Door-Keeper
of the Church of the Holy Sepulchre**

Tel. Resid. 02/6285910
Church 6282025   *Jerusalem*

flight home. What an incredible trip it turned out to be; I will never forget it.

Yes, we had some exciting adventures that layover, not the least of which was our visit to Jericho located in the West Bank. We drove into the middle of Jericho and spotted a wall mural of Yasser Arafat on the side of a building. The crew wanted a picture of themselves standing in front of the mural. I stayed in the van. As they were assembling, I was watching a group of men across the road at a café. They seemed to be upset and were looking our way. Now they were getting out of their seats.

I realized that several of the girls had shorts on, something not tolerated in Jericho. I yelled, "Everyone in the van—now!" We managed to pull away just in time. I headed for what I thought was the road out of Jericho—but it wasn't. We got stuck behind a slow-moving

Jerusalem gates, Stephanie and friends, watercolour by Gord.

truck; the worst part was that we were right beside a PLO training camp loaded with armed soldiers. It seemed to go on forever. Finally we got past the truck and out of Jericho without incident.

THE FINAL YEARS WITH AIR CANADA

We took delivery of the Airbus A330 in October 1999, and I flew it a few times. It was a much better performer than the A340. I must admit that I found out "how much better" on one short trip from Montreal to Ottawa with about twenty passengers on board on a cold day. Normally we used a reduced thrust takeoff if conditions permitted. In this case I could not resist a full thrust takeoff using runway 28. The takeoff roll was only about 2,000 feet and the climb out attitude reminded me of my old CF-104 Starfighter flights.

I enjoyed the senior captain position on the A340/330. However, I made the decision to bid onto the Boeing 747-400 because I simply wanted to fly the Queen of the Skies before I retired. Seniority took second place to bragging rights and the desire to fly the biggest airliner in the world was overpowering.

I am so glad that I made the decision to spend my last two years with Air Canada flying the Boeing 747-400. I am asked all the time, "What was it like to fly?" My answer is, "Beautiful, and just like a very large Piper Cub." The biggest difference is taxiing. You put the yellow taxi line under you instead of off-set to the right because your eyes are thirty-two feet above the taxiway (height of a three-story building).

Looking back now, the 747-400 and the CF-104 are my two favourite airplanes: one is the biggest and the other is the fastest.

I retired from Air Canada on February 1, 2002, because I had reached the mandatory retirement age of sixty. I had given a total of thirty-five years, eight months, and twenty-three days of service. The mandatory retirement age for airline pilots has since been changed to sixty-five. I realize now that some depression set in after I had to give up my airline career. I did not even consider flying again for seven years.

Airbus A330. Photo used with permission.

Boeing 747-400 combos, photo © Gary Gentle.

Abstract watercolour sketch I did to sum up my feelings at a difficult time.

"SANITY 1" THE SKYBOLT

Lamar Steen with his Skybolt, a photo given to Gord by Lamar.

Captain Lloyd Windh and I were experiencing one of those occasional lulls of flight whilst traveling between Toronto and Winnipeg. We were flying a DC-8 during the summer of 1974. The passengers were contentedly munching on snacks and sipping on drinks in the cabin. All was well.

After a sip of his coffee, Lloyd turned to me and said, "Wanna see a picture of the airplane I'm building?"

"You can build an airplane?" I uttered. I was both amazed and impressed. "Sure."

Lloyd rummaged in his flight bag and pulled out a photograph. He smiled and handed it to me. I looked at it and thought to myself What a beautiful aircraft! A thought suddenly soared into my imagination; this might be the answer to what is missing in my life.

It was called a Skybolt, and it had been designed by Lamar Steen, a high school teacher in Denver, Colorado. Hmmm, my inner voice stirred. This looked interesting!

I asked a lot of questions. I did not know that one was allowed to build an airplane! And in one's garage even! Who would have ever expected that such things were going on in basements and garages all over the continent!

We talked about it all the way to Winnipeg, and all the way back to Toronto. I got home to an unsuspecting Sandy, and even before we finally sat down for dinner, I had already shown her the picture. I offered her some rough calculations and told her that I was going to build an airplane in the garage. It would only cost about $8,000 and take about a year. Being such a supportive wife, she said, "Why not? Sounds okay with me." Then we sat down to supper.

It's unfortunate that what we had for dinner that night is now lost to history. In many ways it could be considered a "last supper" of sorts because our lives would never be quite the same afterwards—$8,000? Yeah, sure!

THE BUILD

Sandy and I flew to Denver, Colorado to meet Lamar Steen, designer of the Skybolt, and his wife Dixie. We hit it off immediately. They were really a wonderful, talented, and down-to-earth couple. In 1968, Lamar Steen was a teacher at Denver's Manual High School. He thought his students could learn and apply math, science, and other skills by tackling a challenging real-world project.

Lamar took Sandy and me up on a few familiarization flights, and I flew the airplane from the front seat. We looped, rolled, and pulled a bunch of g's. For me, it really was a case of "love at first flight!"

I both realized and decided that I needed one of these for my mental well-being. We named our Skybolt "Sanity 1." We returned home with a set of plans, and in typical fashion I started the project immediately. When one starts a new project, such as building an airplane from scratch, there are lots of problems to overcome. One of the first problems was the fact that I did not know anything about welding. The fuselage and tail feathers were to be fabricated using 4130 chromium molybdenum alloy steel tubing.

I signed up at the local high school for a grade ten welding class. Halfway through the course we switched to the arc welding portion of the curriculum. I told the instructor that I would rather keep on practicing oxyacetylene welding. He said that if I didn't learn the arc welding process, that I would not be able to receive the diploma. "That's ok with me," I said, "I don't need a paper diploma. I just need to be able to weld thin wall 4130 steel using the torches that I have in my garage."

The various tubes that made up the structure had to be carefully made to fit into a jig. Once the fitting process was complete, then the tubes were tack welded together to form the structure. When the structure was complete, the final welding was carried out, keeping in mind that it had to be square. It was tricky—but I managed.

Another problem was that there were lots of oddly shaped little steel bits that had to be made. They were to be cut first and then shaped into useable parts and fittings. Normally, this required the use of expensive tools and gadgets. I had no desire to invest in expensive tooling, as I was only going to build this one airplane. So—I made a trek around my area to machine shops, and humbly asked if I could rent their equipment. Generally, I received a sly smile and was told, "NO!"

It was a little frustrating, but at last I met an older fellow, a dutchman, who agreed to let me into his shop. He charged me seventy-five cents an hour. Using the plans, I drew all the parts I needed on sheets of 4130 steel, and I then went to his shop to make them. Well—at first, I screwed everything up. I made a real mess of things and beat the hell out of his machines.

He quickly realized what kind of mess I was making of his equipment. He took over and showed me the right way to work the steel. He showed me how to do it more quickly and how to use material more efficiently, and, in the process, how to save his machines. It was a bargain for me—seventy-five cents an hour and experienced instruction thrown in. He turned out to be a huge help in teaching me how to properly work with the 4130 steel.

It took a couple of months of my spare time when I wasn't flying to make most of the fittings. At our home, when guests made queries like "So, what's new?" I would tell them that I was building an airplane. Since it was such an unusual project, they would become very interested.

"Well, I've been at it for a couple of months. Would you like to see it?" There would be a shuffle to the garage, I would proudly turn on the light and lead the guests to a filing cabinet where I would, with great ceremony, withdraw a drawer filled with a myriad of little steel parts. I would beam with pleasure as my friends stood there awe-struck. "That's it? Two months' work?"

"Yep, I'd say. "And I made 'em myself!"

For many months, every spare moment was spent on the airplane. While the fuselage came together in the garage, the wings took shape in the family room. Eventually they would have to be moved into the garage for the fabric covering and the application of the nitrate dope to tighten and stiffen the fabric.

The top wing was twenty-four feet long assembled, and the garage wasn't. I extended the garage by eight feet by building a tar-paper

Gord welding outside the garage.

shack and attaching it to the end of the garage. I moved the garage door to the end of the shack, and I also added heating ducts to the garage so that I could work through the winter. I told my neighbours what I was up to and obtained their collective approval for my "temporary improvement."

It must have been fascinating at times for those neighbours to watch—no doubt with keen interest—the various and sundry fumes arising from the interior of the garage through the exhaust fan. The exotic chemicals and compounds used convinced some of them that the whole thing would disappear in a puff of colourful smoke one day, or that the occupant would soon come stumbling out, overcome by the chemicals within. I was merely painting and doing fabric work on the wings and fuselage.

One of the neighbours was a chemist, and after careful observation he concluded that the place couldn't explode—it was so oversaturated with the stuff that there wasn't enough oxygen left in the air to allow an explosion! Sandy and the kids, mainly to remember what I looked like, would come out to the garage at safe times and help out.

ENGINE AND FINAL TOUCHES

I should mention that Walter Schmidt, a fellow DC-8 first officer, was also building a Skybolt at the same time. He was a "builder's builder" and a solver of all problems. Had it not been for his genius, it would have taken me at least an additional six months to complete the project. I still can't quite figure out how he built his drill press out of an old, discarded cream separator—pure genius! He had a brilliant mechanical and creative mind.

Skybolt upper wing in family room.

Walter and I drove to Bucks County, Pennsylvania in August to pick up our new Lycoming engines from an aircraft parts dealer who had offered us a good deal. Walter was originally from Germany, and he still had a mild accent. During the trip to Pennsylvania, Walter asked me, "Have you ever lost your passport?"

I replied "No, why do you ask?"

"Well," he said, a bit exasperated, "I did, and it is not good if you are German. I had to go and be interviewed. The questions went on and on, then the officer finally said, 'Ok Walter, now raise your right hand, put your left hand on the Bible, and say after me.' I stopped him then and said, 'I can't do that.' The officer asked, 'Why not?' I said, 'I am not a religious person. But I'll tell you what, do you have a Canadian Tire catalogue handy? I have one of those in my hand every day!' "

During the first week of September, the initial rigging of the aircraft took place in our backyard. The bulk of the aircraft was under the patio roof, and the starboard wing and the tail were out in the open but covered with plastic. The tail also hung out over the swimming pool.

On Friday, September 13, 1974, and with the wind gusting to 45 mph, I was busy rushing around securing the plastic that was covering the aircraft. The Ministry of Transport inspector arrived, and he ended up spending four hours crawling all over the aircraft; he checked tolerances and material and construction adequacies. In the end, he certified the aircraft "ready for cover." Whew, what a relief! I guess Friday the thirteenth didn't turn out unlucky after all.

A few days later the aircraft was disassembled. The wings were returned to the family room and the fuselage went into the garage. I must give some credit here: during the building process I recruited Chris Deere, fifteen, my neighbour's son. Chris spent so many hours every day helping me build the airplane that he certainly earned, through his hard work, the title of "Skybolt Crew Chief." His help was invaluable.

Finally, eighteen months after the start of the project, the airplane rolled outside for the first time. It looked very impressive. The neighbours came over to look at it. There it was, all shiny and new with its Lycoming IO-360, 200 hp engine and propeller in place. I was impressed, Sandy and the kids were impressed—and without a doubt the neighbours were impressed. But in some ways, the next part was just as impressive as everything else that had happened with this suburban neighbourhood airplane.

I tied the tail of the airplane to a fire hydrant at the curb and proceeded to run up the brand-new engine. Running up that engine was an amazing experience. We had been living with that thing for a year and a half, and to finally see it out there, tied to that hydrant, and to hear that sound—well, noise really—coming from the engine was rewarding and amazing. Believe me, it really was quite the noise. Unfortunately, the line was drawn when it came to flying the thing off the street of this quiet suburban neighbourhood. The first flight would come later, at a far more appropriate location.

Sanity 1 tied to fire hydrant ready for engine run-up.

(RE) LEARNING TO FLY

The airplane had to be disassembled and towed in pieces to Guelph Airpark where it was reassembled in a T-hangar on the edge of a maple wooded area. Endless hours were spent on the reassembly and final adjustments.

The next big question was—who would fly my Skybolt on the test flight? Who would be capable and competent enough such that I would trust them to handle this most important of flights? Usually, it is not the builder of the machine, and in truth, I wasn't capable of test-flying my eighteen-month-old, raring to go, glossy new family member.

But how could that be? Here we had a competent airline pilot: an ex-RCAF fighter jock who had flown the hottest machine in existence and who now flew a Lockheed L-1011 jumbo airliner as his day job. How could someone, who was so obviously qualified to count

Ready to tow Sanity 1 to Guelph Airport.

Lockheed L-1011, photo © Gary Vincent.

himself in the upper echelons of the aviation community, be unable to capably fly an itty-bitty, little wood, steel, and fabric airplane that he had built with his own hands?

The answer came in two parts: (a) where the wheels were located, and (b) that noisy 200 hp Lycoming engine with its Hartzell propeller. Since I had been flying a great big passenger aircraft, the Lockheed L-1011 Tristar, (a lovely airplane to fly by the way), I was used to rounding out for landing with my eyes about 100 feet above the runway.

My cockpit, an office really, was full of instruments and gadgets; I had tons of high-tech machinery at my disposal, and I basically did everything by remote control. The last time I had flown a taildragger had been more than ten years earlier, and the plane had been an RCAF Harvard trainer.

For those readers who are not overly familiar with airplanes, some explanation is in order. A "taildragger" has the main landing gear up near the front of the airplane and a smaller, steerable tail wheel at the rear. The plane sits on the ground in a nose up, tail down attitude, and this is why it is called a "taildragger." The other type of landing gear configuration, as seen on most modern airplanes, is called "tricycle gear." The main wheels are located slightly behind the

My tail-dragging biplane Sanity 1.

center point of the airplane (the center of gravity) while a steerable "nose wheel" is situated at the front.

This type of arrangement is much more stable on the ground while taxiing, and it allows the pilot more control and visibility. Taildraggers require much more control awareness and input from the pilot than a tricycle geared airplane does. Although an experienced taildragger pilot can control his airplane just as safely as he can a tricycle geared airplane, it is undoubtably an exciting, if not downright foolish, exercise to go cold turkey into a taildragger with nothing but tricycle gear experience.

As mentioned, the propeller was the second compounding factor. An airplane that is propeller-driven is subject to "torque effect". When a propeller is spinning, any force applied to it acts at 90 degrees in the direction of rotation. In other words if the propeller is spinning anti-clockwise, as seen from the cockpit, and the tail is raised, the nose of the aircraft will swing to the left.

This factor's impact is at its strongest at takeoff when propeller rotation is at maximum. That energy tends to force the airplane to swing its nose off centre and if left uncontrolled will cause a quick and exhilarating trip off the runway. The rudder, which is controlled by your feet, is used to keep the airplane straight. Jet aircraft are not affected this way as they do not have propellers.

A tricycle geared airplane is less squirrelly on takeoff since the nose wheel acts as a stabilizing resistance to the propeller torque due to its position near the front of the aircraft. So, to conclude, I was not particularly anxious to strap on a feisty, lightweight, tail-dragging biplane simply for the purposes of macho bravado—especially since I had built the damned thing myself. I knew I couldn't just climb in and go. If I had done so and pulled it off, it would have been great. But if I had done it and damaged the airplane, well, let's not go there!

When I know I am getting in over my head I normally seek help. I got a friend, Fred Thompson, to check me out in his Cessna 120 as it had a tailwheel. Fred is a wonderful guy and I really appreciated it that he had taken it upon himself to check me out in his airplane.

We went out to Malton Airport (now Toronto Pearson International Airport) where it was stored and we did a walk-around inspection. Then came the briefing. Fred noted that the left brake wasn't working too well but that it wasn't anything to worry about; he just felt that I should know about it. (It may have been nothing for Fred to worry about, but I was sure that I wasn't going to be able to fly the airplane without it.)

Here I was, getting out of a Lockheed L-1011 and into this bitty, little Cessna, which was a wild animal on the ground as far as I knew, especially with a useless left brake. I just knew something would happen!

Fred had a good amount of taildragger time and was vastly experienced as a pilot. He convinced me that it would be all right. We taxied out to runway 32 (yes, dear readers, there was a day that you could fly a Cessna 120 out of Toronto International). The run-up went fine, the brakes held okay, and we were ready to go flying. The tower cleared us for takeoff.

Well, I applied the power to takeoff on that huge runway. That's when this vicious little airplane decided to dart off for the edge of the pavement! The runway was 250 feet wide; someone who had known the airplane would probably have been able to get it airborne within just those 250 feet. But there I was—heading for the weeds.

It just got away from me! The tower called and asked if we needed any assistance while Fred frantically tried to regain control. I couldn't help it; I just broke out laughing it was so funny. Fred got the airplane back on the runway and, after declining the tower's offers of assistance, continued the takeoff. By now I had regained some of my composure and we decided that my learning might be enhanced away from the distractions of a busy international airport.

We headed for Brampton, a small rural airport about twelve miles away. I took the controls on the way up to Brampton and when we got to the field, we joined the circuit for runway 14. Then Fred told

Fred Thompson's Cessna 120. Photo © Fred Thompson.

me he wanted me to land there! It was about one-tenth the size of the runway at Toronto; it looked like a damn sidewalk! Here I was: an experienced L-1011 pilot who was used to being seated 50 feet above the runway on touchdown; now, I was being expected to land this vicious little taildragger on a piece of sidewalk that wasn't even as wide as the cabin of the airplane that I normally flew!

I thought Fred was just kidding, but I broke out in a cold sweat when he told me to quit stalling and land the thing. This turned out to be the trickiest bit of flying this old fighter pilot had done in a long while. A very humbling experience started to unfold. I just knew that the Cessna would want to turn around and bite itself on the tail as soon as we had touched down—but there was no way out now.

I came in on a nice easy approach, and, with Fred talking me down throughout, I managed an acceptable landing—much to his relief and amazement. I pulled off several competent (more or less) landings on the sidewalk. In doing so, I learned what I had to, both about myself and the taildragger. It was going okay.

Sometime later, we were positioned at the end of the runway; we were ready for another takeoff. All of a sudden, Fred opened the door and stepped out of the airplane.

My eyes opened wide in alarm. "Where the hell are you going?" I croaked.

"You are doing just fine," answered Fred. "Go ahead and take it around a couple of times."

"I'll kill myself. I'll bust your airplane!" I exclaimed.

"Nah, go on," said Fred.

Let us pause for a moment here and reflect upon the situation. I had logged about 4,000 hours in various airplanes by this point. This included the hottest fighter in the world and one of the largest, most unbelievably complex transport aircraft ever built. I was totally at home in them. Yet now, at the side of a rural runway in an airplane that weighed less than one of the wheels of a 1011, some crazy man was telling me to take the thing up in the air by myself.

As I sat there, the thought occurred to me: for eight or nine years I had not flown an airplane by myself. There had always been somebody else in the cockpit with me! I was a product of my environment. I had been removed from making solo decisions. As a first officer I was often being told what to do. I had to fly the same way as everyone else. I was conditioned. So how was I supposed to just leap into the air all by myself—in somebody else's airplane?

I lined up on the narrow runway, took a moment and a breath, and applied full throttle. The little Cessna rumbled down the field twitching a bit from side to side, but I was able to control it easily enough with the rudder pedals under my feet. This became easier once I was airborne. The airplane was a solid flying machine, and I flew it around the circuit with no problem—but I was thinking all the while about the landing to come. On final approach I reduced the throttle and glided toward the runway. The airplane was rock solid all the way down. My concentration was intense as I got closer to the touch-down point. With the ground rushing past in my peripheral vision, I began the flare, pulling the control column back ever so smoothly. "Chirp" went the tires on the pavement, with a tinier "chirp" as the tailwheel touched a split-second later. I had to be alert on the rudders, but it was nothing unmanageable.

It was probably one of the hardest flights I had ever made, even with all my experience. But I am so glad I did it. It felt very good. I was right at home again. This was the something that I had been missing. I had found it again in that Cessna 120 on that hop around Brampton. It started to come back—the magic of it all. I smiled to myself and took off and did it again! Piece of cake! I now had enough confidence to test fly my Skybolt.

SANITY 1 FIRST FLIGHT

With the initial experience in the Cessna 120 under my belt, I did about three hours' worth of high-speed taxiing in the Skybolt at Guelph. It gave me a small feeling for what the airplane was like—at least what it was like to sit in and manipulate the controls.

On June 26, 1975, the Skybolt had its final Transport Canada inspection; it was declared airworthy. On the morning of June 27, I was at the head of the line at the Ministry of Transport offices to apply for my flight permit. By noon, I was westward bound on the freeway for Guelph (yes dear reader, it used to be possible to get things done that fast). By dinnertime, the few remaining snags had been remedied and all was ready. It was now eighteen months since I had begun the impossible. The moment of truth was upon me.

To add to the Cessna 120 time, I had arranged for a few quick circuits in a Citabria first, while the Skybolt patiently sat waiting for me on the ramp. At 8:00 p.m. I strapped into my new biplane Sanity 1 and taxied slowly out to the runway. Bob Little, a friend and ex-RCAF pilot, taxied out with me in a Cessna 172, as he was to act as my chase plane. The final checks were completed and there was nothing else left to do but to fly. I lined up on the centreline and slowly applied full power. The airplane started to move. This was one of the greatest moments of my life!

I got my tail up and accelerated to 100 mph. It didn't take long. When I pulled back on the stick she instantly leapt up at a steep angle. I settled into a normal kind of climb at about 80 mph and 1,200 feet per minute up. It was such a great thrill! The poor old Cessna 172 was left far behind during the climb. When I levelled out, I noticed that the oil temperature was climbing beyond normal limits, so I turned back for an immediate landing on runway 14.

I flew her on to the runway at 80 mph since I had not checked the stall speed performance. It was a bit fast, and some hairiness was added by the onset of a vigorous tail wheel shimmy. There was plenty for my feet to do during the roll-out to keep her on the runway. At 8:30 p.m. the engine cowls came off and the oil lines to the cooler were blown clear. During this process, pieces of rubber came out—the culprits that had been blocking the flow. Everything was buttoned back up. By 9:10 p.m. I was lifting off again, because I wanted to do a stall check and fly slow. I hoped that she wouldn't need to land fast all the time. At 60 mph she stalled in a gentle straightforward manner. I rushed back to the airport to beat the approaching darkness.

This landing was much better at a slower speed, but the tail wheel shimmy was still there (the problem was later solved by replacing the tail wheel). It became dark shortly thereafter and I put the airplane away in my T hangar. A small celebration was in order. I went to bed that night with a grin that remained on my face for about a week.

COMPETITION AEROBATICS IN THE SKYBOLT

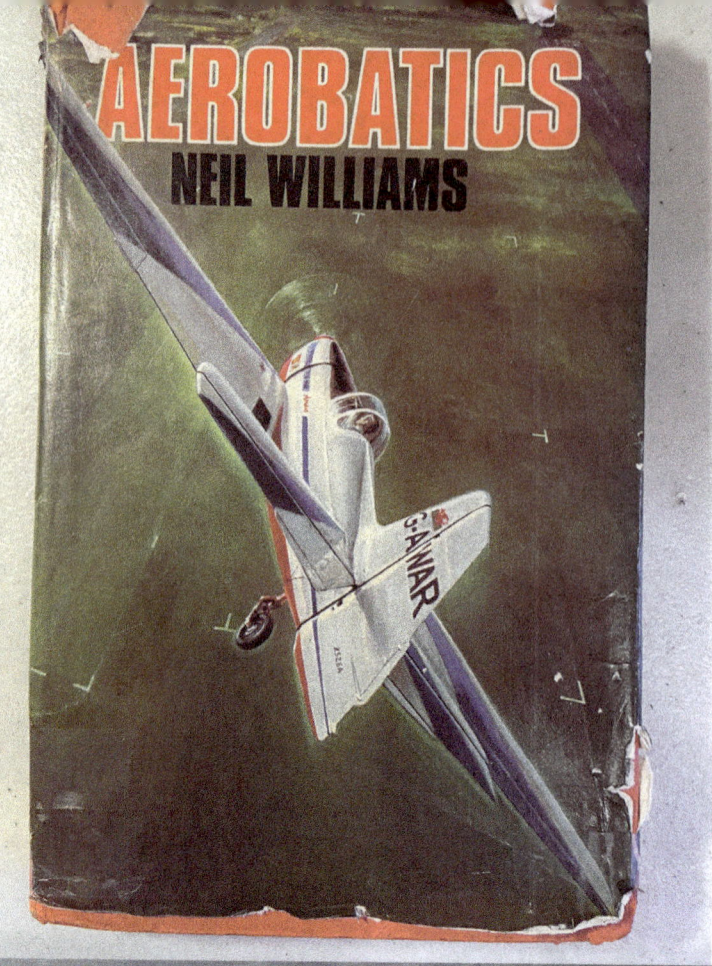

My own dogeared copy of Neil William's book, my aerobatic bible.

My Skybolt, Sanity 1: co-winner of the 1976 Keith Hopkinson Award for best homebuilt in Canada.

During the autumn of 1975, hopefuls for the Canadian Aerobatic Team gathered in Picton, Ontario. They were there to choose their best—those who would compete at the World Aerobatic Championships, which were to be held in the USSR during the summer of 1976.

I showed up there in my Steen Skybolt. I didn't fly—I just watched.

Initially I thought those guys were all out of their minds. They were flying upside down and pushing lots of negative g's. I was soon surprised to discover that it fascinated me. Eventually, I came to the realization that I just had to learn how to do it. But nothing in the RCAF (or Air Canada for that matter) had prepared me for this kind of flying.

I bought a book on aerobatics written by Neil Williams, a British aerobatic champion. I'd sit in the airport coffee shop reading it. Then I'd go fly the Skybolt to experiment with what I had read.

I never did have any formal aerobatic instruction; I'd just go to a safe altitude, scare myself silly, then return to the coffee shop and read the book some more before going out again. I wouldn't recommend this method to anyone; it takes too long, and it can be quite scary! However, I had discovered that "something" that I had been missing. Challenge, excitement, and just plain fun.

GETTING THE SKYBOLT READY FOR AEROBATICS

Transport Canada's flight permit for the Skybolt had a list of restrictions, and one of these was that aerobatics were prohibited. Officially, aerobatics is defined as any maneuver where a change in the attitude of an aircraft results in one of the following: a bank angle greater than 60°, an abnormal attitude, or an abnormal acceleration not incidental to normal flying. In plain language it means that you are not allowed to turn the airplane upside down.

Some people refer to aerobatics as acrobatics, but those people "know not of what they speak!" Here is the difference. It is possible for aerobatic pilots to do acrobatics because they don't need an airplane to do acrobatics. If they were so inclined, they could do a couple of backflips before they climbed into the airplane. Then they would be classified as acrobats. Technically, they could then be called acrobatic, aerobatic pilots. I have never met one of them, but I suppose it is possible. I digress.

The Skybolt was designed to do aerobatics, but within certain limitations. These limitations were accepted in the US where the airplane had been designed. However, they were not accepted carte blanche in Canada. To be allowed to perform aerobatics in Canada, the aircraft had to be put through a test flight program and evaluated by approved pilots and engineers. This was the case back in the 1970s, although I understand that current regulations are not as stringent.

Fortunately, the Experimental Aircraft Association of Canada (EAAC) had already established a technical committee to conduct these evaluations. Two engineers, who also had pilot's licenses, and a qualified test pilot from the National Aeronautical Establishment (a division of the National Research Council) made up this committee:

Bill Roderick, Stan Kereliuk, and Doug Laurie-Lean. They were assigned this duty in my case, and they were based in the south hangar at Ottawa International Airport. All I had to do was deliver the Skybolt to them.

On October 1, 1976, Sandy and I arrived at Ottawa International in the Skybolt. Some flight testing was carried out by the committee over the next couple of days and then we returned to Guelph. Final testing was carried out by Stan Kereliuk from May 7 to 9, 1977 in Ottawa. The flight test report was finalized by the EAAC Technical Committee, submitted to Transport Canada, and approved almost immediately. I was very thankful for the tremendous effort of both the committee and Transport Canada for their sense of urgency.

The first aerobating that I did, legally, was at an aerobatic practice weekend on May 21, 1977. It was a competition without trophies;

Aerobatics Canada in Ontario was very active in 1977.

experience was its only prize. The idea was for new pilots to have an opportunity to participate in something that was like a competition, and to be given competent critiques by judges and experienced pilots. It was a kind of seminar for aerobats, where they would be able to get an idea of their place in the scheme of things. They would be told what they needed to work on, how to improve their performance, how to prepare for future competitions, and other things.

The intensity of true competition might have been missing, but there was plenty of incentive to do your best. The prize was a realistic evaluation of your performance and a clearer understanding of the somewhat complex world of the aerobatic competitor. I had a wonderful time that weekend with the Skybolt and came to the realization that I was going to get serious about competition aerobatics.

TRUST, BUT BE SURE TO VERIFY

By July I considered myself ready—so much so that I entered the advanced category at the Canadian Open competitions at Centralia, Ontario. There were three competitors in the category.

My competitors were both flying the zippy little Pitts Special single seater, and I had the heavier, two seat Skybolt. Once in the air the tension faded, and I went through the routine satisfactorily. I looped and rolled and climbed and dived, and I went from positive to negative g as the maneuver came up on the Aresti card. (This card is based on the Fédération Aéronautique Internationale (FAI) standards document [the Aresti catalog]. The catalog is used to specify the various aerobatic maneuvers that are allowed during an aerobatic competition).

As I curved into land at the end of my sequence, I was a bit tired and sweaty, but quite satisfied. I thought I had done a good job—maybe even beaten somebody. I paced a bit while I waited for the posting of the results. When they were posted, I was third of three. In another other words, I had come LAST in my first ever contest!

I was devastated! However, I was prepared to accept the results. I had flown to the best of my ability, and I was ready to learn from

Open Cockpit Skybolt.

the experience. However, when I realized how close the scores for first and second were, with my score being so much lower, I was left wondering. My total score was only about one third the total of the others and that didn't seem right; I was sure I had done better than that. Something clearly was missing, and I had to find out what.

After the trophies were presented, I asked if I could look at the score sheets to find out what I had done wrong, and to see if I had left something out. I discovered that by some error, the score I'd been given had only included the first page of my score sheets. The last two pages had been forgotten or misplaced when my scores had been added up.

I roughly added up the other two pages and got quite excited as it showed that I had unquestionably placed second and might even have placed first. Then it got a little complicated. I pointed out these new facts to the competition director who was smiling warmly to himself on the success of the event. He did the math and conceded that I had indeed placed first.

The existing first place finisher was from the US. To avoid what might have become an "international embarrassment," the contest director decided to let him take his first-place title home. I changed trophies with the second-place finisher, who was not too happy to now be in last place. On my hangar wall hangs a plaque reading, "1977 Canadian Open Advanced Category, First Runner Up,"—material evidence of my very first competition. There is a note attached: TRUST, BUT BE SURE TO VERIFY!

THE FITNESS OF THE PILOT

In late July of that summer of 1977, Sandy and I flew the Skybolt to Medina, Ohio, to enter the Ohio Open Championships. We were prepared for an enjoyable weekend of competition.

It must have been close to 100°F when we landed at Medina. We were glad to finally be there; the ride had been hot and bumpy and being on the ground was something to be desired. Just as we touched down, the left tire blew. The airplane lurched off to one side and wiped out that side's brake. Then it lurched to the other side, tore off that brake, and left the runway. It had all happened very quickly.

There we sat on the side of the runway at Medina, Ohio, with one flat tire, two busted brakes, and the hot sun beating down. Our day was starting to go sour.

The organizers were as helpful as they could be. They rearranged the schedule so that I could fly in the advanced category as late as possible. This gave me time to make repairs. Cursing and muttering in the humid Ohio air, I wrenched nuts and bolts and changed tires, while covered in grease and sweat. I worked on the wheels and brakes, and occasionally listened—looking skyward as the competition went on around me.

When it was finally all back together in working order, someone handed me the Unknown sequence that I would have to fly. I quickly studied it. Around the same time one of the officials came by and told me that they would help push the airplane to the runway so that I could relax for my flight!

By this time, I was getting frustrated. I know that they were trying to help. But—if their idea of relaxed meant me walking out to the runway while I tried to cram the Unknown sequence into my brain while somebody else pushed my airplane—well, it just didn't go over with me well right then.

I was grimy and dripping with sweat when I was asked by my friend Glenn Biederman, "Are you ready to go Gord?" I nodded, climbed into the hot cockpit and prepared to start up. Glenn looked at me strangely. "You gonna take your parachute?" he asked. I looked back and saw my parachute on the horizontal stabilizer. I wearily climbed out and put it on.

At last,—I was in the air and going through the routine. I was doing a rolling turn when something suddenly came off the floor and flew by my face. It was my navigation supplement book. I grabbed it and stuffed it into my flying suit. While I was still turning and rolling, something else flew by and I recognized it as my wallet. I didn't catch it, and it instantly disappeared.

There was a canopy over the cockpit, so I didn't have to worry about it going overboard, but it must have gone somewhere, I thought! I was hot, greasy, and tired. My wallet containing credit cards, money, and licenses was floating around the airplane. I was not having a good time. As might be expected, I didn't do very well that day.

When I finally landed after the routine, I just walked away from the airplane. It was five minutes before I remembered the wallet. I found it in the tail after opening the inspection covers. It was hanging over one of the rudder cables! I didn't take any trophies home from that one. I did, though, take home my wallet, some valuable experience, and a firm and painful lesson in mental preparedness: the fitness of the pilot, mentally and physically, is just as important as the condition of the airplane itself.

ENGINE UPGRADE, ENGINE FAILURE

I learned another important thing from those early competitions: the Skybolt was at an obvious disadvantage when flying against the lighter, more nimble Pitts Special. Some changes had to be made to the Skybolt to get more performance from her.

The season was not yet over. I purchased a 260 hp engine to replace the original 200 hp model. The engine change was completed by

August 29.

The Canadian National Aerobatic Competitions were scheduled for Carp, Ontario on September 18. Intense training filled the next couple of weeks. I tinkered with the new engine on the ground and practiced aerobatics with it in the air.

September 12 was a nice sunny day, and I was up practicing northeast of Guelph. The bugs were out of the new engine and there was time for just practice.

I did a three-quarter loop with a snap-roll on the way down and then shoved the throttle forward for power. Nothing happened. No power! This was a big problem. I was about 1,000 feet above ground and urgently looking for a solution.

I suddenly remembered a little airstrip just off to the left on a diagonal line. I turned left, scanning for the strip; it was difficult to see. I finally spotted it and headed for the fence at the end of the runway, which was just coming into view. I barely managed to get over the fence and I made a very firm landing going up the side of a hill.

I had to stop quickly because, at the last second, a horse appeared out of nowhere, trotting down the centerline of the runway. I got the airplane stopped within about 600 feet. When I got out, the horse was nowhere to be seen. This all happened very quickly; I was just operating on adrenaline.

After the excitement of the engine failure and landing, my energy quickly drained away into near depression. Here I sat in the middle of a field with a dud airplane and the nationals less than a week away. I still had lots of practice to get in. What in hell could be wrong with the engine? It hadn't failed completely; in fact, it was still chugging over at about 800 rpm.

I shut it down and opened the cowling. In short order I found the problem. The throttle linkage had separated; a cotter pin was missing. The throttle was able to open to idle power only. I had either forgotten to put the cotter pin in, or I had not put it in properly during one of my numerous engine adjustments. About this time, I noticed someone sitting on a tractor a couple of hundred yards away and looking back toward me.

I had seen the tractor plowing a field alongside the runway as I had been landing. Since the airplane's engine had been at low power, I suspected that the tractor driver had not heard me land. I waved and beckoned for the farmer to come over, and the tractor turned around and started in my direction. "So, if it isn't the flying chainsaw," the tractor driver said. "Nice of you to drop in."

"Well, I hadn't really planned on it," I replied, "My engine quit and there wasn't any other place to go."

"Oh," said the farmer," before continuing, "Wanna drink?"

"No thanks," I replied, "I gotta get this thing flying again."

"Well, ya don't mind if I have one, do you?" he said, pulling a flask out of his jacket.

"Not at all. Do you have any tools?" I asked.

In short order the tools appeared, and, with the farmer sitting on his tractor sipping whisky, I fixed the throttle connection. In short order I waved to the farmer and took off. I went back to practicing right away and then headed back to the airport. After all, I had to prepare for the national championships.

THE SKYBOLT'S FINAL CHAPTER

When I arrived at Carp, Ontario, to enter the competition, I had put twenty-seven hours on the new engine in twenty days. I entered the most advanced "unlimited" category and I managed to fly to a second-place finish. In the interest of clarity (and honesty), I should point out that there were only two of us competing in the unlimited category. Second place sounds so much better than last place.

I am, as far as I know, the only person to ever fly a Skybolt in an unlimited competition. Some people thought that it wasn't the right thing to do: to enter unlimited at the Canadian Nationals after having only competed twice before, but that's what I felt I had to do to move forward. I just jumped into the world of aerobatics with both feet. I do not regret it.

I had nothing to lose (except the contest), and I needed the experience.

With my son Glen. He was 13 years old at the time.

This level of competition takes a phenomenal amount of effort and energy. To get to the upper levels it takes experience, and experience is only gained by doing. There was no other way I could have done it.

This turned out to be my final competition with the Skybolt. I knew that if I intended to continue competing at that level, I had to have a Pitts Special. Adding power just wasn't going to solve the performance problem. The 260 hp engine was heavier, and the center of gravity had changed. The airplane didn't fly the same; in fact, I had to add about twenty pounds of lead to the tail to off-set the heavy nose to get the thing to fly comfortably.

The lead in the tail made it even trickier to handle on the ground, and really, all that extra weight defeated the purpose of the additional power. It was the design of the airplane that was the obstacle. It was designed for intermediate level aerobatics at best and it was a lot nicer to fly with its original 200 hp engine.

I sold my Skybolt, Sanity 1, to my good friend Mac McGladdery the day after the Canadian National Championships ended. I saw it after takeoff at Carp. It looked like a flying haystack with hay streaming from the wheels and tail—apparently, it had been a hairy takeoff!

I had occasion to fly it one final time at Mac's request. He asked me to retrieve it from Springbank, Alberta where it had just been repaired after a landing accident. Mac had flown it out west and stopped in Moose Jaw. A friend of his had claimed that the brakes were not the proper installation, so he changed them from a remote hydraulic reservoir system to two individual brake reservoirs located on the brake pedals. On the next landing at Medicine Hat, Mac ground-looped the airplane causing significant damage.[16]

I arrived in Springbank, found the aircraft in repaired condition, and set out on the first leg back to Ottawa. My first landing was at Medicine Hat. It was what we call in the business "a very hairy landing"; the machine wanted to ground loop, but somehow, I managed to keep it on the runway. I taxied up to the fixed-base operator (FBO, the firm running the airport), shut the plane down, and discovered the source of the problem—the new brakes!

To apply full brake, you had to extend your foot out and push down, instead of forward which was the normal procedure. When you tried to apply brakes in what you'd think would be the normal way, they simply would not work. It was impossible for the brakes to function normally. This was not a good thing. I determined that they could be fixed by welding on a length of one-quarter inch bolt. Fortunately, I convinced the owner of the FBO to let me use his welding torches to weld up the extensions. I tested out the brake extensions and much to my delight they worked perfectly.

The next day I departed for Regina. It just wasn't meant to be that day. There was an electrical problem, so the radio failed. I needed a radio to get into Regina, so I decided to land at Moose Jaw Municipal. The visibility was not the best, and I was having difficulty finding the airport. So, there I was, no radio, no electrical systems, poor visibility, and getting low on fuel. This all added up to a very bad situation. But it all could be fixed by an unauthorized landing at RCAF Station

---

[16] A ground loop is an aviation term referring to an uncontrolled, sharp turn or pivoting of an aircraft on the ground, often resulting in damage to the aircraft. This phenomenon typically occurs in tailwheel (taildragger) aircraft but can also happen with tricycle-gear aircraft under certain conditions.

Moose Jaw which was easy to find.

I was just north of the field, and I noticed that both runway 29 circuits were full of Canadair CT-114 Tutor jets. These are training aircraft, and they were doing touch and goes. I noted the traffic on the north runway and determined that I could slip in and land right after a Tutor had completed a touch and go. It worked perfectly; I slipped in between Tutors, landed on runway 29R, and exited the runway at the first taxiway.

I taxied for a bit and then the engine quit. The military police (MP) showed up with flashing lights. "You can't land here, sir. You need prior permission to land," he said.

"I understand that sergeant, but I have had an electrical failure and need fuel."

"Sorry sir, you can only land if you have an emergency."

So, I tried again. I said, "Mayday! Mayday! Mayday! I need gas!" I received all the help I needed in very short order.

After several more owners and some very interesting experiences, Sanity 1 is still flying in Syracuse, New York, as of 2024. Philip Stone is the owner.

Sanity 1 now owned by Philip Stone in Syracuse NY. Photo © Philip Stone.

WAC 80 AND LADI BEZÁK

The first FAI World Aerobatic Championships (WAC) were held in Bilbao, Spain in 1960, and a Czechoslovakian pilot named Ladislav (Ladi) Bezák was its winner.

Ladi had worked as a test pilot for the Zlin factory in Czechoslovakia. Zlin was the maker of light two-place aircraft.

With a growing interest worldwide in civilian aerobatics, it was not unusual at the time for governments of many countries to encourage, or at least not discourage, those who had shown an ability to bring glory home in this unique sport. After all, the Cold War was at its height, and rivalries between nations, east and west, were a fact of life.

Ladi obviously was just such a person. He had made repeated requests to the authorities in his then communist nation for an aircraft of his own with which he could practice. He was stolidly refused, although he was permitted to possess aircraft parts.

Inevitably of course, he soon had enough parts. He was then able to assemble a complete aircraft of his own. The authorities seemed unwilling or unable to notice this assemblage of parts flying around in connected formation, with Ladi at the controls. Some form of institutional blindness must have been in effect, I assume.

It was ultimately unfortunate for them that they took no notice of this, because in 1971 Ladi Bezák took these assembled parts, filled with his wife and three sons (it was a two-place airplane) and flew it west to Austria. There are apocryphal stories of low-level dodging of MiG-19 fighters and border defenses but suffice it to say that the Bezák family safely made it to the west unharmed.

In 1979, Ladi was at an aerobatic competition in New York state, and I was there also. I was excited to be able to meet this living legend of the aerobatic world: the first to hold the title of World Aerobatic Champion, the man who invented the spectacular Lomcovák maneuver (it translates as headache), and the daring escaper from behind the Iron Curtain.

Ladi was a brilliant aerobatic scholar; however, the difference between brilliance and insanity is a very fine line! For instance, in the interest of keeping the weight down in his Zlin aircraft, the instruments had been simply painted on the panel. When driving his

Mercedes, he had determined that if he accelerated to one hundred mph, turned off the ignition, allowed the car to coast until fifty mph, and then do it again, he would save on fuel.

I had never realized what it meant to be a "man without a country" until I met Ladi Bezák. At that time, he was living in West Germany on welfare, and he was facing plenty of red tape issues regarding his resident status. He had problems that I had no inkling of at the time. In West Germany he was living as a squatter. He had moved into an abandoned house and lived there with his wife and three sons.

He wasn't short of enemies, either. Someone put sugar in his gas tank a few times and his beloved Zlin was seized and chained up in the UK.

Ladi's escape from Czechoslovakia with his family, 1971.

After meeting him in New York, I wanted to get Ladi to visit Canada; I worked my buns off getting a visa for him. Eventually he was able to come to Canada, and he stayed with us for a while. He taught me a few things, and everything was going fine until his visa was about to expire—then he had to leave the country. I suggested that he apply for a visa extension to allow him to stay a bit longer.

The immigration folks said, "No problem, just sent him back to West Germany," (where he was a resident at the time), "and we'll give him another visa to visit Canada." Somehow, that didn't seem particularly efficient to me. But—if we took him to Buffalo, New York, he could apply for an extension of his visa there—it just had to be done from outside of Canada.

We drove down to Buffalo and entered the USA at the Peace Bridge.

The abandoned house Ladi and his family moved into as squatters.

Ladi's modified oil heater designed to extract all possible heat.

Before leaving Canada, I made sure that we were following all of the rules, and I was assured that there would be no trouble getting back into Canada.

We sat in the office of the Canadian Consulate in Buffalo, New York, from 10:00 a.m. until 3:00 p.m., at which point somebody said, "Bezák?" When he stood up, they took him away. They were not nice about this at all! When Ladi came out, they pointed at me and said, "You, you're next." They wanted to know what I was up to. I said that I wanted to get Ladi's visa extended, so that he could stay in Canada a bit longer. "Why?" they asked.

"Well, he's helping the Canadian Aerobatic Team train for the World Aerobatic Championships."

They got excited: "Aha, he's working in Canada illegally."

"He's not working, he's just giving us advice."

"He's being paid!" they insisted.

"No."

"What do you mean, 'No'?"

"He's not getting anything for doing it."

"Where is he staying?"

"At my place, with my wife and I."

"Is he paying you to stay?"

"No."

They got excited again: "Aha! Then you are paying him with room and board."

"What?"

"He is not entitled to work in Canada. He is helping you and you are paying him by letting him stay for free with you. Therefore, YOU are an accomplice, and aiding in bringing people into the country to work illegally!"

This was not going at all as I expected. What was going on? Why were these bureaucrats putting up such a fuss? What did they have against Ladi? I was confused. Eventually the officials decreed that Ladi could go back into Canada if I promised to put him on an airplane to West Germany at the first opportunity. I agreed and we headed back for the bridge. I had asked the consulate folks to phone ahead to the customs office at the bridge to explain what was happening, and they had agreed to do so. However, when Ladi produced his documents at the bridge, the customs officer stared at it for a moment, looked the two of us over, and motioned, "Over there!"

We were shown into a room and another grilling started. "Tell us what you are doing." I explained to him what had been going on. The officer looked me in the eye. "What is your picture doing on his passport?"

I was totally at a loss. The officer showed me the passport. I saw a well-handled passport with a younger-looking Ladi. There could be a sort of resemblance between us, maybe if you squinted? I replied: "That's not my picture. It's him, only younger."

"Let me see your passport."

"My passport? I don't carry it with me to cross this border. I'm a Canadian citizen."

"You have no way of proving that!"

The guy was right. I was about to get thrown out of my own country. I pulled out every piece of identification I had, and grudgingly, after a phone call to the consulate, the customs officer let us pass.

After Ladi went back to West Germany, Sandy and I and a few others raised a bunch of money and put on a concerted effort to get him back to Canada as a landed immigrant. We even had an apartment for him when he came back, plus an old car that had been donated to him. I placed an appeal in a newspaper article in the Toronto Sun hoping to find Ladi a job, and a couple of Czechs who had a machine shop near Toronto Pearson Airport answered and said that they would hire Ladi as a machinist. I invited them to the house to discuss the situation.

What a strange event I thought, as we swapped stories while sitting on the floor in front of the fireplace. The brothers had both been

MiG-19 pilots in Czechoslovakia in the 1960s and I had been there in West Germany on the other side as a CF-104 nuclear strike pilot at the same time. One of them had been jailed for flying under a bridge in Prague.

The brothers hired Ladi as a machinist and I remember his first day on the job—or almost on the job. We sent him off to work but it wasn't long before he returned. I asked him what the problem was, and he said, "The police would not let me go to work!" I asked him why and he told us that the police said that the car was too noisy due to a hole in the muffler. I told him all that had to be done was to repair the muffler and the police would not bother him. Then came the phrase that we, the entire Canadian Aerobatic Team would grow tired of hearing: "Who pay this?"

Ladi and his son's arrival in Toronto in spring of 1980 with their new visas.

TRAINING THE CANADIAN AEROBATIC TEAM

In early 1980, Ladi Bezák was back in Canada (legally). He took on the job of training the Canadian Aerobatic Team for the world championships which were to be held later that year. It would be a major effort for the Canadians as a team, but there was lots of enthusiasm and boundless optimism. We were prepared to take on the world.

Ladi's training program was intense. I jumped in with both feet and did everything that he said, without argument. I had confidence in this aerobatic master. It turned out to be quite an experience.

Charts of our blood pressures were kept, and what we ate and drank was monitored. They even tried to determine such things as what

The Pitts at the Erin Gliding Club. How it looked at the 1980 World Championships.

the best time of day was for each pilot to train.

Ladi was very tough minded and regimented. When we went somewhere, he would wipe the doorknobs in the hotel rooms with disinfectant so that we wouldn't catch anything. He had us exercising and following his instructions like a military unit. Despite the trappings of strictness imposed on the team, I recognized that Bezák had a brilliant aerobatic mind. His reservoir of knowledge and experience was a valuable source of information for me, and for everyone on the team.

Ladi was almost as free with good advice as he was with orders and restrictions. I was learning an awful lot about the technical aspects of aerobatic flying, and I believed that all the regimentation that went along with it was necessary. I didn't know any other way of going about it, so I gave it all I could. It was a very good try, but for me it all came apart during that sunset flight at the World Aerobatic Championships in August.

1980 WORLD AEROBATIC CHAMPIONSHIPS

I had been feeling so positive about my performance up to the World Aerobatic Championships and I could foresee nothing preventing me from getting into the top ten at least.

The weather had been rainy most of the day and we had been spending our time doing what was known to us as the "Bezák Dance,"—actually a pretty good training exercise. World Championship aerobatic flights take place inside an aerobatic box in the sky that the judges watch. The minimum altitude to be flown is 300 feet.

In the Bezák Dance, the pilot walks around inside this area on the ground which represents the box. You hold your arms out like a kid playing "airplane" and go through the sequence. It helps to visualize things from the inside out, instead of looking at a maneuver from the outside in like you do when you use a model airplane to demonstrate, or when you use your hands.

A total of fifty-one pilots from ten countries flew in the competition, which was held on August 17-30, 1980. The Canadian team consisted of four pilots: Frank Jenkinson, Bill Kennedy, Gerry Younger, and me.

A couple of guys had flown their sequences earlier, but due to the weather the aerial activity had been mostly limited to airshow flying and keeping the spectators from getting too bored.

It looked like the day was going to be a wash out for our team, so some of the guys had started to get into the beer. Suddenly, word came down that we had to provide a member to fly. I was really the only one prepared to go, even though it wasn't my slot on the schedule. It would have been embarrassing for the team not to send someone, and I figured that I was in fine form, so I volunteered.

It was the Unknown sequence; the competitor is given the card a set amount of time before the flight. They have to go through the routine in their mind. Actual practice is not allowed. I studied the sequence and made sure that both I and my Pitts were ready.

With that calm, intense feeling of controlled excitement that one feels at a time like that, I taxied out and took off. Conditions were now perfect; the air was as calm and smooth as it can be on a summer evening. The sun was just down below the earth's rim and a warm glowing light reflected off the clouds around the horizon. I got into position and began the routine.

Everything was going quite well, and it was now about halfway through the entire sequence. At the top of a hammerhead, while still going vertical, I suddenly lost the flow of the sequence and couldn't remember the next manoeuvre. Now this was not normally a major problem because the sequence card is taped to the instrument panel for just such a moment. But, due to the low light of the evening and the location of the card, it was in deep shadow and I couldn't read it. That moment imprinted itself on my mind. To this day I can still put myself in that cockpit and relive that feeling of total helplessness.

My mind scrambled frantically for the next step, and I came up with "do a roll." As I rolled, the light changed and was able to take a quick look at the sequence card. In the feeble light, I saw that I had done the wrong maneuver. In aerobatic competitions, especially world class events, it is not unusual for first and second place scores to be separated by fractions of a point. When a maneuver is out of sequence, it is awarded a zero. I had just zeroed the roll.

It was a major blow to me. The instant I saw the card I knew that I had lost a bunch of points. It had so much of an effect on me that I had to break off and leave the sequence. That cost me another 300 points. At the top of the hammerhead, I was in seventh place with an excellent chance of keeping that position, and even improving on it. But following these errors, I dropped to twenty-first position.

I had been so keyed up all day. I had been going through my mental exercises and the "Bezák Dance." I had been preparing and preparing and preparing. It turned out that I had, in fact, over-prepared. When the moment of truth had arrived, when I had had to call on that something extra—I had drawn a blank.

The aerobatic box in the 1970s. Illustration by Nick Hill.

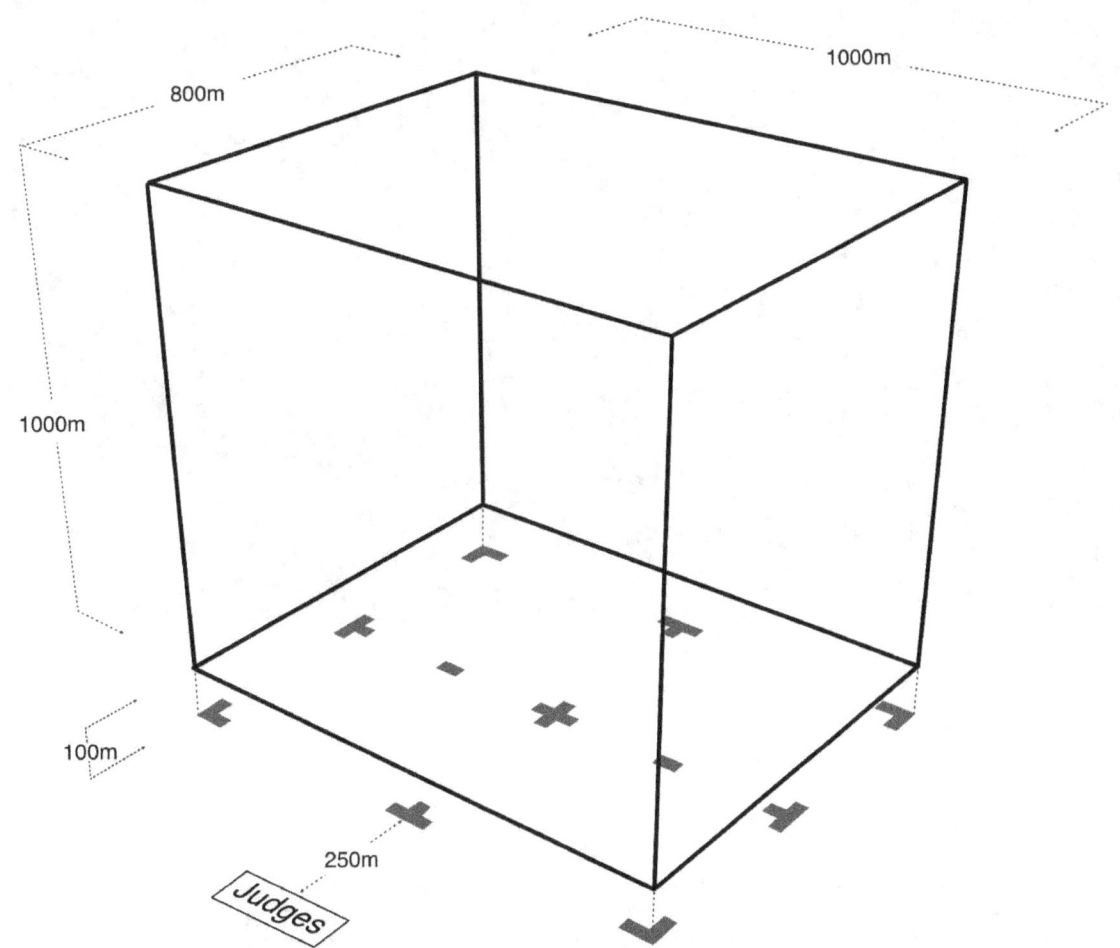

The four pilots on the 1980 Canadian Aerobatic Team are pictured together at Oshkosh. From left to right: Frank Jenkinson, Gord Price, Bill Kennedy, and Gerry Younger. Their standings were forty-third, twenty-first, fifty-first, and thirty-fourth, respectively.

Such is the life of the competition aerobatic pilot. The intensity of concentration leaves you no time to even swallow for six or seven minutes. The true competition is with yourself. I've been as high as you can go and as low as you can go in this life. This was one of the lows.

THE ULTIMATE PITTS

Gord and the rebuilt Pitts-S1S at the Erin grass strip practice field, watercolour by Mc-Donald.

A friend of mine, Glenn Biederman, had recently purchased a partially completed Pitts Special project in 1976. I went over to look at it one day. I poked around a bit and remarked on just how much work had to be done to get it flying. "Ya wanna buy it?" Glenn asked.

"Sounds like a good plan!" I said. I took it home and got to work. It wasn't long, though, before I realized just how much work and money it was going to take—especially money. I went back to Glenn and said, "How would you like to buy half a Pitts project?"

"Sure!" he said, and together, we finished the airplane.

The test flight took place at Guelph Airpark on April 26, 1978. It was a very pretty airplane, red and sexy, with a 180 hp Lycoming engine. It was a standard Pitts, nothing fancy. I flew it for about an hour around the airport and had no problems. I refueled, took off again, and headed east for some more flying. When I was at 1,000 feet above ground, and flying straight and level, the engine quit—DEAD! As they say, the silence was deafening.

I was over a gravel pit at the time. I looked around for a place to land and spotted a little field at the seven o'clock position, between the gravel pit and some trees. It was the only possible landing spot, and it didn't look quite long enough; however, it was all there was. It took about forty-five seconds to touchdown. I side-slipped over a fence and set it down in the field as quickly as I could. The grass was damp, and braking was minimal. I slid across the field with my feet pressing down on the locked brakes with as much force as I could muster—but it was to no avail. I smacked into an unfortunately well-built split-rail and stone fence.

It got very noisy as I hit that fence. Let's just say it was exciting for a few moments! When everything stopped crashing and rotating, my vision came back. The nose was buried in a swampy bit of ground, which was the only wet spot around, and there was steam coming off the engine. I thought it was smoke at first and I expected flames to leap up at any moment; I smacked the quick release on the seatbelt, bolted out of the airplane, hit the ground running, and leapt over a fence! Luckily, it didn't catch fire.

I stood there and looked at my broken Pitts sitting on its nose in a mud-hole. I then realized that I was still wearing my tight-fitting parachute. Adrenaline had helped me to leap over that fence while still wearing the thing. Off in the distance I saw a farmhouse, so I headed for it.

I knocked on the door, and a very surprised lady opened it and said, "What happened?"

"Well," I said, with the parachute now over my shoulder, "I've just crashed my airplane in your field over there and I would like to use your telephone to get some assistance."

The immediate response was, "Would you like a smoke?"

"No thank you," I said to her, "I quit five years ago."

"Then would you like a drink of whisky?"

The first Pitts crash.

"Yes please," I happily answered, as we headed for the kitchen and a phone.

Subsequent analysis indicated that the fuel pump had failed. It was going to be another busy summer.

On the first of July, just over two months after the first test flight, I flew the airplane on its second test flight. I put in two hours right over the airport. The airplane had been totally rebuilt and had had some modifications done to it that made it fly even better than before. It now had a streamlined cowling and spring aluminum landing gear.

On July 14 it was Glenn's turn to fly it; he had never flown a Pitts, so we wanted to be sure that all the bugs were worked out. The plane was on a large, wide grassy runway used by the Caledon Gliding Club, so there would be plenty of room if he found any ground handling

Our Pitts S-1S rebuilt and ready to fly, watercolour by McDonald.

Ron Bull/Courtesy of Tor

THE CANADIANS
ARE GOING !

World Aerobatic Championships. Oshkosh, Wisconsin Aug. 17-30, 19

Canadian Aerobatic Team poster 1980. Photo Ron Bull, Toronto Star.

problems on takeoff or landing. Glenn climbed into the cockpit—excited but confident.

He taxied out slowly and took off. It was a warm, hazy day and there were many gliders around. On his first landing approach Glenn had to overshoot to avoid a glider, then he had to do it again on his second landing attempt. He flew away from the field for a bit to let the glider activity die down; he wanted everything to be perfect for his first landing. Sandy and I and Glenn's wife, Peggy, were sitting around watching the activity.

We waited patiently for the little red biplane to reappear. A full half hour passed. You can imagine what was going through my mind. We had just spent two intense months re-building this airplane, and now I didn't know where he was. I was thinking the worst. Peggy didn't seem too concerned; she just sat there knitting. I think it was Peggy who coined the phrase "Soaring is boring."

I got to the point where I just couldn't stand it anymore. I announced that Sandy and I were going for a little flight in the Aeronca Champ. We took off and started looking in every field for a little red airplane. It had to be somewhere we reasoned, but we found nothing and headed back to the Caledon Gliding Club.

Glenn had since telephoned and explained that he had become disoriented in the haze; he had wound up not too far from the gliding field at the Orangeville Airport. He needed gas, but Orangeville didn't have any. I loaded up a couple of five-gallon jugs in the Aeronca, flew over to Orangeville, and landed on the rough, very narrow runway. I taxied up to Glenn who was standing beside the Pitts.

"Glenn," I said, "we went to the Caledon gliding field so you would have those big wide runways, and here you come zipping into this place with that skimpy little runway and put it down slick as can be—and with a fifteen mile an hour crosswind. That is very impressive!"

Glenn shrugged as he put the fuel in. "I didn't have much choice—I needed fuel." He cranked up, flew back to Caledon, and dodged gliders to land on that nice, big, wide, grass runway.

For the rest of that summer, Glenn and I flew our Pitts in numerous practice sessions and competitions. I spent a lot of time grinning to myself. This airplane was a competitor. Glenn was quite happy with

CANADA'S AVIATION JOURN[AL]

airborne

JUNE / 1980 $1

Aerobatics: poetry in

Man versus

All you should know about

'80 Piper

On the cover of Airborne Magazine.

the airplane as it was, and his dream did not include international competition. Mine did.

Glenn recollects some of those times:

> *The partnership worked out really well at first. We were both getting to know the airplane and Gord was a great one for tinkering and adjusting stuff to make the thing fly better. And we'd go to the same competitions and share expenses. It was great while it lasted.*
>
> *But our interests started to diverge.*
>
> *Gord was constantly trying to improve the performance: make it more streamlined, add fairings, change the rudder—stuff like that. He had unlimited energy and aptitude for this kind of thing, and I just didn't. It got to the point where I'd practically have to treat the airplane like a new machine whenever he made some kind of change, like checking out in it all over again. You could see that Gord had developed a hankering for something of his own design. It was inevitable that we would have to dissolve the partnership.*

It was done without animosity and then I was free to poke at and fiddle with whatever I wanted to on the airplane. I competed, tinkered, and practiced—and tinkered some more. By the summer of 1980, I had what I considered to be a chance of placing in one of the top places in the upcoming World Aerobatic Championships. The airplane was trimmed and squeezed into top form.

One of the things that I took away from the 1980 World Aerobatic Championships was that my Pitts was not able to do a proper vertical roll, or present very well to the judges. Ideally, a vertical roll will be in the center of a vertical line with equal distance lines before and after the roll. This was not possible in my Pitts. The roll rate was a normal 180° per second and the engine was 180 hp. To solve the problem of non-equidistant lines before and after the roll, I had the option of doing one of two possible things—adding a more powerful engine or increasing the roll rate.

Adding a bigger engine meant adding more weight. That in turn meant an increase in wing loading. An increase in wing loading would result in a decreased ability to go around corners without experiencing a high-speed stall, which would create excessive drag and make the improvement counterproductive.[17] Besides, I had already used this solution on the Skybolt, and the increased weight had adversely changed the flying characteristics of the airplane. On the other hand, I could try to increase the roll rate; this could be accomplished with design changes and only a minimal increase in weight. I decided to opt for the increase in the roll rate, and I set about redesigning and building new wings for the Pitts.

I hadn't been a welder or a metal fabricator, but I had learned. I also hadn't been a competition aerobatic pilot, but I had learned that, too. I was not an engineer, but now I planned to learn what I needed to do.

In this case, I used the same airfoil and dimensions as the existing Pitts's wings, but instead of using rounded and tapered tips, I squared them off. The ailerons were basically doubled in size to become full span ailerons.

The ailerons were fabricated from aluminum instead of wood. They were made fifteen percent thicker than normal rib depth so that they reattached some of the separated airflow over the wing, a good thing. The trailing edge was about three-quarter inch thick. This effectively moved the aileron center of pressure backwards which in turn reduced the pressure required on the control column to deflect the ailerons. In other words, it reduced the stick pressure.

The Pitts utilizes streamlined stainless-steel flying and landing wires as a structural component of the two wings. The wires are attached to the front spars of the wing. The increased roll rate put an additional twisting stress on the wing. To neutralize this additional stress, additional landing and flying wires were added and they were attached to the rear spar. This stiffened the structure and prevented

---

[17] A high-speed stall occurs when an aircraft's wing exceeds its critical angle of attack (AoA) even at high airspeeds, resulting in a sudden loss of lift and a significant increase in drag.

any breakage.

These changes were all good; however, I had to know: would the wing be able to tolerate the increased stresses from the improved roll rate? To answer these questions, I turned to the EAAC Technical Committee that was made up of engineers from the National Research Council. I received a solid lesson in structural analysis. These were the days before computers were widely available, but with their guidance, and a calculator, pencil, and graph paper, I was able to complete a structural analysis of the wing.

After a review of my analysis, the EAAC Technical Committee sent a report to Transport Canada. They in turn approved the new wing design for aerobatic flight. The day finally came to test fly the new wing. I was apprehensive since this was a real test flight. It was one of the most exciting and fulfilling flights of my life. It was hard to believe the results: I had doubled the roll rate!

My Pitts now rolled at 360° per second which was unheard of at the time. One other benefit was the rapid roll rate at a speed that was just above stall speed. The ailerons were in the prop-wash, and this now made them effective at zero airspeed. This was a very handy feature for aerobatics performed in a competition. On the negative side, I was disappointed at the snap roll characteristics. It didn't really want to snap.[18]

I was flying a DC-9 at the same time that all this was going on and I noted that there was a stall strip on the inboard leading edge of the DC-9 wing, close to the fuselage. Should a stall happen, the stall strip would ensure that the inboard part of the wing stalled first, making it more controllable. Hmmmm, I thought, what if I put a stall strip on the outboard portion of my new wing?

I duct taped an eight-inch piece of aluminum angle to each of the lower wings. Bingo! It worked like a charm and restored the snapping ability to the aircraft. I was so happy that I added two more strips on the upper swept wing. The life of a test pilot can sometimes be too

---

[18] A snap roll is an aerobatic maneuver commonly performed in aerobatic competitions and airshows. A snap roll that involves a rapid, high-speed roll of the aircraft around its longitudinal axis. It is essentially an accelerated stall where one wing stalls before the other, causing the aircraft to spin quickly.

exciting.

Now with the four stall strips duct-taped on to the four leading edges, I took off, climbed straight out to 1,000 feet, and started a turn. The Pitts immediately snapped—with hardly any back pressure. I checked it out again, but yes, there was a problem. It would snap well but would not fly straight and level well. I gently nursed the airplane around the pattern and landed. Seeing that adding the upper stall strips had not been a good idea, I quickly removed them.

The new wing was really something special. I built it originally for the basic purpose of improving my own personal airplane and for getting an edge on the tough competition that I would face. Competing in these international events was expensive, but it now became my hope that this new wing might just help pay for some of it.

THE HOME OFFICE

Ultimate Aerobatics Ltd. was incorporated July 1, 1981. When I first decided to build an airplane, I dove in: I learned welding and woodworking, and whatever else was needed. But as I will share more about in a later chapter, I learned that building a company was much harder than building an airplane.

The "factory" for the wing fabrication was the hangar at Guelph Airpark where I kept my Pitts. There was a pile of wood in one corner and the airplane in the other. One man worked on turning the wood into wings. I helped when I wasn't in the DC-9 cockpit, or in "the office" in the breezeway at home. I shared the office with the dog. Every time the kids came home from school and opened the door all the papers and the dog hair blew around until the door closed.

I finally got fed up with all the papers flying around; I had my eye on the guest bedroom. Sandy was not totally happy with the idea, but I thought that I was more important than the guests, and we didn't have that many anyhow, so I moved in. However, when we did have guests, we now had to put them in the kids' room and make the kids sleep on the couch. So—it really wasn't working out very well.

There was, in this house, a living room which can best be described as a museum. It was filled with all kinds of interesting stuff, but no one actually lived there. Guests were just shown through on a tour of the house and then led into the family room where socializing took place. It seemed a shame to me that this lovely space was pretty much uninhabited. If I could just turn that museum into an office, I reasoned, then the kids could come off the couches and the guests could go back into the guest room, and everything could go back to normal.

We came close to a divorce on that one. Sandy was not going to give up her museum. She preferred the idea of me going back out to the breezeway with the dog and returning things to normal that way. Sandy made the mistake one weekend of going off skiing and leaving me at home unsupervised. My son, Glen, helped me to lift the desk and we carried it from the guest room into the museum. The thing must have weighed 400 pounds. Sandy was not a big lady so we knew

On our way from Frankfurt to Baden Soellingen. Photo © Gord Crawford.

that she wouldn't be able to move it once we got it in there.

I added a gigantic cork board to the wall and converted the place into my office—dubbing it the "Ultimate Office." There was a bit of fuss when Sandy came home, but she accepted that the new office was there to stay. As the saying goes: "Give and take, a marriage don't break."

1982 WORLD AEROBATIC CHAMPIONSHIPS

The 1982 World Aerobatic Championships were held in Spitzerberg, Austria. A team was put together to represent Canada which included myself, Frank Jenkinson, and Bob Lavigne.

I arranged for Air Canada to transport our airplanes from Toronto to

Taxiing out at Baden Soellingen. Photo © Gord Crawford.

Gord on the way to Spitzerberg, Austria. Photo © Frank Jenkinson.

Our cross country route from Frankfurt to Spizerberg and return.

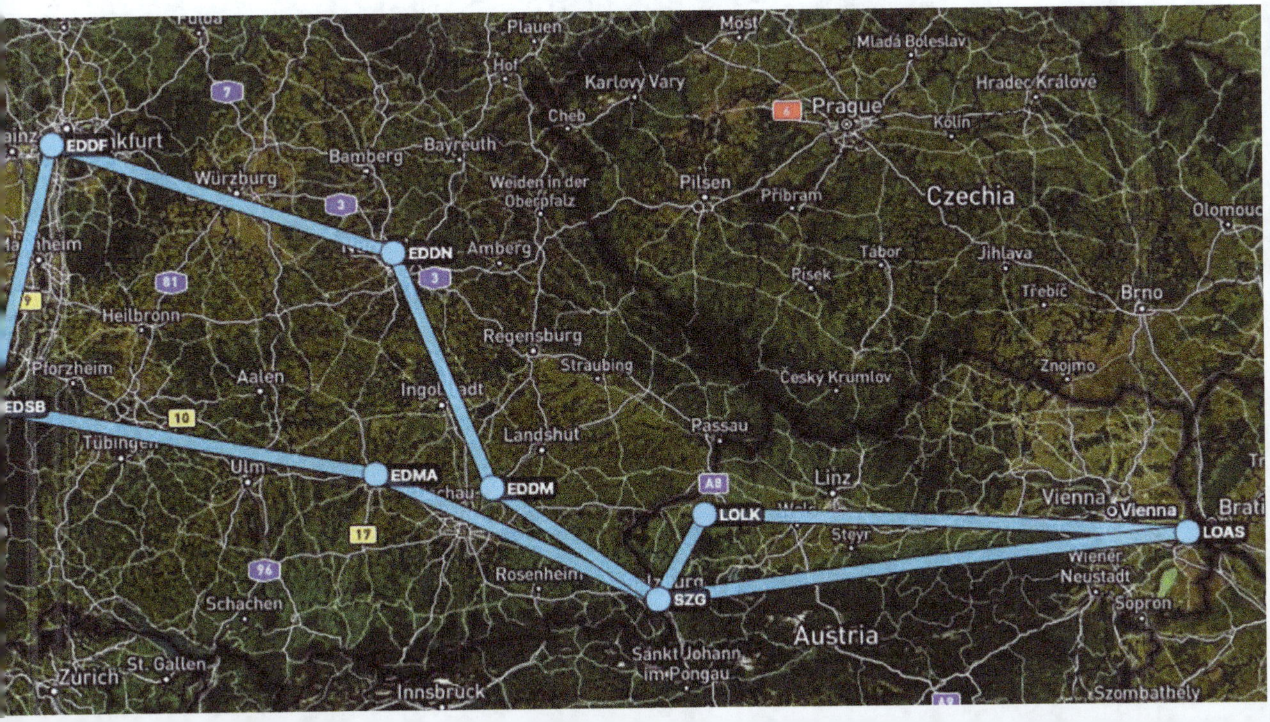

Frankfurt as a sponsorship. A big thank you goes out to Air Canada Vice President of Flight Operations Charlie Simpson for making it happen. The three airplanes were flown into Toronto Pearson on July 23, disassembled, loaded into a DC-8 freighter, flown to Frankfurt, and finally assembled in the Lufthansa hangar there. Then they were flown down the Rhine Valley to Baden-Soellingen, my old RCAF CF-104 base.

What a great time we had there: practicing for three days from July 27 to 29. I even got to put my Pitts in my old CF-104 Quick Reaction Alert hardstand! All the CF-104s had been deployed elsewhere because they were doing some repair work on the field; we had the entire airfield and staff to ourselves! Surprisingly, we had some noise complaints! The local population was used to a different type of noise.

The 1982 Canadian Aerobatic Team (L-R): Frank Jenkinson, Gord Price, Bob Lavigne.

First westerner to fly the YAK-50. Photo © Gord Crawford.

We flew to our official practice site, the Ried-Kirchheim Airport on July 3, and we practiced there from August 1 to 6. I remember that to monitor my heart rate, I was wired up for my flights by the team doctor, Gord Crawford. We discovered that pulling 6 g's and pushing -5 g's caused my heart rate to vary from 160 bpm to 40 bpm, and that the cyclic change took four seconds.

We flew in the WAC 82 contest from August 7 to 21. Of the Canadians I placed thirty-sixth, Bob Lavigne finished forty-third, and Frenk Jenkinson sixty-sixth. Our performance was disappointing for sure; however, we took home the satisfaction of having overcome countless obstacles and we gained a life experience that few people will ever attain.

The highlight for me was flying Victor Smolin's Yak-50. It was so exciting to be the first Westerner who was offered this opportunity in the midst of the Cold War—especially considering that I had been a NATO nuclear strike pilot only sixteen years previously. I was so impressed with the Yak-50 that thirty years later, in 2011, I bought the prototype Yak-50 which had been built in Moscow, at the Yakovlev Design Bureau. That is a story I will tell in another chapter.

We flew to Munich on August 22 and Frankfurt on August 23, where the Pitts was disassembled and airfreighted to Toronto by Air Canada. After reassembling it in Toronto, I flew it home to Guelph on the sixth of September. It took forty-five days on the road to fly in the 1982 WAC. A total of twenty hours of flying time was put on the Pitts.

One of the things that I learned is this: if you want to fly world level, competitive aerobatics—you must be willing to surrender your life. These events took tremendous effort and lots of time out of an already more than busy schedule.

When I finally sold the Pitts in September of 1985, it had accumulated 600 hours in about 2,100 flights over seven years—most of them flown by myself. Glenn Biederman flew it quite a bit, followed by Roger Hadfield. Stan Kereliuk, a test pilot for the EAAC Technical Committee, flew it with the Ultimate Wing installed to get Transport Canada approval for aerobatic flight. Other pilots who flew it were Bob Lavigne, Eric Müller, Michel Brandt, Richard Goode, Victor Smolin, Brian Becker, John Hilton, Wayne Quistberg, Clint McHenry, Bob Herendeen, and Larry Ernewein.

A Pitts Special is an aircraft specially designed and developed for aerobatics. It is not like a Cessna 150. It is almost always flown to the limits. Things bend and break—hopefully slowly. The engine is not babied. You are operating at full power or idle. You could almost use an on-off switch for a throttle. That's at the very core of the sport (religion?) of aerobatic flying.

From my perspective, the 80s were golden years of competition aerobatics. I was in the company of truly great aerobatic pilots like Leo Loudenslager, Kermit Weeks, Henry Haig, Jurgis Kairys, and Walter Extra. They were not only outstanding aerobatic pilots, but also aircraft designers and builders themselves. While I may not have scored as well as they did, I was fortunate to have been able to enjoy their company.

There were lots of others of course like Manfred Strössenreuther, Victor Smolin, Clint McHenry, Charlie Hillard, Gene Soucy, Eric Müller, Patty Wagstaff, and Patrick Paris—to name just some of them. However, they were not designers and builders—they were simply outstanding aerobatic pilots.

A BAD WEATHER LANDING

I would estimate that for every hour the Pitts was in the air, there were more than three hours of maintenance. The cost of competitive aerobatics in time and money was very high, especially if there was a landing accident. Unfortunately—due to bad weather—my good friend Larry Ernewein, while ferrying my Pitts home for me, had to land in a field in Michigan.

Larry was building a Pitts of his own with my Ultimate Wing. We had worked out a deal that was mutually beneficial. He worked for me at the Ultimate factory in his spare time—learning all that he could about the new wing's construction methods. He also flew my Pitts with the new wing and gained valuable flight experience for himself and for the airplane. Soon, Larry was tapped to ferry the airplane

Front view of the Pitts after the crash.

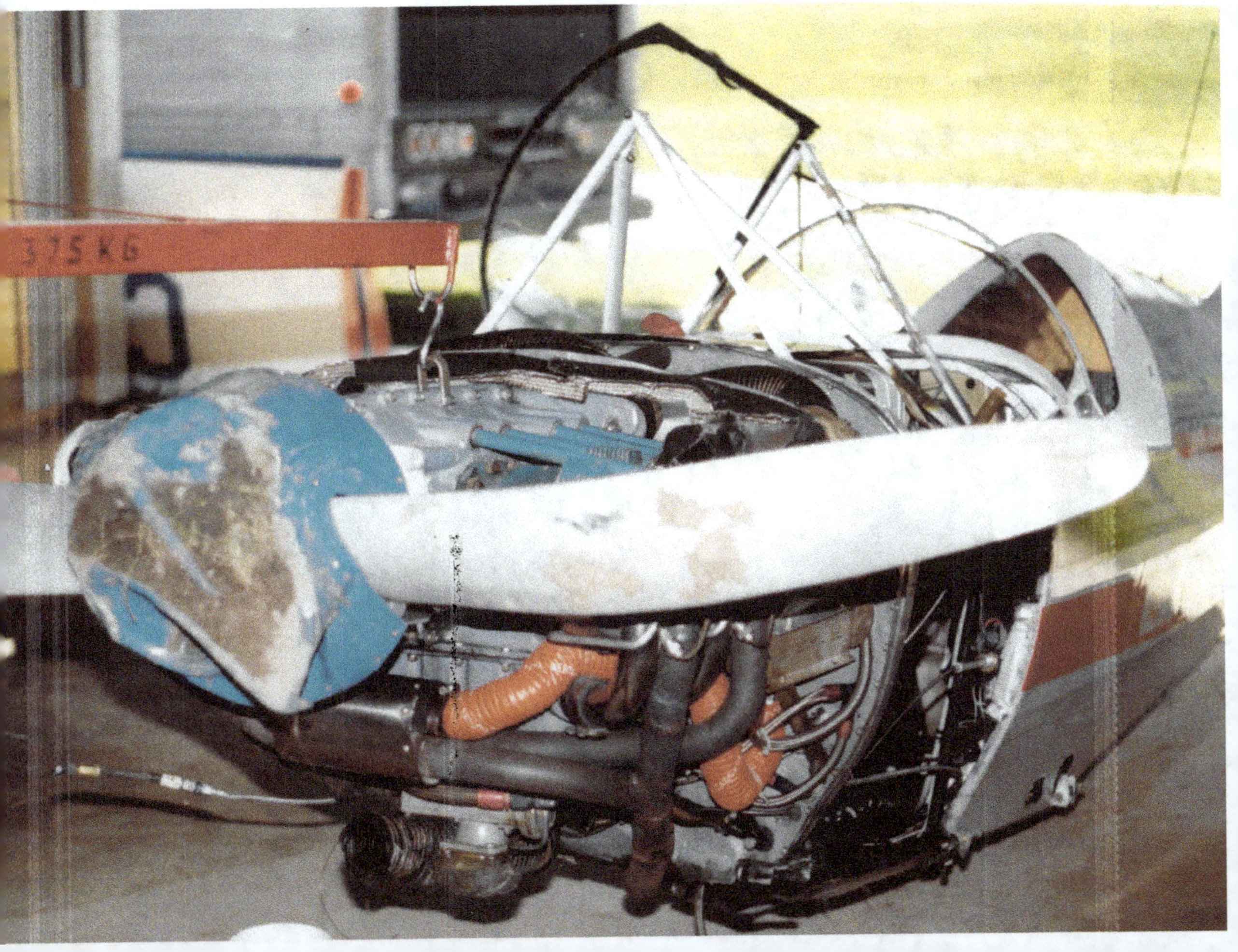

from place to place where I was entered in various competitions.

I have always maintained that the most dangerous part of competition aerobatics was getting to and from the contest. IFR in aeronautical terms means instrument flight rules; however, my aircraft had little instrumentation so IFR to me meant: I Follow Roads. It worked well in most cases; however, in low visibility situations surprises occurred: radio towers popped up in the middle of four-lane highways and tunnels suddenly appeared as you climbed up a hill while following a winding four-lane highway.

Cross country flying in aerobatic airplanes can be tricky. I have landed in half-mile visibility, experienced thirty knot crosswinds with driving rain, and in one case taxied at high speed into an open hangar to get out of torrential rain and hail.

In July of 1984, the airplane was needed in Guelph to prepare it for the major Oshkosh Fly-in and Convention at the end of that month. Arranged by the Experimental Aircraft Association (EAA), it is held

Close up view of the Pitts after the crash.

annually in Oshkosh, Wisconsin, and it attracts aviation enthusiasts from around the world.

Larry had recently ferried the aircraft from a competition at Sandusky, Michigan, to another in Calgary, Alberta. He now planned to fly it back from Calgary to Guelph. Larry was no longer in Calgary, so he hopped on a jet and flew there. With the experience of the problem free, day-and-a-half flight to Calgary from Sandusky fresh in his mind, Larry was confident of being back in Guelph within two days.

The airplane was equipped with the "Extend-A-Range" upper wing fuel tank which allowed for a flying range of almost four hours. This cut down on the time spent on the ground caused by the need to re-fuel every couple of hours, and on a long trip across the continent it effectively increased the groundspeed over a day's flight. The first night Larry made it to Winnipeg and wound up sleeping in a fuel truck; that would have been a less than restful night.

The following day he went from Winnipeg to Thunder Bay, fueled, flew north of Lake Superior to Sault Ste. Marie, and fueled again. Due to a slowly moving warm front across Georgian Bay, the route along the north shore of Lake Huron and Georgian Bay was going to be dicey. He decided instead that he would go south into Michigan, cut across the border at Sarnia, clear customs at London, and then head home to Guelph. The front was in the London area as he took off from Sault Ste. Marie, but it was moving eastward and the weather in London was improving. He estimated about three and a half hours to London, so the front was likely going to be well to the east by the time he got into the London area.

The forecast for northern Michigan was scattered clouds at about 4,000 feet, and visibility five to six miles in haze. He contacted various ground stations for weather updates almost constantly during the flight, and he listened in on other aircraft along his route. Everything seemed to be just fine up ahead, and though London's weather wasn't quite as good as he had hoped, Sarnia's was quite fine. He climbed to 7,500 feet and he was now on top of the haze layer which seemed to end at about 6,000 feet.

Larry found visibility superb well above the haze. In fact, about one hundred miles away, around Bay City, Michigan, well ahead and slightly to his left, was the top of the only thunderstorm in the area. He could see it quite clearly and would be able to easily avoid it. As he got closer to the storm's top, he was in contact with the radar at Bay City and they advised him of the position and size of the cell of the storm. He chose to descend and navigate around the storm instead of staying at his current altitude and flying visually around the top.

There is a certain comfort in being in sight of the ground when one is in the vicinity of questionable weather and flying by visual rules. It seemed like a very simple navigational exercise to fly around the thing; visibility in the haze was easily five or six miles, and the area of the storm was well enough defined.

Larry decided to stay north of the cell since it seemed to be travelling somewhat southerly. If he stayed to its north, he'd be able to fly out to the shore of Lake Huron and simply follow the shoreline down to Port Huron and Sarnia; he knew the weather there was fine. If he went south of it, there was no telling how far he might have to go to clear it and then there would be the added concern of becoming involved in the traffic around Detroit and Selfridge Air Force Base.

Larry was flying along quite happily at about 1,500 feet with visibility still in the five-mile range. He was cruising at about 145 mph, so things were going by speedily but manageably. He was aware that the extend-a-range tank would soon be empty—it had been about two hours since his last fuel up. Visibility gradually started to worsen, and a light drizzle began.

Slowly everything started deteriorating. He was following a road which coincidently led straight into Sandusky. It was a comfort to Larry to see the Sandusky Airport below; it would be his haven if the conditions became much worse and he had to turn back. As he passed the airport, he was at 1,000 feet and visibility was about three miles. He decided to follow the highway that was running west to east, straight out to the lake. The lake by this point was only about twenty miles away. He then planned to follow the shoreline down to Sarnia where he knew the conditions were good. It was perhaps forty miles to Sarnia from where he'd arrive at the lake shore in less than half an hour.

At Carsonville, between Sandusky and the lakeshore, visibility dropped and the ceiling closed in. He was at about 500 feet with visibility maybe a couple of miles. He kept thinking about that good weather ahead in Sarnia, not really considering the actual localized conditions.

A thunderstorm is a type of mini-cold front. As it travels across the countryside on a summer's day, it causes the temperature of the air around and in front of it to drop. Most of you reading this can recall such a thing happening during a summer storm. Add to this the fact that Larry was flying toward Lake Huron, and the air temperature near the water was less than that over the land. Temperature and dewpoint were quickly coming together.

As noted, the airplane was totally unequipped for any kind of instrument flying. Having only an airspeed indicator and an altimeter as flight instruments meant that Larry had to be in visual contact with the ground to continue safe flight. As he followed the road to the Lake Huron shore, the ceiling kept coming down, visibility kept decreasing, and a misty wet sort of fog was forming ahead.

He was about 300 feet above ground and visibility was down to about a mile when he decided he had to turn back to Sandusky. Just as that thought was passing through his mind, he saw bubbles going down the gas line from the wing tank indicating that it was nearly dry. Reaching down, he quickly switched tanks to prevent the slightest hesitation in fuel flow to the engine. When he looked back up, he was stunned to see that the fog had now completely engulfed him. He immediately dove toward the ground and levelled off at about one hundred feet. He clung to the thought that no one would build a transmission tower in the middle of the highway and he knew that he had to keep the center of the highway in view. By this time he had slowed down to 130 mph; he was heading straight for Port Sanilac, a town that sat on the edge of Lake Huron. Suddenly he was able see the town looming through the fog ahead. An idea started to form in his mind on how he could make a safe turn.

He followed the highway the rest of the way to Port Sanilac, and he continued to follow it as the town flashed by him below. Finally, he reached the lake. He knew that the time had arrived to make the turn, but there was a big problem. Visibility in the murk over the lake was non-existent. There was no horizon, real or artificial, to use as a reference for the turn. He had to do it on airspeed, altimeter, and luck alone. Larry later told me:

> *That is where I came very close to dying. I flew right out to the lake because I knew there would be no obstacles out there, but imagine what it was like over the lake in the fog in an airplane with no instruments other than an airspeed indicator and an altimeter. It was hairy. I almost stalled and spun in. I was very close to meeting my maker!*

But he didn't. He managed to get turned around and he headed back up the highway toward Sandusky. While he had been struggling with the fog around the lakeshore, it had oozed off to the west and there now appeared to be no break in it over the Sandusky highway. The thought of landing on the highway and getting out of this situation became quite appealing.

Every time he lined up to descend to the highway, however, a set of headlights would appear coming towards him out of the fog. (He found out later that this might have been a blessing in disguise since the road was crisscrossed every few yards with wires that he wouldn't have been able to see!) With visibility down to about one-half mile, he was running out of options. It was quite clear that the airplane would be on the ground in very short order—one way or another.

Larry wanted to put it down while he still had some sort of control and some choice in the matter. He had spotted a long green field near Sanilac; it was an image that he had filed away in his mind as he had zoomed past. It seemed to be the only suitable landing site anywhere around and he decided to go for it. He did another 180° turn and headed east back toward Sanilac and the field that he had seen. He found the field without any trouble. It seemed to be long and smooth, and there were no wires across it. Everything was looking good.

He commenced a circuit. As he flew downwind, he checked the field and saw that it was probably 2,000 feet long with houses along one side. There were no obstacles on the approach—everything seemed to be perfect. He came in over a fence at about seventy mph indicated airspeed. There was no wind to cause the plane to drift. Everything was looking great. Because visibility was rapidly getting worse, there was obviously not going to be any opportunity for a go-around—this landing attempt would be it.

What happened next happened very fast.

The airplane touched down perfectly, but within a fraction of a second the main landing gear dug into the soft moist earth and the airplane literally somersaulted. It went up on its nose and completely flipped over one more time before coming to rest again on the propeller.

It turned out that this area of Michigan had experienced rain for about a week—all the land had become completely saturated with water. It was known by local pilots that this phenomenon of "instant fog" was quite common under these circumstances. In fact, within the previous ten years, three other airplanes, all flown by non-locals, had done the same thing in the same field! If Larry had known at the time that he hadn't been the only transient pilot to make such an entrance, it might have provided a miniscule amount of comfort to him.

He stood in that soggy Michigan field beside my busted airplane, and surveyed the damage. He was grateful for the integrity of the structure of the airplane. He was not injured in the slightest, and the cockpit area was not damaged. There was a tragic part to the story, however. An observer, a resident of one of the nearby houses, ran toward the airplane with a fire-extinguisher. He was an older gentleman and unfortunately his heart was not up to the excitement. He had a heart attack. This being a small town, the fire department was on the scene immediately. They proceeded to give him CPR, but unfortunately, the elderly gentleman did not make it.

Larry still feels quite upset about that. Despite whatever rationalizations he could make, it was hard for him not to accept some responsibility for the loss.

The aircraft was rebuilt over the winter and flew again in March of 1985. I flew the Oshkosh Airshow again along with several other competitions. I finally sold the airplane to Buck Wagnon, the doctor of the US Aerobatic Team. I delivered it to Buck in Oklahoma on September 14, 1985.

Tim Taylor from Louisville, Kentucky, currently owns the Ultimate Pitts that I built in 1978—forty-six years ago. It was last rebuilt in 2011, and, as far as I know—it is still flying.

The Ultimate Pitts in Oshkosh 1985 after rebuild #2.

The Ultimate Pitts as seen in 2023. Photo © Carmelo Turdo.

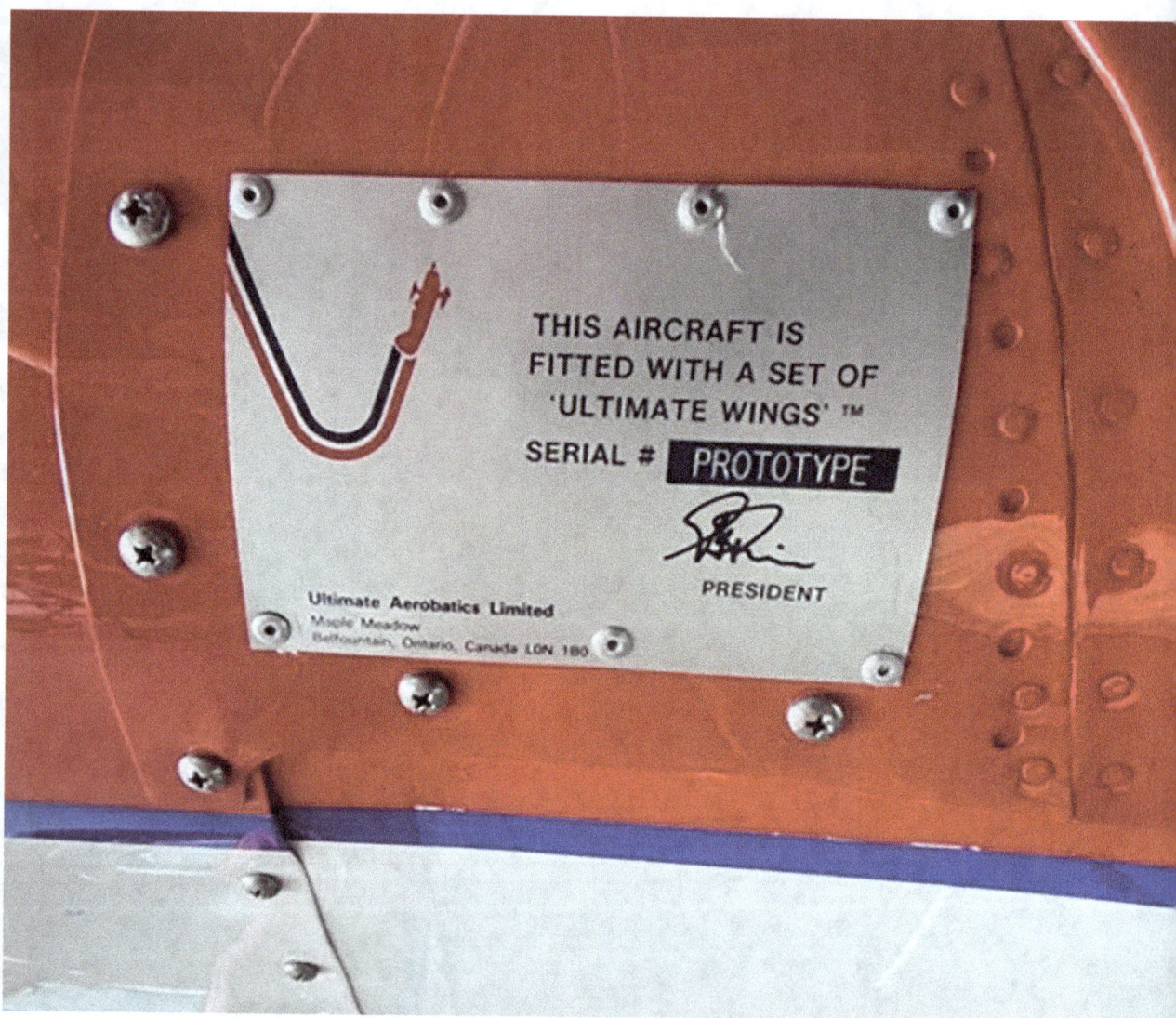

Ultimate wing placard. Photo © Carmelo Turdo.

WORLD CHAMPIONSHIP
AEROBATICS

Hilton Masters group photo 1983, from L–R: Gene Soucy, Henry Haigh, Kermit Weeks, Frank Fry, Gord Price, Christian Schweizer, Jerzy Makula, Michel Brandt, Eric Müller.

After having flown in the 1980 and 1982 FAI World Championships, I flew four more WAC events. This gave me a total of six.

I was invited to fly the Hilton Masters of Aerobatics in Mesa, Arizona, in November 1983. The nine pilots were from five countries: the US, Canada, Switzerland, Poland, and Australia. Each pilot was guaranteed $1,000. First prize was $10,000, second $5,000, and third and fourth $1,500. The contest director was Don Taylor of Cumulus Productions Inc.

This was a unique contest in that three brand new Pitts S-2Bs were provided for the pilots, and you never knew which airplane you would fly. The most important factor was that the judges did not know who was flying, so the "halo effect" was removed.

In addition to these unconventional rules, one more was added. Competitors were not allowed to watch another competitor fly unless they had already flown. This had the effect of forcing every pilot to fly in unknown wind conditions. Normally everyone watches

Rank	Country	Pilot	Airplane	Score
1		Weeks, Kermit A	Pitts S-2B	14657.50
2		Soucy, Gene	Pitts S-2B	14650.80
3		Schweizer, Christian	Pitts S-2B	14314.00
4		Haigh, Henry	Pitts S-2B	14265.00
5		Fry, Frank	Pitts S-2B	14113.70
6		Price, Gordon	Pitts S-2B	13970.60
7		Müller, Eric	Pitts S-2B	13625.90
8		Makula, Jerzy	Pitts S-2B	12740.00
9		Brandt, Michel	Pitts S-2B	9567.90

the first pilot to determine where the wind is coming from and how it affects the flight.

Each pilot did three flights: the Known Compulsory, The Unknown, and the Free Style. I placed sixth.

A TRIP TO AUSTRALIA

In 1984, I was one of twelve pilots from seven countries who were invited to fly in the Philips World Aerobatic Challenge in Australia. This was a huge effort for Sandy and me, but it was the chance of a lifetime to experience Australia like no other. The Ultimate Pitts was flown to the Tamiami Airport in Florida on January 8. It was disassembled in Kermit Week's hangar, loaded into a container,

Loaded into the truck for transport.

trucked to Jacksonville, and finally shipped to Melbourne, Australia.

Sandy and I eventually caught up to the Pitts in Essendon, Australia. That's where we put it back together on March 9. The left aileron had been damaged in transit and had to be rebuilt. After a test flight on the tenth, I flew to Ballarat on the eleventh. I flew twenty flights in Ballarat and we left for Schofields on March 18. On the way we stopped in Wagga Wagga and Bankstown. I felt like a gypsy. What a great time we had with a twelve-plane formation and not everyone speaking English. The contest consisted of the wildest manoeuvres that I had ever seen.

What is not written in the results is what happened to Betty Stewart. Betty did not bring her Pitts from the US and instead borrowed a homebuilt Pitts in Australia. One of the complicated manoeuvres called for an outside snap roll on a diving vertical line. I remember

In Kermit's hangar, ready to go to Australia.

standing there watching with Henry Haigh as she did about three snaps down instead of one. I was ready to turn my head, not wanting to watch her auger in, when she finally pulled out, just missing the ground. What had happened? No one would have ever known if she had hit the ground.

This was a homebuilt Pitts and the builder had left a small gap between the bottom tube of the rudder pedal and the plywood floor. Her heel had gotten caught in the crack and the toe of her running shoe had been caught on the diagonal tube that runs by the fuel tank. This had immobilized her foot and jammed on the rudder. That was a very close call.

We had a great time in Australia for a month, and we even managed to talk the police out of a speeding ticket. I remember seeing a sign at a lion safari park, "Poms on bicycle admitted free!" ("Pom" being

Group photo Australia. Top row L-R: Victor Smolin, Kermit Weeks, Chris Sperou, Henry Haigh, Gord Price, Bottom L-R: Eric Müller, Sergio Dallan, Richard Goode, Frank Fry.

the Australian nickname for immigrants from Britain.)

The trip home from Wagga Wagga to Essendon was one to remember. We were a twelve-plane formation. I was flying formation on Henry Haigh, and I suddenly realized that we were going sideways. A major front had gone through and the wind had really picked up so the drift was extreme. I do not remember the windspeed, but it took lots of power to get to Essendon's runway 18 and to put it on the runway. I took the power off once I was over the runway. The airplane stopped and four people who had been waiting for me on the side of the runway grabbed the wingtips and tail to walk me in. Cross-country

Rank	Country	Pilot	Airplane	Score
1	 🇺🇸	Weeks, Kermit A	?	7755.00
2	 🇨🇭	Müller, Eric	?	7542.00
3	 🇦🇺	Fry, Frank	?	7511.00
4	 🇺🇸	Haigh, Henry	?	7459.00
5	 🇨🇦	Price, Gordon	?	7362.00
6	 🇦🇺	Selvey, Geoffrey	?	7267.00
7	🇸🇺	Smolin, Victor	?	7144.00
8	 🇬🇧	Goode, Richard	?	6929.00
9	 🇦🇺	Sperou, Chris	?	6913.00
10	 🇮🇪	Dallan, Sergio	?	6611.00
11	 🇦🇺	Beard, Mal	?	6431.00
12	 🇺🇸	Stewart (Everest), Betty	Pitts S-1S	6222.00

Route from Melbourne to Ballarat to Sydney to Melbourne.

flying can be exciting!

The airplane was disassembled and air freighted to JFK in New York City, where on April 22, I put the airplane together. You haven't lived as a pilot until you have taxied around JFK in a Pitts Special! I was in a taxi lineup right behind the British Airways Concorde. That by itself was exciting enough!

The procedures are complicated at JFK, and I had limited avionics and radios. I am not sure if they had ever seen a Pitts at JFK before. They issued me a complicated clearance that I could not comply with, so I said, "Unable that, just give me a takeoff clearance. I'll stay on the deck, and you will never see me again!"

The reply came: "Charlie Golf November Oscar Delta, cleared for takeoff, goodbye and good trip." I immediately took off and stayed below one hundred feet all the way to the west side of Lower New York Bay. The Ultimate Pitts had left Guelph for Australia on October 23, 1983, and returned on April 22, 1984—182 days later.

HILTON MASTERS OF AEROBATICS 1985

I received an invitation to fly in the 1985 Hilton Masters of Aerobatics; the competition was to be held in Homestead, Florida, in December 1985. Obviously, Hilton must have been pleased with the results of the 1983 Hilton Masters of Aerobatics production. There were to be ten days of practice followed by two and a half days of competition, videos, and interviews. The prize money was to be the same as it was in 1983, but with the addition of bonuses for the winning of individual flights.

Pictured on page 221 is my Hilton "Unknown" sequence card as drawn up for the day of flight using Aresti aero cryptographic symbols. If you are interested in an exercise, I suggest that you photocopy my sequence card and follow along with your finger as we fly the flight together. I will try to put you in the cockpit with me to help you understand the intensity of competitive aerobatic flight.

Note: This exercise involves following a complex aerobatic flight sequence using Aresti aerobatic symbols, and may not be easy for everyone to grasp. So don't worry if the details seem overwhelming. However, if you wish to learn more, please visit https://www.fai.org/news/understanding-aresti-figures-aerobatic-competition.

Pitts model S-2B.

First, I will translate the Aresti symbols for you—manoeuvre by manoeuvre. There were seventeen aerobatic maneuvers in the sequence, and the flight time was about ten minutes. Bear in mind that this "unknown" flight had not been practiced nor had I seen anyone else fly it. Also, the judges had no idea who was flying the airplane that they were judging. This was the truest form of competitive aerobatic flying that I had ever seen.

#1. Starting in level positive flight, ½ of an 8 point vertical roll with a negative recovery.

#2. An inside snap roll on an inverted diving 45-degree line, starting from inverted level flight and ending in inverted level flight.

#3. A hammerhead turnaround with an inside ½ snap roll in the middle of the down line, starting from inverted level flight and ending in positive level flight.

#4. An inside loop, starting from positive level flight and ending in positive level flight.

#5. A hammerhead turnaround with a ¾ inside snap roll on the upline, starting from positive level flight and ending in negative level flight.

#6. A 4-point roll on an inverted climbing 45-degree line, starting from negative level flight and ending in negative level flight.

#7. A ¾ inside snap roll on a diving vertical line, starting from inverted level flight and ending in positive level flight.

#8. An inside hexagonal loop with each corner being 60 degrees, starting from upright level flight and ending in upright level flight.

#9. A ½ outside snap roll on a positive 45 degree climbing line, starting from upright level flight and ending in upright level flight.

#10. An upright 360 degree turn with 2 rolls in the opposite direction to that of the turn, starting from upright level flight and ending in upright level flight.

#11. A "belly up" tailslide, starting from upright level flight and ending in negative level flight.

#12. A ¼ roll on a vertical upline, starting from inverted level flight

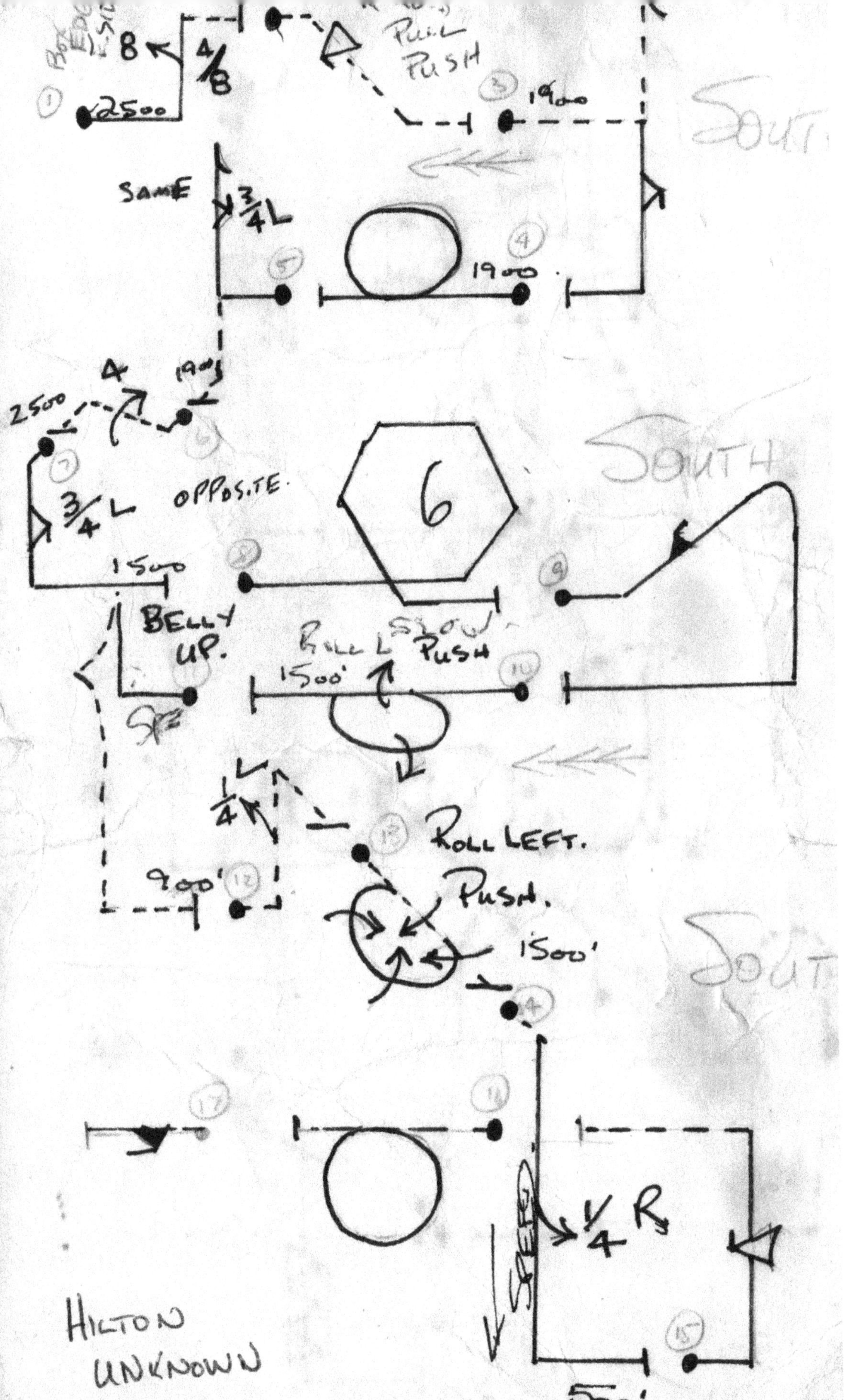

Box
EDGE
E-SID

8   4/8

① 2500

Pull
Push

③ 1900

SOUTH

SAME   3/4 L

⑤

1900   ④

4   1900

2500   →

⑦ ⑥

3/4 L   OPPOSITE.

6

SOUTH

1500   ⑧

⑨

BELLY
UP.

⑩   SP

ROLL L   SLOW
PUSH
1500'

⑩

1/4 L

ROLL LEFT.

⑬   PUSH.

900' ⑫

1500'

⑭

⑰   ⑯

1/4 R

STEP

HILTON
UNKNOWN

⑮

500'

and ending in inverted level flight.

#13. A 360 degree turn with 4 rolls in the same direction as the turn, starting from inverted level flight and ending in inverted level flight.

#14. A ¼ vertical roll on a vertical downline, starting from inverted level flight and ending in upright level flight.

#15. An inside snap roll on a vertical climbing line, starting from upright level flight and ending in inverted level flight.

#16. An inside loop from the top down, starting from inverted level flight and ending in inverted level flight.

#17. A ½ outside snap roll on a horizontal line, starting from inverted level flight and ending in upright level flight.

Full power is used throughout the sequence except at the top of the tailslide when idle is used to let the airplane fall backwards.

Here we go, flying the sequence... imagine where we are in the sky, and what we are doing.

The first manoeuvre must be placed on the downwind edge of the box at a predetermined altitude to allow for the predicted energy decay throughout the sequence of manoeuvres. In my case I elected to start at 2,500 feet on the north edge of the box with as much speed as possible.

Three brisk wing wags to signal the start of the flight, ensuring level flight to start, pull +6 g's to vertical, swiftly rolling right 22.5 degrees, stop, right, stop, right, stop, right stop after the ½ roll pause to draw a crisp vertical equal to line before the roll then pull to the horizontal, keep nose up, flying a level line inverted now, maintaining altitude, not too far, eating up the box, pull the nose down now, on a 45 degree down line, a good hard pull to precisely stall the airplane and snap roll 360 degrees, recovering upside down on an inverted 45 degree line. Draw a short line equal to the line before the snap roll, then push to level flight inverted.

I should now be at 1,900 feet upside down with good speed, coming up on the south edge of box. Give a good -3 g push to hit a vertical line and hold it until the airspeed is almost zero then kick the left rudder to pivot the airplane back to a vertical down attitude using aileron to ensure no roll, draw a bit of a line, a good pull on the elevator to stall the airplane and induce a right roll using rudder but immediately stop it since only ½ a snap roll is required, then a +6 g pull to horizontal.

Going downwind now at 1,900 feet, before the middle of the box, a gentle +3 g pull to create a large round loop, flying it over the top inverted, gently, since there is a headwind here on top of the loop, continuing the loop, making it round and recovering exactly where the loop was started with lots of speed and then right into a +6 g pull to vertical so as not to exit the box on the north side.

Hopefully, I am positioned on the east side of the box in anticipation of the upcoming ¾ roll to the left which will mean 90-degree flight to the right in inverted flight.

Once on the vertical line a quick pull and kick with left rudder to do a ¾ snap roll to the left, losing speed rapidly now ... waiting for the airplane to almost halt, another quick kick of the left rudder to pivot the airplane through a hammerhead stall back to vertical down, gaining speed then a very good -3 g push to the horizontal. Hit the horizontal line then push again to a climbing 45-degree line and do a 4-point roll while climbing on a 45-degree line with equal distance before and after the roll, then pull to the horizontal. Now I am inverted and cross box, make an easy pull to a vertical down line before exiting the box on the west side. Draw short vertical line, kick the left rudder while aircraft is stalled doing a ¾ snap roll to the left. Draw a short line on bottom, then make a good pull and I should be at 1,500 feet on the west side of the box heading south as fast as the S-2B will go.

Now heading into wind, middle of the box, pull up 60 degrees for the first side of a hexagonal loop, another 60 degrees then horizontal flight across the top, pull down 60 degrees then another 60 degree pull to the horizontal, back in the middle of box at 1,500 feet, pull to 45 degrees up, draw short line, then a 'God awful' -3 g negative push and a kick with left rudder and right aileron with a recovery almost before the start in order to do an outside ½ snap roll while still climbing, but now inverted on that 45 degree line, then an easy pull to complete a 5/8 loop back northbound and upright ready for a toughie, a 360 degree turn with 2 rolls—opposite to the direction of the turn.

I elected to turn right while rolling left, which means pushing the left rudder to turn left but using right aileron to roll right and the rate was important to be consistent. Which means for every 10 degrees of heading change there is to be 20 degrees of roll. Finishing the turn and rolls on a north heading and trying to accelerate in level flight from that draggy manoeuvre is difficult. So, using a gentler pull to the vertical and before going out of the box at the north end and setting up for a tailslide to keep the belly up and maybe cheating a bit negative on the way up to ensure the belly of the aircraft is up during the transition to vertical down flight. (Better to lose a few points than zero a manoeuvre.) Slowly bring the power off so as not to rotate ... then slide backwards ... belly-up ... flop over and vertical down, gaining speed aiming for 900 feet above ground, a good -3 g push to end up in level inverted flight southbound.

Hopefully I am hugging the east side of the box then another -3 g push to the vertical, a ¼ roll to the left and a gentle pull to the horizontal, now inverted, travelling cross box, and accelerating in inverted level flight to do another rolling 360 degree turn. This one is with 4 rolls, one every 90 degrees of turn, only the rolls are in the same direction as the turn which in this case rolling left and pushing forward start the rolling turn. The turn is completed after 360 degrees with the roll rate being 4 times that of the turn rate.

Now coming up on the edge of the west side of the box, make a gentle pull to the vertical, trying to accelerate on the downline as much as possible while rolling 90 degrees to the right then a good pull and transitioning to level flight at 500 feet above ground (remember, 300 feet is bottom of box). Speed is high and there is a danger of exiting the box to the south so a quick +6 g pull to the vertical, a short vertical line then a 360 degree snap roll (which really slows the S-2B down), keep it going vertical till almost out of airspeed, a gentle pull over the top ...without sagging, maintaining level flight inverted, then a gentle pull down doing an inside loop from inverted to inverted and making it round regardless of the different speeds being flown in the loop, back to level inverted flight then a sharp push with jab of rudder and immediate recovery to carry out a one half outside (negative) snap roll.

And that is the end of the sequence. The intensity of the concentration leaves me no time to swallow.

The results of the contest were based on the total score from five different flights. For the Known flight, everyone received a copy of the manoeuvres to be flown in a certain sequence and practice was allowed. For the Freestyle flight, pilots designed their own sequence, and practice was allowed. The two Unknown flights were designed by the organizer and given to the pilots the day before those flights; however no practice was allowed. The final flight was the "Four Minute," where each pilot flew for exactly four minutes in a no holds barred approach to impress the judges. All types of manoeuvres were allowed—including tumbles which were not listed in the Aresti catalogue.

All flights were flown in the "Aerobatic box" and any excursion

Rank	Country	Pilot	Airplane	Score
1		Soucy, Gene	Pitts S-2B	11504.90
2		Price, Gordon	Pitts S-2B	11276.20
3		Weeks, Kermit A	Pitts S-2B	11271.50
4		Haigh, Henry	Pitts S-2B	11137.20
5		Kynsey, Peter	Pitts S-2B	11107.80
6		Paris, Patrick	Pitts S-2B	11049.70
7		Müller, Eric	Pitts S-2B	10845.00
8		Schweizer, Christian	Pitts S-2B	10796.70
9		Celliers, Peter	Pitts S-2B	10713.90
10		Fry, Frank	Pitts S-2B	10296.70

outside the box incurred a penalty which was deducted from the score. Excursions below the bottom of the box (300 feet), resulted in disqualification. The box was clearly marked on the ground, so the pilots knew exactly where to fly.

Much to my surprise, I placed second at the 1985 Hilton contest. I consider this to be my best performance in competitive aerobatics. Second place to Gene Soucy is okay with me, and this was the only time I scored better than my heroes Kermit and Henry.

1988 WORLD AEROBATIC CHAMPIONSHIPS

The fourteenth FAI World Aerobatic Championships were held in Red Deer, Alberta, in 1988. My last flight out of Red Deer before that event had been on October 31, 1961, back when it was called RCAF Station Penhold. I had just completed my Basic Flying Training on the Harvard trainer.

At that point in my life, I had had no idea that I would be flying out of Penhold twenty-seven years later in the Ultimate 10-300S, an airplane that I had designed and developed to fly in the world championships! Although it was not the first airplane that I had created that had been to Penhold. I had built a model of the Harvard using brown paper and 2x4s for our RCAF Training Course 6016.

The design concept for the Ultimate 10-300 was sparked by the Tournament of Champions which was a model airplane contest in Las Vegas sponsored by the Circus Circus Casino. Since the monoplane models were always winning the contest, Bill Bennett, the owner of the casino, offered 15 percent bonus points if a competitor flew a biplane. With this aim in mind, I worked with model builders Bob Godfrey and Don Lowe on the concept, and I built the full scale 10-300S. I eventually gave the model rights to Carl Goldberg Models, which produced a model of my aircraft that turned out to be a best seller.

I worked with the Ultimate Aircraft Corp team that I had put together to design and develop the 10-300S as a competitive aerobatic aircraft capable of winning the World Aerobatic Championships. I showed up at WAC 88 to do just that. That plan did not work out as I had hoped.

RED DEER
ALBERTA
CANADA

JULY 31 —
AUGUST 13

1988
WORLD
AEROBATIC
CHAMPIONSHIPS

RED DEER INDUSTRIAL AIRPORT

WAC 88 poster.

It was one month before I was scheduled to fly to Red Deer, Alberta, and I was practicing an aerobatic sequence directly over Guelph Airport. I was on a vertical down line and I pushed seven negative g to a horizontal line. On the horizontal line I was 500 feet above ground and ready for another push to the vertical. Suddenly I did not feel well, in a way that is hard to describe.

I rolled upright immediately; then I lost my vision! I could not see! I thought to myself, You are going to have to jump out! Then I remembered that I was not wearing a parachute (a questionable decision that I had made earlier to save weight). So, I was forced to stay aboard. I had little to work with. I could see light above, and darkness below. I could hear the engine. So basically, I could keep the aircraft level.

As I worked on that plan, I started to see colours, but the world was still spinning. Gradually the spinning started to slow—not stop—but

RCAF Graduating course 6016 Penhold with model that I built. Circa 1961.

Gord in the RCAF, Penhold Alberta, 1961.

slow. I flew around the airport area hoping that my vision would continue to improve. Somehow, I managed to get the airplane lined up with the runway and I set up a slow rate of descent. I landed with the spinning still there and taxied to the hangar. By the time I got to the hangar, the spinning had stopped. It seemed like my world had just ended. Now what? I thought.

I was standing in the bathroom at home several days later when it happened again. I hung on to the bathroom vanity. "Sandy," I yelled, "Come here and check my eyes!" She confirmed that both of my eyes were uncontrollably and rapidly flicking back and forth. I had a doctor friend pull some strings and I was in Ottawa the next day at the National Defence Medical Centre.

I underwent a myriad of tests and a scan. The results were inconclusive. However, the feeling was that a hair in my inner ear had broken and that it was disturbing my inner ear fluid. The solution was rest. Right! How could I rest when I had to practice for WAC 88? But the

The Ultimate 10-300S during the flight test program.

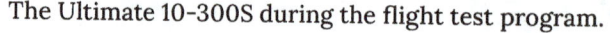

decision had been made—no practice for thirty days; that would give me only one week to practice just before the World Championships.

My mechanic, David Lea, and I flew to our designated practice airport in Camrose, Alberta, a week before WAC 88. (David owned an Ultimate 10-200). The practicing began. I avoided negative g's for a couple of days when finally David said, "Price, when are you going to turn the $#@!ing airplane upside down?" I slowly started with some of the negative manoeuvres. I never exceeded four negative g.

On a sad note, David Lea and his girlfriend, Lynda, were killed in a head on collision while riding his motorcycle in Ontario in September later that year.

I managed to get through the contest without having a recurrence of the eye problem—my new main goal. One claim to fame was that I believe I had my longest tailslide ever (I must have been doing sixty knots backwards). After the tailslide, I found that I had to change the control inputs to fly level because the rudder was bent! Fortunately, I didn't have to break off and I managed to complete the flight. As an extra bonus, the Soviets were kind enough to let me fly their Sukhoi 26M. It is a beautiful aerobatic machine.

A fellow by the name of Stanislav, who wore "coke bottle" glasses and was from the Sukhoi Design Bureau (a Russian aircraft manufacturer), approached me about my airfoil design. I found him studying it very carefully. He noted that the Soviet pilots were complaining about their existing wing. I don't know if they changed their design because of my design, but he indicated that it would solve their problem of snapping "too good." I guess that was a sign that the Cold War was slowly winding down.

WAC 88 was the last competition that I ever flew in. My Ultimate 10-300S was eventually sold to Joann Osterud, who was then a well-known American aerobatic pilot. In a strange turn of events, she would go on to crash that plane. Apparently, she attempted an inverted ribbon-cut and flew it into the ground upside down. But it was a strongly built airplane. Immediately after crashing, she climbed out of it and then—none the worse for wear—apologized to the audience for missing the ribbon. Unfortunately, that was the end of that airplane, and of her aerobatic career as well.

I take my hat off to all aerobatic competitors, but especially those who take up the challenge and fly unlimited world aerobatics. It is a test of yourself—by yourself. As a bonus, you get to meet lots of highly motivated people! The tremendous commitment of time, energy, and money is a true test that only a few can pass.

WAC 88 Red Deer Alberta. Photo © Brad Price.

WAC 88 Red Deer Alberta. Photo © Brad Price.

Gord flew this Soviet Sukhoi 26M at Red Deer WAC 88.

Canadian team pilots Guido Lapore twenty-seventh, Lloyd Beaule fortieth, Randy Gagnon thirty-fourth, and Gord Price twenty-first with Jay Hunt in the background. Photo © Brad Price.

OUR HOME SWEET HOMES

Our wedding day 14 July 1962.

Sandy and I have had more than our share of homes since our marriage on July 14, 1962. We have moved a total of twenty times—and not just local moves but in some cases moves to entirely different continents. All the moves perfectly dealt with situations as our lives evolved. After all, the only thing for sure is change. We have been very fortunate in that our family unit has been able to make positive changes to meet all of the life challenges that have been presented to us.

EXETER, ONTARIO

Our first home was a small two-bedroom apartment in an apartment building in the southeast part of Exeter, Ontario. It was conveniently very close to RCAF Station Centralia. We were only there for three months, but I remember it being party central, and the place where Sandy's dad, Jimmy, gave up smoking after one severe party.

I also vaguely remember letting my buddy from Cape Breton, Jerry Cameron, use our apartment's washing machine. I recall that he used to drink a bottle of Emu 999 (a fortified wine) while watching his clothes go round and round. I'm sure it kept him amused.

CHATHAM, NEW BRUNSWICK

From Exeter we moved to Chatham, New Brunswick and rented a studio apartment with a pull-out bed from the Duffy family. It was not what you would call a fancy place. It had a communal bathroom in a cold breezeway that was attached to the main house, but we survived there for about six months. Young love is much different than old love—the warmth of that first passion can make up for any amount of outside distraction or inconvenience.

Despite its shortcomings, it was good for the budget. Plus, we were busy making a baby! We were, however, delighted when the upper one-bedroom apartment became available, and we snapped that up immediately. What a treat it was not to have to unfold the bed every night! We remained there for five months while I finished the F-86 Sabre transition course.

COLD LAKE, ALBERTA

In Cold Lake, Alberta, we rented a house from Bill and Betty Ross. Bill was my T-33 instructor in Portage and had already transferred to Baden-Soellingen on 422 Squadron. The house was in the Permanent Married Quarters (PMQ) area on the base and was perfect for our short stay in Cold Lake, and for us to get used to our sweet new baby girl Stephanie.

LICHTENAU, WEST GERMANY

After four different living quarters in less than two years, it was off to our big European adventure, and a new home in Lichtenau, West Germany, with the Mehlhorn family. We rented their brand new

Our upper apartment in Lichtenau, West Germany 1964.

two-bedroom apartment which was perfect for us given that Frau Mehlhorn treated us like family.

Several happenings come to mind here. This was a time before disposable diapers, so Sandy was always busy processing the diaper parade. We had a small Hoover high spin rate clothes washer that did a nice job of spinning all the diapers together into a giant knot. It was a tedious job, but Sandy faithfully untangled them. Once untangled they were hung from the clothesline in the attic to dry. In the winter they would just freeze into little boards, so instead they were spread around the living room to dry. The apartment was heated with an oil-fired stove which burped black soot on several occasions.

One burp occurred when we were drying the diapers. It was quite a chore cleaning that mess up! There were a lot of sooty diapers!

In June of 1965, our son Glen was born at the hospital on the base and the diaper parade doubled. We were hoping for a boy to round out the family, so we were ecstatic when Glen arrived. Lichtenau was to us our first real home and when it came time to leave there were a few tears. It was like leaving your family behind.

TORONTO, ONTARIO

In May of 1966, our family of four flew on a Canadair CC-106 Yukon transport to Trenton, Ontario, Canada—courtesy of the RCAF. Our brand-new, maroon, 1966 Oldsmobile Delta 88 was waiting for us. We had used our pension lump sum payment of $8,000 to pay for it.

CC-106 Yukon. Photo RCAF.

Our first home back in Canada was a brand-new three-story townhouse rental, in the Jane and Finch neighbourhood of Toronto. We soon learned that having the bedroom on the third floor was way too much exercise, earning it the nickname "The Vertical Condo."

I suppose it could be seen as fortunate that the local sewers backed up into our basement less than six weeks after we moved in, a rather serious problem that allowed us to break our lease. The only downside was that we had unpacked all our belongings and had had our new furniture delivered and assembled. Oh well, onward and upward!

MALTON, ONTARIO

We had been looking at a new development in Malton, Ontario, which was as close as you could get to the airport. I approached my dad with the brilliant idea that we should buy a house instead of renting one. But there was a problem. We didn't have any money. So, armed with all sorts of information about the house we were looking at, I approached my father. "$20,500! For a semi-detached house? Are you out of your mind? That's an outrageous price!"

So, I approached Jimmy, Sandy's dad, and he said, yes—he would loan us the down payment. That was the financial boost that we really needed to get into the housing market, and we moved into a new and very muddy subdivision on the east side of Malton.

We were so excited! Our very own house! I set about organizing the backyard and built a beautiful brick barbecue using leftover bricks that I scrounged from the construction sites around us. It was a masterpiece! We finished the basement with a beautiful little bar. I really enjoyed all this construction activity.

However, we did have the typical new home purchaser problems— like items that were not finished. In our case, I had been all over the contractor to clean up twenty outstanding items, but all I was getting from him was lip service, so I tightened the screws. I bought a 4 x 8 foot sheet of plywood, painted it white, and in black paint wrote up the twenty items to be completed—itemized one to twenty in big dark letters. To get to the sales office, prospective purchasers had to drive right by our house, and as the sign was erected on our front lawn, they couldn't miss it.

To ensure that our campaign continued around the clock, a couple of spotlights made it really stand out at night. I remember setting up a two-four of beer and some chairs on the veranda just to watch the action. Popcorn was supplied and we, along with some neighbours with similar problems, watched the show.

The developer was in London, England. I received a call from him. "Gordy! I have spoken to the contractor. Don't worry, all the outstanding items will be completed for you. Please take the sign down."

"As soon as everything is done Bob, I will remove the sign," I told him. "As a matter of fact, as the items are completed, I will draw a line through them to show progress."

Bob was not happy. Apparently, the sign was affecting his sales negatively; what a surprise! Within two weeks all the outstanding items were completed, and I removed the sign from our front lawn.

GEORGETOWN, ONTARIO

We enjoyed our home in Malton for several years but saw an opportunity to move into a very comfortable four-bedroom detached home with an attached garage on the end of a cul-de-sac in Georgetown, only thirty minutes from the airport. We paid $24,250 for it, which was less than what we sold our semi-detached Malton home for.

Out of all our homes—this one is the family favourite. Stephanie and Glen were five and three years of age, respectively, when we moved in. Sandy and I had decided that we would invest in cottage-like features for this home rather than buying a cottage, so we didn't have to waste time and money travelling. It was one of our best decisions, and the main reason it is an all-time family favourite.

To make the backyard into a summer wonderland, we put in a 20 x 40 foot heated swimming pool and surrounded it with a concrete block wall to keep the wind out and the heat in. The only help I had was from a couple of airline buddies, Dale Horley and Ted Strachan, who had a swimming pool company. I did all the block and concrete work myself. We didn't have the money to hire a contractor, so I was it. The pool became the unofficial neighbourhood centre.

One issue I faced was my increasing beer expenses, so after some trial and error, I found a solution: brewing my own beer. Initially, I ended up with either sweet, flat beer or cloudy beer that sprayed everywhere upon opening. While it may not have matched the world-class German beer we enjoyed overseas, it was at least economical.

I was flying to London, England, at the time and came across a beer making kit with a five-gallon polyethylene keg with a spout. It utilized a carbon dioxide cartridge (which was costly), the tap was above the sediment layer, and it poured a good pint of beer. This was the start of the experiment. The end product was superb. I bought

Uplands Court Georgetown.

a total of five of the five-gallon kegs, an old refrigerator, and a large commercial bottle of CO_2 with a regulator. I then drilled a hole in the side of the refrigerator to allow the CO_2 hose to be attached to the keg which sat in the fridge.

To get a pint of beer you simply opened the refrigerator door and turned the spigot on the keg 90° for a perfect pint. I significantly lowered the cost of providing beer to the neighbourhood. However, it was so successful that some wives complained that the boys were drinking too much. That was easily fixed. I changed the mash recipe and lowered the alcohol content to two percent. Having five kegs made it simple to keep rotating them and this provided an endless supply of beer. Another house specialty was elderberry/chokecherry red wine. Our house white was apple, elderflower, and banana. We were quite the little producers.

We enjoyed that home immensely for eight years, but then decided to move for a variety of reasons. A big factor was that Sandy's mom, Blanche, had had a severe case of spinal meningitis that had left her totally deaf. Sandy's dad, Jimmy, was looking after her and had been forced to retire. They were living in Rochester, New York, about a 260 km drive from Georgetown and a long way away should they require help. We decided that we would have an architect design a home for us that would include an 1,800 square foot apartment for Blanche and Jimmy.

A young Stephanie.

Our Summer Wonderland in Georgetown.

Glen and Stephanie.

Our 20' x 40' swimming pool.

BELFOUNTAIN, ONTARIO

We purchased a lot in an upscale subdivision in Belfountain and began construction in April. In preparation for the move, I pre-built all of the kitchen cupboards, a range hood, and the bathroom vanities in the garage in Georgetown.

It was a lovely house and it worked out well for Blanche and Jimmy. The kids loved the fact that their grandparents were always there to bail them out when they got into trouble. The apartment was over top of both a three-car garage and a workshop. The workshop produced a myriad of products—the two most significant being my Pitts S-1 and Sandy's Clipped-wing Piper Cub. Yes, I built my wife Sandy an airplane! I felt it was cheaper than a divorce (just kidding).

Our house in Belfountain.

Sandy unloading 4130 Chromoly steel for her Piper Cub.

Sandy in her Clipped Wing Cub.

Clipped Wing Cub I built for Sandy.

We lived in Belfountain for about eight years, but travelling to Guelph Airpark almost every day got us thinking of moving again.

ROCKWOOD, ONTARIO

We found ten acres just south of Rockwood and built a beautiful house overlooking a valley. It was close to Guelph Airpark which was to make life a lot easier, since Ultimate Aircraft Corp (UAC) was now consuming all of our spare time.

While building the house I had a conversation with someone from the town about putting a second house on the same lot, basically a Granny flat. There was no provision for it in the local bylaws, so the answer was "No Way." On one visit from the building inspector, he commented on how nicely secluded the property was. It was true. The tree line between us and the road made it impossible to see the house or any of the property.

Once our final building inspection was completed, we poured a large concrete pad adjacent to the house. It was big enough for a house to

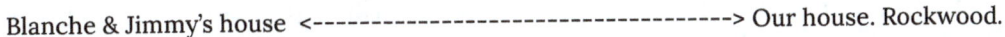

Blanche & Jimmy's house <--> Our house. Rockwood.

fit on—if you wanted to.

On a very snowy day with very poor visibility, two trucks showed up—each with half a house. It did not take long to put the house together. Blanche and Jimmy lived in it for the rest of their lives, and we were all very happy.

This is where the story takes on a sad note. We had had, up to that point, so many highs in our life that I guess it was inevitable that something would go wrong. And ultimately, this would become one of the most difficult chapters of our lives.

By this time I was not just flying airplanes, but I had created a business to build them. We were producing some good products, we had buyers, and everything was going well. But as it is for any enthusiast who tries to turn their passion into a business, problems develop that they could never have foreseen. Ultimate Aircraft Corporation ended up having to declare bankruptcy, and since Sandy and I had guaranteed all the loans—we also had to declare bankruptcy.

I (fortunately) still had a good job with Air Canada which I was desperately trying to hold on to. We had built our home close to the airport where we kept the airplane, but the mortgage on the house was twelve percent at that point and we simply couldn't afford it. I went in to meet with the bank manager and requested a reduction in the interest rate. He said, "Well, a deal is a deal. That's too bad." What a disaster!

Blanche and Jimmy had recently died, along with Sandy's uncle. Worst of all, we had also lost Cory, our granddaughter, Stephanie's daughter, at the age of five weeks. She had never left the neonatal clinic in Hamilton's McMaster Children's Hospital. We moved Blanche and Jimmy's house to Sandy's sister's farm, and then we moved out and left our empty house for the bank.

On the last day, as we were cleaning everything out of the house, the bank manager called and said, "Maybe we can make a deal."

But I told him, "It's too late. The house is empty now, and it is all yours."

Our house in Boca Raton.

BOCA RATON, FLORIDA

I don't remember much at all about the house that we rented in Barrie while we were trying to figure out how to carry on and recover. My dad came to the rescue this time; he loaned us enough money for a down payment on a house in Boca Raton, Florida. It seemed like a good idea to get away and to somehow put everything back together.

The Boca Raton house worked for a year while we consulted with a residency lawyer to come up with a recovery plan. The complete change and the warm climate were good for us. Ideas started to flow as we healed. Then a stroke of good luck occurred.

Our old next-door neighbours, George and Margaret Howie from Georgetown, suggested, "Why don't you come to Bermuda? We have a house and residence there. We can get you permission to live in Bermuda. All you need is an annual letter of approval."

So, the adventure in Bermuda began, and life became fun again.

HAMILTON, BERMUDA

Our first home in Bermuda was a one-bedroom apartment on Point Shares Road on the west side of Hamilton. It was small but quite luxurious. We had a scooter for transportation—an adventurous way to get around during tropical rainstorms. We were starting to feel alive again.

Bermuda rain gear and the scooter.

Then another stroke of good luck hit. There was a fellow who was building a beautiful house in Southampton, Bermuda, with a view over the Great Sound. He had run into financial difficulty, but if he could obtain additional income by getting someone to sign a lease for five years, then the bank would lend him the money to complete the house. We were offered a five-year lease at a very good price. We signed it, and moved in shortly thereafter.

SOUTHAMPTON, BERMUDA

The Southampton house was spectacular; it was just what we needed to recover emotionally from the recent series of disasters. We hosted many parties there for the Air Canada staff in Bermuda and the staff of the Norwegian Cruise ship *Dreamward*. The rest of the time I played golf or attended parties on the *Dreamward* with Sandy! Yes, they were probably the best years of our lives.

The *Dreamward* made weekly trips between Boston and Bermuda. They were in Bermuda for three days during midweek. I frequently played golf with the captain, first officer, and the food and beverage manager at various golf courses around the island—thanks to complimentary passes. The crew needed transportation, and that

Red dot was the location of our Bermuda house for five years.[19]

was me since I had the car. It was an ideal situation.

Sandy and I also attended quite a few captain's dinners on the ship. On several occasions we dined in the captain's quarters when he and his wife felt like a less stressful meal.

There is a vast difference in stature between an airline captain and a ship's captain, I observed. When the captain of the ship is ready for coffee, he simply glances imperiously at one of the stewards hovering nearby and it is done. I can attest to the fact that airline captains do not receive the same sort of treatment. In fact, in some cases I had to return to the galley and make my own coffee, because the flight attendants were busy looking after our passengers.

Upon arrival to Bermuda the ship would first dock in St. George's, at the north end of the island. After a day there they repositioned the ship to Hamilton Harbour in the middle of the island. Sandy and I were invited on board the ship for the repositioning to experience "the world's shortest cruise." It was a very exciting experience.

Since we lived in Southampton (a long way from St. George's), we commuted on a scooter. With Sandy hanging on behind me, we motored through the chilly morning air. We rolled up to the boarding

[19] "Bermuda," Google Maps screen shot, January 2024. https://www.google.ca/maps

Bermuda house, gouache painting Gord.

ramp of the *Dreamward* and they were waiting for us in the dark. They pulled the scooter onto the ship, closed the loading door, and ushered us up to the bridge where everyone was quite busy casting off. The ship sailed through the Town Cut at St. George's with only a few feet of clearance on each side of the massive ship. We sailed down the west coast of Bermuda and finally docked in Hamilton Harbour. Parallel parking a cruise ship takes some expert talent.

After the ship was secured to the dock, we joined the captain for lunch and a couple of glasses of wine in the dining room. After lunch, the crew rolled our scooter off the ship, Sandy and I jumped on, and away we went—home for a nap. We had a great life in Bermuda!

We were members of the Riddell's Bay Golf & Country Club, and I frequently golfed there with other members, friends, and of course the crew of the *Dreamward*. But sometimes I golfed alone.

One of those days was a memorable one: April 27,1997. I showed up at the course and teed off. There was no one else around, which

Elbow Beach, Bermuda, watercolour Gord.

was not unusual for a Wednesday morning. As I walked down the seventh fairway, I noticed that there seemed to be more police sirens and yelps than usual. In fact, they were getting louder and closer. It seemed to me that they were very near the golf course. Maybe they were even on the golf course!

I had just putted out the seventh hole when I looked to my left and saw flashing lights coming down the fairway! Those vehicles then veered off to the left. Hmmm very strange, I thought. Then a motorcycle with a flashing light came flying down the fairway; it was aiming right for me! I headed for the woods and stood there as he pulled onto the green. Yes—right onto the green!

"Did you see some police cars come this way?" he asked.

"Yes, they went that way," and I pointed towards the ninth green.

"Thanks," he said as he gunned the motorcycle. The rear wheel spun all the way across the grass, leaving a trail of mud and a very damaged

Middle Road, Bermuda, watercolour Gord.

green. I still didn't know what was going on, but it seemed to me to be a good idea to skip a few holes and to head for hole number thirteen.

I played up to number seventeen, and was headed for the tee off on eighteen, when I was stopped by a police officer. He said, "Sorry sir, you can't be in this area."

"What's going on?" I asked.

"There has been a bank robbery," he explained. "We have the suspects cornered in the woods there." He pointed just to the right of the nineteenth fairway.

"Ok then," I said.

I went over to the fifth fairway and from there walked back to the clubhouse. On the way, I noticed lots of police with guns drawn— some had machine guns. When I got back, I received a bit of an ovation from a crowd that had assembled on the clubhouse balcony. They had been watching the drama unfold. Apparently, I had been the only golfer on the course that day.

It turned out that the Somerset Branch of the Bank of Bermuda had been robbed. Three men had burst into the bank—two of them brandishing pistols. No one had been hurt in the robbery, although one shot had been fired into the ceiling. A fourth man had remained outside but he had joined the other three when they had fled the bank with a large amount of money that had been taken from the boxes of two tellers. They had made their getaway on two scooters which they had taken to a boat that they had positioned nearby. Crossing the Great Sound, they had landed at the golf course where I happened to be golfing.

YOUNGSTOWN, NEW YORK

By this time, I was flying the Boeing 747-400 to Frankfurt and London. The schedules were such that I was not home very much. We had already decided that we would move to Scotland when we retired, so we did not want to return to Canada as residents. Instead, we found a beautiful little one-bedroom apartment in Youngstown, New York—an easy commute to Toronto to finish out my final years with Air Canada.

It was nicely finished, had in-floor heating, and was located right across the Niagara River from Fort George. It provided a spectacular view of the Niagara River. We were located just above the yacht club. Two years later we moved to Scotland, a real-life adventure for us.

CULLEN, SCOTLAND

Both Sandy and I have some Scottish blood in us, but it was very strange how we were drawn into living in Cullen, Scotland.

The original plan was to find a little cottage by the North Sea and settle in as retirees. Somehow, the plan changed, and we bought a very large building, 27 Grant Street in Cullen. It was a large house with an attached chemist shop.

We felt very at home as we settled in, and we were immediately accepted into the community. We joined the Family History Society in Aberdeen and set out to find our relatives. In a twist that's a bit spooky, we discovered that Sandy's grandmother and my grandmother were both born just outside of Aberdeen in Old Machar; in fact, they had lived on the same street. We also found out that Sandy's great-great-grandparents were buried twenty minutes from our house and mine were buried just forty-five minutes away. No wonder we felt at home!

We completely renovated 27 Grant Street and the old chemist shop. It was great therapy for me as I tore the building apart—right down to the four-foot-thick rubble walls, as they called them. The chemist shop floor was taken back to the mud and completely done over. When the renovations were completed, it was converted to a self-catering apartment and was awarded gold star status with the Scottish Tourist Board.

During a visit to Scotland, Stephanie announced to us that she had recently quit her job in sales, had completed a bartender's course,

27 Grant Street, Cullen, Scotland.

and was now working in a bar back home. She even worked for free at the three different pubs in Cullen to gain some Scottish pub experience for the future.

She told us that it was not all that great working for someone else behind the bar until two in the morning and that maybe, one day, she could own her own pub and we could call it The Dam Pub, which you'll read more about in an upcoming chapter. The Dam Pub sparked a move back to Canada in 2007.

DYERS BAY AND MEAFORD, ONTARIO

We sold 27 Grant Street in Cullen for a good price and took up residence in our cottage at Dyers Bay. I had a very large garage/ workshop there to keep me busy making biodiesel from used restaurant oil.

In 2015, we moved to our current home on five acres in Meaford, Ontario to be closer to shopping and medical services as we grew older.

Our little paradise in Dyers Bay.

Our home on a five-acre lot in Meaford.

THE ULTIMATE DISASTER

I was consumed by Ultimate Aerobatics Ltd. and its successor, Ultimate Aircraft Corp., for a period of about ten years. Sandy and I literally put everything we had into my vision. In the end we lost everything in what became known to us as "The Ultimate Disaster," and we were forced to start over from scratch.

It is a very difficult subject for me to talk about, and in fact my self-protection mode has blocked out a great deal of the events to the point that I simply cannot remember them all.

Fortunately, Jim Morkill was employed by Ultimate Aircraft Corp. as a welder while he was attending the University of Guelph. In addition to being a very good welder, Jim also had a very good memory. He wrote "Destiny by Design" as a project while attending business school; a shortened, edited version of which is included here. It sums up "The Ultimate Disaster" perfectly, while saving me from having to re-live the nightmare by writing about it.

DESTINY BY DESIGN

Gord Price and Ultimate Aircraft Corp.

Presented by J. A. Morkill

April 5, 1992

Award-winning aerobatics pilot Gord Price designed and built several sets of wings for his homebuilt Pitts aircraft in 1978, and it wasn't long before there was commercial interest in them. It was almost by accident that people were hired to speed up the building process, and soon a substantial market developed for these specialty items.

Gordon began to wonder what the possibilities might be of purpose designing, and building, a high-performance stunt aircraft from the ground up. He knew that he wanted to win the world championship, and with his typical focus, energy, enthusiasm, and "never say never" attitude he set about to determine the machine specifications that would be requisite to maximizing his flying ability and winning the competition.

He determined the optimum machine characteristics and [began] designing a 300 hp bi-wing aircraft from scratch. Although this began as a labour of love, the economic realities of the situation demanded that the venture sustain itself financially, thus the need for commercial interests. On the advice of others, at the same time he undertook to design and develop a 100 hp biplane that would become the selling tool for all other designs, and be more marketable than a pure competition airplane. This aircraft proved to be very successful in all respects except power, so a 200 hp version was designed, built, tested and offered for sale as well. Both were available as drawings, kits or completed, and several intermediate forms as well.

Gord still wanted to build the 300 hp competition airplane and used most available company resources to this end. However, by mid-1986, there was only half a fuselage and one set of wings in rough form. The prices of the completed airplanes ranged from $30,000 to $90,000 depending on the options chosen, and many were ordered, mostly in kit form.

It quickly became obvious that the company would need an infusion of working capital and skilled employees if progress on the 300 was to continue. Both were acquired in mid-1986, and the company atmosphere was one of excitement, anticipation, trust and commitment.

By June 1987 though, the atmosphere had changed to one of anxiety. The 300 was still under development and using up a lot of free cash. Even though business in the 100 and 200 series was brisk enough to keep most employees busy on other things, Gord quite often seemed over-stressed. No one was quite sure how the 300 was going to get built and developed in time for the 1988 world championships.

Throughout this entire period, Gord and his wife Sandy performed virtually all administrative and marketing tasks by themselves. Although they did get help from time to time, the workload was enormous.

By August 1987, the 300 hp airplane was built and flying. Company resources were used to the fullest extent to accomplish this, and everyone was proud of the finished product. Now all that had to be done was to refine and develop the machine for Gordon, a skilled and ready pilot, to be competitive at a world-class level. This was easier said than done.

The first problem was money. There was very little of that available, and new sources were not obvious. The second was that existing customer orders were now in a rush state, having been delayed by pushing on with the 300 project. The third was that the constant stress was beginning to tell on Gordon's (and Sandy's) physical, emotional, and marital health. Lastly, few new orders were being placed. There was no formal marketing program to sell the products, although brochures and a price schedule were available for those who wrote, or phoned in.

As the fall of 1987 progressed, the situation worsened, and creditors began turning up the pressure. The first several months of 1988 were very difficult and Gordon and Sandy had to face the chilling task of laying off all their employees.

Soon afterwards Gordon discovered that while his competition airplane was everything he had hoped, his own physical and emotional health did not permit him to sustain the high level of negative G forces (-7 G's) required to win a world championship.

This meant that he would not have his most potent marketing tool available to him, his flying skills and a world championship. Gord flew in the world championships in 1988 anyway and placed 15th, "with one eye glued to the G meter", knowing that if he exceeded negative four G's he could black out and possibly crash and die.

This was not a purely selfish gesture, as both Gord and Sandy were committed to the company and felt responsible for their former employees. He believed that his company might have been saved if by some miracle, he was able to win despite the handicap.

They now found themselves having to declare bankruptcy [both corporate and personal], as well as attempt to mount an effective legal defense against their creditors and customers who all wanted a piece of the rapidly shrinking pie that was Ultimate Aircraft.

Legal fees were rising, and his immediate personal liability ranged in the neighbourhood of $400,000 which he didn't have, with a further $330,000 invested by friends and family for which he and Sandy felt responsible.

To add fat to the fire, Gordon was booking off work regularly for stress-related concentration loss. Gord felt that as a senior pilot for Air Canada, it was his responsibility to be alert and focused while flying, something which in those business circumstances had become increasingly difficult. This meant that he was unable to earn a predictable income from Air Canada.

As of this writing in 1992, Gordon and Sandy are in the process of launching their own lawsuits against various individuals and companies, having successfully fought off most of the financial and legal attacks over the last four years. Their personal finances are in shambles, but Gord is still employed with Air Canada and Sandy has work.

They have both negotiated the emotional roller coaster that characterized the last four years of their lives, and have come out wiser and more philosophical than they went in.

Completed 10-100 airplane.

THE PRODUCTS

Here are some of the products that we developed at Ultimate.

The 10-100 was a marvelous airplane, but it was tough to fly in airshows because of the limiting horsepower. I managed to fly the Capital Air Show in Ottawa with it on July 1, 1986, or 1987, I think. I remember that lack of power made it tricky to maintain altitude and to fly over the Ottawa River behind the parliament buildings.

The trip in the 10-100 down to the Sun and Fun Airshow in Lakeland, Florida was another story. It took place in a skidoo suit with chemical

"We build the wings for you!"

The Ultimate Wing

Complete Ultimate Wing Kit

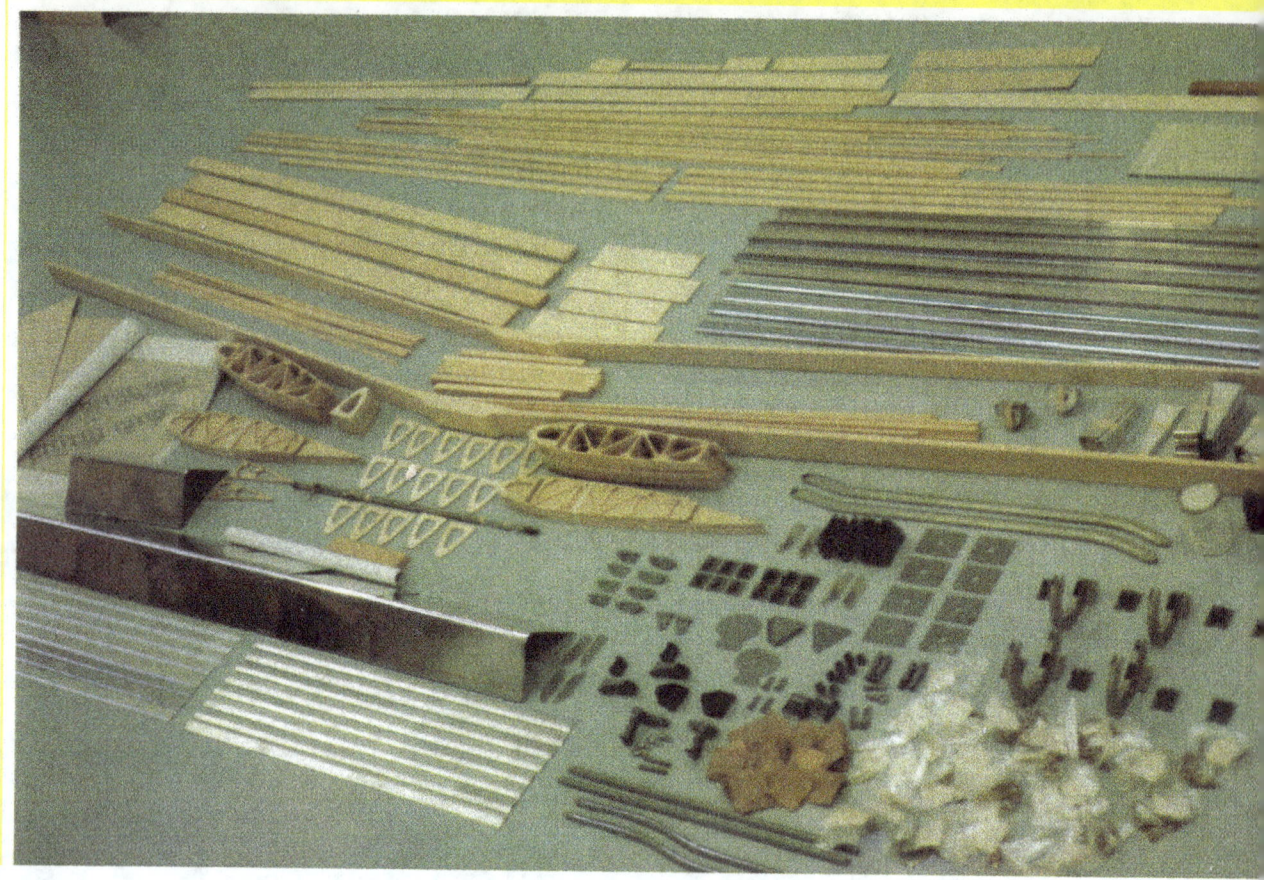

"You build a wing from our kit."

Complete Ultimate 10-100 kit.

Aerobatic Fuel Tank

Safest, best-performing main tank built. Internal header tank is always full, allows cough-free inverted flight. Tank is filled with EXPLOSAFE metal foil which makes it **explosion proof** and cuts down on fuel slosh. Tank and cap completely finished in white acrylic enamel, ready for installation. Fits Pitts S-1 and most other aerobatic airplanes.

Order Numbers:
22 US Gallons.....................1012
18 US Gallons.....................1013
Flop Tube for above tanks........1012A

Extend-A-Range Fuel Tank

Extra cruising range with minimum drag penalty, cuts out fuel stops. Tank straps onto top wing in 5 minutes, can be plumbed into main tank or to a fuel selector. Contains EXPLOSAFE foil - explosion proof, slosh resistant. Mounting straps & hardware included. Finished in white acrylic enamel. Order:

9 US Gallons (Pitts S-1)...........1009
15 US Gallons (Pitts S-1)...........1010
18 US Gallons (Pitts S-2, Eagle 2)...1011

Innovative fuel tanks.

Custom Fuselage

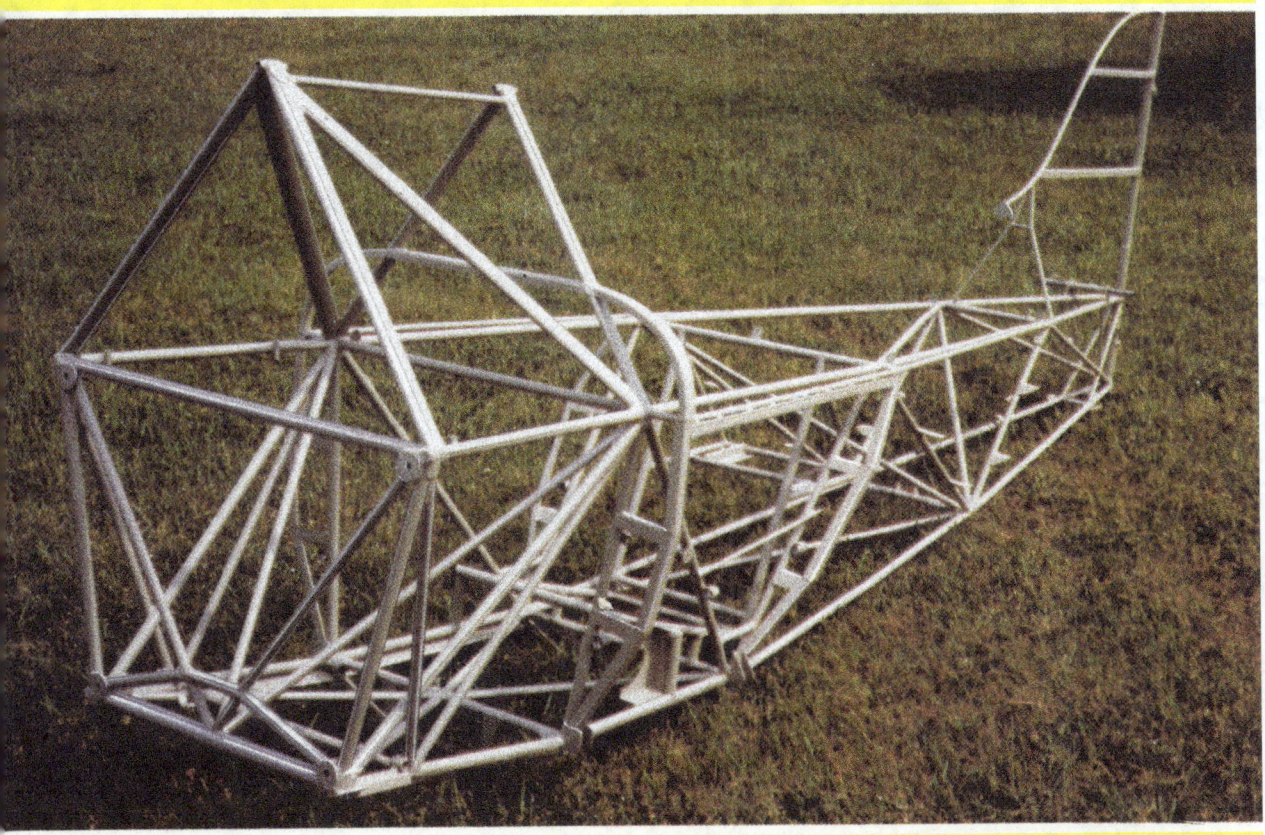

el a little cramped in the cockpit? your pitts can be custom-fitted to size! The ULTIMATE Fuselage can xtended up to 8-1/2'' to provide extra ort without any sacrifice in euverability.

Fuselage is jig-built of 4130 Chrome Moly steel tubing, oxy-acetylene welded to ensure stress relieving. Light weight with strength and guaranteed accuracy.

Order Number. 1019

Welded fuselage, custom fit.

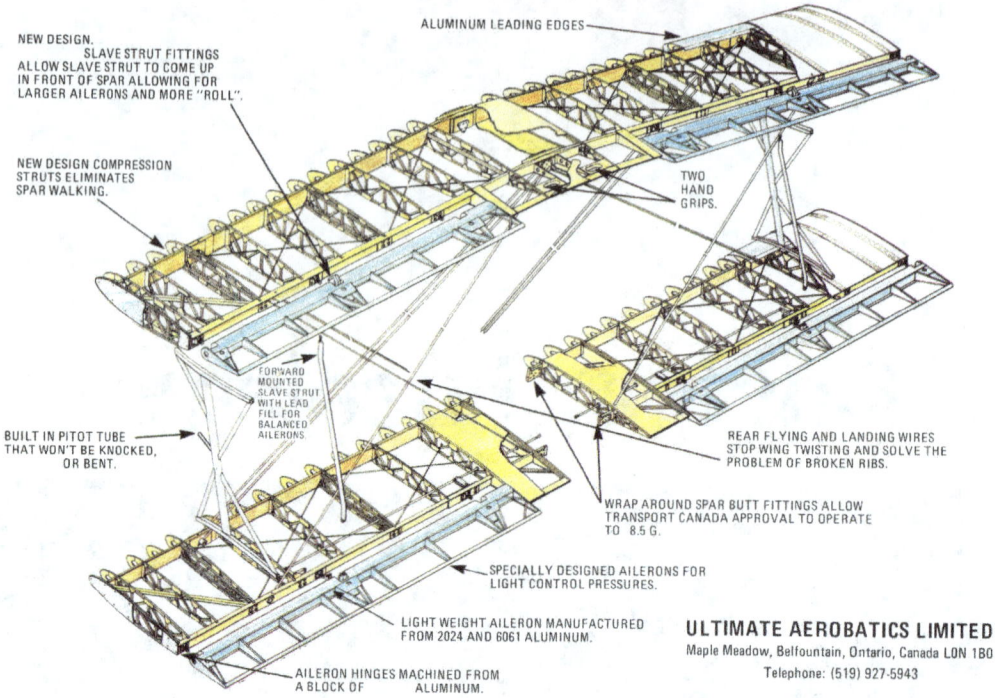
"Exploded view" of the Ultimate Wing.

hand and foot warmers and -30° temperatures (some stuff I don't miss). When I flew that show, I managed to eke out three vertical rolls before beating a hasty retreat for speed from the top of a hammerhead because the airplane was going to stall. It rolled at 360° per second, and it was a real performer on one hundred hp, but as I say, it was quite difficult to fly and to conserve altitude with due to its lack of power. But I guess I can't have everything, as all airplanes are a compromise.

The 10-100's landing attitude (and the pilot's associated lack of visibility over the nose) contributed to a mid-air landing accident which resulted in some serious injuries to a friend of mine, Reg Tustin. It happened on final approach to Guelph. A Cessna 172 was on a long final approach and Reggie was in a tight circuit. The Cessna was behind the 10-100's nose which blocked it from Reg's view. Reg landed on top of him. We all learned a lesson from that one—move

The Ultimate 10-100 prototype on runway at Guelph after a midair collision with a Cessna 172. Photo © Marc Ranger.

the nose around on base and final circuit legs, and assume that it is hiding someone.

The 10-300 was designed for the judges. We then had to make it fly for the pilot. The long lines gave it the same visual characteristics of a monoplane. If you were straight, there was no doubt. If you were five degrees off, there was no doubt. With a Pitts you could fudge a few degrees because it was stubby, but the judges never accepted it for drawing crisp straight lines because of the visual fudge factor.

On the other hand, the full scale 10-300 series is longitudinally stable which is a disaster for the aerobatic pilot, but a delight for the licensing authorities. The stick loads were unbearable without some sort of assist. Our solution was the integrated control system which provided for 5° full span aileron (flap) movement opposite to the 30° elevator deflection. Pull back, and the ailerons droop. Push forward and the ailerons go up—and presto!—the corners were sharp and

Ultimate 10-300s, shipped to Finland.

stick loads were manageable.

The snap roll is essentially a horizontal spin. To spin, the airfoil must be stalled. A high-speed stall after inducing a skid makes the airplane "snap." Flaps reduce the stalling speed, so in effect we have a contradiction. We try to stall by pulling or pushing, but the effect is counteracted by the action of the flaps which is trying to prevent the stall. So, does it (the 10-300) snap well? Yes.

For a positive snap, a good sharp pull satisfies the judges as they see the positive pitching of the nose. Then you ram the stick into a forward corner (removing the lift) and the rate of rotation is magnificent. It took a little to get used to, but it was a fabulous snapper.

I have a final word of advice for all test pilots: be cautious and stay over the field. I was always very cautious when testing, and it paid off several times.

Also: the airplane will not kill you, but sudden contact with the ground will. Come close to the ground only on landing. I have a lot of dead friends.

SUMMING IT UP

The early 1990s were a tough period for me and my family. There were at least three or four very traumatic years that we had to endure. I would have to say that that time was the lowest of the low for me. Essentially, we went from me being at the top of my aerobatic career—I participated in the 1988 World Aerobatic Championships and I flew at the Canadian International Air Show. CIAS—to having to sell my Ultimate 10-300S aerobatic biplane.

Ironically, you need an awful lot of money to go through bankruptcy—money we didn't have. What was worse was that I couldn't afford a lawyer of my own. I was at the mercy of an aggressive lawyer representing a customer who just wouldn't let go, and it made my life very, very difficult.

Sandy and I were forty-nine years old when we experienced The Ultimate Disaster, and essentially, we had to start over from scratch. I lost my RSPs, I lost my sense of self-worth, and I even lost a lot of friends—but I did learn a lot of lessons as well.

I discovered (the hard way) that in business, if you can't convince an absolute stranger to invest money in your company, then it's not worth it. Don't try to get friends and acquaintances into your business, because that's the surest way to lose them. It was a tough lesson to learn, and one that has helped to guide me ever since.

Ultimate 10-200 owned by Glenn Biederman and Les McInnes.

A FEW HEART-STOPPING EVENTS

Gord, walking the Ultimate 10-200 to the Oshkosh Airshow flight line.

Anyone who flies will have a story to tell that goes like this THERE I WAS, JUST ABOUT OUT OF GAS, AND I THOUGHT THINGS COULD NOT GET ANY WORSE, AND THEY DID!

Been there, done that!

Flying an airplane is different than driving a car or operating a boat. It's the third and fourth dimensions that you're dealing with that ultimately complicate everything. Not only must you contend with the whole UP and DOWN thing, but the equation is also further complicated by GRAVITY! Here are a few of the hairiest moments that I experienced as a pilot.

NO GAS, NO FLY

I was flying the Oshkosh Fly-In Airshow one time in Joe Underwood's brand-new Ultimate 10-200 aerobatic biplane, and I was on the way up to perform a hammerhead turn around when the engine coughed. That was very unusual. The next manoeuvre was a loop with a couple of negative snaps on top. Just before I snapped, the engine quit. It stopped: nothing, nada, silence! The prop had suddenly stopped spinning.

Was I surprised? YES! Was this a problem? NO! I was flying directly over runway 36, so I just landed uneventfully. I discovered I had run out of fuel. But the question was, why?

Aircraft performance is optimized by keeping the weight down, so loading the minimum amount of fuel is the normal procedure. Before my flight I had been in the airshow line-up, in the grass, just off the taxiway. The fuel truck driver asked if I needed fuel. I had checked the fuel sight gauge and it showed that I had sufficient fuel. "No thanks," I said.

The problem was that the tail of the airplane was sitting in a ditch. Since the airplane was not in a level position, the sight gauge was giving a false reading and it showed that there was sufficient fuel on board. Lesson learned.

THE INEVITABLE CRASH

Life was a blur in the eighties, and my memory of those years is a bit foggy, but some events are still vividly with me, including this one. I was set to fly the Orillia Air Show in the Ultimate 10-200 prototype, but my schedule was going to be very tight. The airplane was in Ottawa and nearing the end of some testing by the EAAC Technical Committee.

I jetted to Ottawa, picked up the 10-200 and flew directly to Orillia, Ontario for the air show, arriving just in time for the briefing. After the briefing, I pre-flighted the airplane and was ready to go when launched.

I took off at the scheduled slot time and went right into the aerobatic sequence. Everything was normal and proceeding as planned. Halfway through the sequence, I pulled up to a 45° line and entered Bezák's Lomcovák maneuver—just as he taught me. I then coaxed it into an inverted flat spin, and got it to wind up pretty good; this was to be followed by the recovery.

Throttle off, stick back, and neutral ailerons. That's when the stick jammed! It would not move fore or aft. I could not stop the inverted spin. This is where time slows down in your mind, but your thoughts and actions are occurring quite rapidly. I thought this was it; after everything I'd done and experienced, I'd finally reached it—the end.

Ladi Bezák had once given me some advice about crashing when it appears inevitable, "Put the airplane into a flat spin and use full power to slow the rate of descent!" I know a lot of you readers may disagree and I am not saying that I agree either, but it is an interesting theory, right?

I was over a forest. As per Ladi's advice, I advanced the throttle once again to full power and prepared to hit the trees—inverted and spinning—but at a slower rate of descent. The big decision having been made, I returned to survival mode.

I started banging the stick every which way to dislodge whatever was jamming the controls. It worked! The controls were freed up. I closed the throttle, stopped the spin, levelled out, did a 180° turn, landed, and taxied up to the ramp. No one had any idea what I was

Dan Marcotte's Ultimate 10-200 inverted —Photo Jean-Pierre Bonin

doing or why, and I wasn't talking.

I jumped out of the cockpit, and it felt like I was walking a foot up in the air with all the excess adrenaline in my body. I calmly walked to the back of the aircraft and checked the "see through" inspection panel in the tail. There it was, problem solved! A set of keys was hanging over the elevator bell crank. I walked away. Again, I said nothing.

I learned later from someone trying to track them down that one of the test pilots back in Ottawa had lost his keys. I just wish I had known this before the flight.

READY TO JUMP

On another occasion, I was practicing individual manoeuvres over a lake east of Fergus, Ontario, in the Ultimate Pitts. I had pulled up to the vertical when the stick violently jumped out of my hand. I thought the airplane had exploded. I opened the canopy, while still going up, and prepared to jump.

Testing the Ultimate wing for the Pitts S-1.

I then noticed that the stick was going back and forth at a high rate but that it was slowing down. I grabbed the stick and managed to slow the oscillations even more. I could get the oscillations to stop at about 60 mph. The trim tab cable had broken, and the trim tab was flopping up and down and causing the aircraft to violently oscillate in pitch.

I was about fifteen nautical miles from the airport at this point. By holding the stick steady with my knees, and if I did not exceed 60 mph, everything was fine.

It was a long trip back to the Guelph Airport. Once I got in the landing pattern, I sped up and the oscillations returned. On final approach, the aircraft was pitching up and down vigorously. However, as I slowed down in the round out, the pitching stopped, and this allowed for a normal landing.

The US/Canada border is the dark line that follows Kelly Rapids. Sully is in Quebec. [20]

AN ACCIDENTAL BORDER CROSSING

After flying the Yak-50 in the 2016 Restigouche Air Show in Charlo, New Brunswick, I headed for Rivière-du-Loup, Quebec. There was some pretty bad weather enroute, so I tried to go around it to the southwest. I passed by Edmundston, New Brunswick, thinking that if I got into trouble, I could always go back and land there. I was pushed farther west by the weather.

Finally, I decided I didn't like the looks of what I had to go through to get to Rivière-du-Loup, so I started to turn back. Just then I noticed an abandoned airport directly below me. Hmmm, maybe I should land there. Maybe Edmundston weather is deteriorating so I should have a look.

I pulled the power off and dove for the airport. I flew a precautionary approach to check out the runway. It looked ok—not perfect—but ok. I landed, missed a couple of potholes, taxied back to the button of

[20] US/Quebec border," Google Maps screen shot, January 2024. https://www.google.ca/maps

The Tailslide. Photo © Kevin Prentice.

the runway, and shut the engine down. I called Flight Service using my cellphone and told them that I was down safely, but not at my destination. I asked them to close my flight plan.

"Where are you?" I was asked.

"I don't know. It's an abandoned airport. I'll wait here for a few hours, then head off for Rivière-du-Loup." I got out the maps—only to discover that I was in the US! I was south of Quebec, by about 1,800 feet.

Since I was flying a Russian airplane that was easily identified by its red stars, I fully expected the border patrol to arrest me. Fortunately, they never showed up. I waited out the weather for two hours, and then uneventfully flew on to Rivière-du-Loup.

SIX SECONDS OF TERROR

The scariest event that I have ever experienced happened on June 14, 2020, in my Yak-50 at the Owen Sound Airport. Six seconds of terror! To this day when I drive by, I can still visualize what the crash site would have looked like

It was only the second flight of the season; I had flown the Yak once nine days prior. There was no one there—no air show crowds or announcers. It was just me and my Yak-50.

To properly frame this story, dear reader, you must understand that my flying style is different from that of most other pilots. A regular mid-season flight, to me, would entail fifteen minutes of aerobatics, starting after a takeoff roll of about 200 feet, accelerate to 130 mph then maybe a snap roll, a hammerhead, or a 5/8 loop—it depends on what sequence I am working on.

This being only the second flight of the season, however, I chose to climb up to 1,000 feet before beginning some gentle aerobatics. The reason I added a safety margin of about 800 feet of altitude for the manoeuvres that day was because my comfort level was not quite yet "up to speed." That decision saved my life.

At about seven minutes into the flight, I pulled up for a tailslide.

Normally I would pull up from 100 to 200 feet, but for the reasons I mentioned, this time I pulled up from 1,000 feet.

I eased the power back to idle as I neared the top of the climb; the nose started to go right. To bring it back, I put on some left rudder. The airplane stopped, and I started going backwards; I switched to right rudder. I ended up with full right rudder on as the airplane flopped over nose down. The six seconds started.

I went to remove the full right rudder during the flop over, but I could not—it was jammed. The airplane started spinning and it was rapid. I pushed on the left rudder as hard as I could. Nothing. I pushed so hard I thought I would snap something. I banged the rudder pedal with my left foot. Nothing!

I looked at the spinning ground. It was coming up rapidly. THIS IS IT, I thought. Then, for some reason I pushed on the right rudder, which was already fully on, and then went back and banged the left rudder. It released!

By now, the spinning had become really fast! Besides stopping that rapid spin, I was fully aware of the next problem—a high-speed stall with a flick roll into the ground. I got the spin stopped. The airspeed was low because the airplane was stalled. The good news, though, was that the airspeed was increasing. Unfortunately—this was at the expense of altitude. Altitude that I did not have.

I now faced the last dilemma. If I pulled too hard, to avoid hitting the ground, the airplane would stall and flick into the ground. If I didn't pull hard enough, the airplane would hit the ground at a higher speed but in a level attitude. Somehow, I managed to pull just hard enough to miss the ground and not flick-in. How that happened I will never know, but I am very grateful to whoever helped me to gauge that pull.

How low was I? I'll never know that either, but it was very close. Had I hit the ground no one would have known why, and speculation would have been rampant. I flew a standard landing pattern and landed. There was no one else at the airport.

The next day in the maintenance hangar, I and my mechanic, Guy Doherty, tracked down the problem. First, we could not duplicate the jammed rudder. The rudder was free to move normally. However, we could hear a slight clicking sound when we moved the rudder with the rudder pedals. The investigation, which included a video of the pushrod interference, revealed that a pushrod that went from the rudder pedals to the differential brake valve was bent slightly. When it moved, the end of the rod rode up over a hydraulic fitting. However, it (annoyingly) moved freely, and we could not duplicate the jammed rudder.

We suspected that the reverse air loads from the application of full right rudder during the tailslide, in combination with the bent rod, caused the control jam. The control rod was straightened, the aircraft test flown, and everything was ok. I will freely admit, however, that it took me a few flights to get my confidence back completely.

THE BUCKET LIST DONE

I think everyone should have a "Bucket List"—that wild assorted cluster of things you absolutely must do before you inevitably kick the bucket. You only go through this life once—why leave some necessary things undone? I'm no different, and despite the extraordinary compilation of things that I had managed to do in my long and certainly never boring life, there were still a few challenges and accomplishments that had remained unfulfilled.

FLYING THE CF-104 AGAIN (76 YEARS OLD)

On April 11, 1966, I had taken what had been my last flight in an RCAF CF-104 Starfighter. But I always thought, wouldn't it be wonderful to fly that incredible machine just once more?

It would be a dream come true, and when I say dream, I literally mean it. Even today I still dream of flying various airplanes that I have flown in the past such as the CF-104, the Vickers Vanguard, and the Boeing 747. In the case of the 747, I am (in the dream at least), the only octogenarian still flying at Air Canada. Sometimes they have me flying the Vanguard instead of the 747, probably as some sort of punishment, I assume. In my CF-104 dreams I never get to fly it. As I stand on the ground watching all my old friends go streaking across the sky, I'm left continually asking: "When is it my turn?"

Rationalization is a wonderful way to surmount the biggest of problems. My favourite is "You can't take it with you," and of course I'm referring to money. You can, however, take memories with you (although, I suppose whether you can take those memories with you to the other side is still a mystery). In fact, you sometimes even get to enjoy old memories while you are alive. So anyway, that's how I justified spending $25,000 to fly the 104 once again at age 76. And now you will understand why (among many other reasons) I married Sandy!

Think about it—what if I had procrastinated and had waited to make sure that we had had enough funds to look after us in our seventies, and then a number of years later decided that we were well enough off to spend the money when I was in my early 80s? Then I might have been ready financially, but waiting for a hip replacement, with my ever-growing arthritis restricting my movements. And, possibly not as sharp as I was at 76 (the jury is still out on that one). There are always more things to deal with as you age.

So the next challenge was, where do you go to fly a 104? Let's face it, like me, Starfighters are vintage, and there was no guarantee that one was available to fly. There is one in Norway, but they can't fly it because they cannot get parts for the Lockheed C-2 ejection seats. There is one in Holland, but because of their rigid anti-pollution laws, it is my understanding that they can't even start its smoke-belching J-79 engine.

Starfighters Inc., located at the Kennedy Space Center in Florida, came to the rescue. It wasn't cheap, but if I ever wanted to strap on a Starfighter again, I knew that this was probably my only option. (I believe you can still fly with them today, but when I last checked the price had doubled.)

On Sunday, June 3, 2018, Sandy and I were up at 1:30 a.m. to catch the

Gord and the Starfighter in 2018.

8:00 a.m. flight to Orlando, Florida, from Toronto Pearson Airport. We rented a car in Orlando and drove to our hotel in Port Canaveral. On Tuesday we drove to the Cape Kennedy Badging Center to get our documents. Security is naturally very tight at Cape Kennedy; we had to be preapproved to even show up at the gate.

Starfighters Inc. is headquartered in the NASA hangar. In 2018 they had eight beautiful 104s—including two ex-RCAF machines (numbers 850 and 633). One of their Starfighters is an F-104B that once belonged to the King of Oman. It is the only two-seater 104 to ever be equipped with a 20 mm Vulcan cannon. The rest of the fleet are the Italian model produced by Fiat, the newest of which is a 104S with an improved engine producing 17,900 lb. of thrust, up from the original 15,900 lb.

The initial briefing consisted of getting the paperwork out of the way, and receiving the manuals, fitting boots, flying suit, g-suit, and Mae West life jacket.

After donning the Mae West, this was followed by a review of the safety equipment and a checkout in the Martin-Baker ejection seat, which was new to me. Its leg restraints on were quite different from the Lockheed C-2 seat that I was used to, being a thick garter that went through two loops—one attached to each leg. These were then plugged into the seat.

I think the Martin-Baker seat is a better seat overall with its zero-zero[21] capability, it's bigger than the Lockheed C-2 but I will still complain that it is built for people smaller than me. Also, the parachute is part of the seat making the seat bigger so there is less room in the cockpit.

The Martin-Baker seat also has a very complicated process to hook everything up, which made me wonder how on earth they would be able to scramble on alert if ever called upon. If you had to depart the aircraft in a hurry while it was still on the ground, it was also a rather detailed process, the steps for which I've outlined below:

1. Make the seat safe. This is done by rotating a plate on the front of the seat between your legs. It is to disarm the seat just

---

[21] These can be used at zero airspeed and zero altitude.

in case your foot accidentally catches the ejection ring — not advisable.

2. Detach the leg restraint straps by feeling for and then finding the small rear moving latch on the lower left side of the seat. This releases the straps from the seat (crisscrossed).

3. Remove the safety pin from the parachute sandwich (quick release) which is on the right side of the quick release.

4. Rotate the quick release to its "release position" from locked. Squeeze the sandwich with both hands and the belts release.

5. Undo the oxygen hose on the left lower side.

6. Disconnect the dingy cord attached to the left side of the Mae West.

7. Unlatch the canopy using the lever on the right side.

8. Use two hands to open the canopy to the left.

9. Climb out, trying to not pull the seat ejection handles over the head rest.

10. Jump to the ground. Good luck!

I met Rick Svetkoff and his brother, John, at our hotel on June 5, the day of the flight. I then followed them to the hangar at the Kennedy Space Center to discuss the flight. I was asked if I wanted to do a Mach 2 run and said, "No thank you." (There really is no sensation of speed, so going that fast is really a non-event.) I said I'd rather just do circuits to experience the low-speed handling characteristics, and to see if I could still handle the more difficult aspects of flight.

I briefed the flight with Rick, reviewed the seat procedures again, and I handed in a written test to satisfy the Federal Aviation Administration (FAA) requirements. The airplane was in the hangar, out of the blazing sun, and it was HOT!

I climbed up and into the rear seat of the Italian F-104C in a manner that was not the way I used to do it—when I was fifty pounds lighter, and much more agile. Caution was key here, especially since we were using a step ladder for entry. I stood on the seat and then eased myself down into it. The volume that my extra fifty pounds took up, plus the decreased cockpit space available due to the larger Martin-Baker seat, indicated to me that the strap-in process was going to take some time.

Thank goodness for capable crew chiefs! They helped me make all the necessary connections and after about fifteen minutes, and the loss of about five pounds worth of perspiration, we were ready to go.

I had familiarized myself with the cockpit already, and to me it all looked as I remembered it. We were towed outside to the ground air supply and started up. The sights, sounds, and smells brought back a flood of memories. We taxied a short distance to the button of runway 33 (15,000 foot long, plus 2000 foot of good overrun) and did the run-up. It was classic and again, just as I remembered. It would have been nice to do the takeoff myself, but realistically it was just not possible given the fifty-two-year lapse since my last flight, so I just savored the experience and probably got more out of it that way.

We were cleared for takeoff and away we went: brakes off, full military power, good acceleration, outboard for burner lite-up, better acceleration, then full forward into max burner and, YES, the acceleration I remembered! And the air conditioning was wonderful!

From there everything happened fast. We rotated at about 180 knots, airborne, gear went up and 300 knots before I knew it, into a left turn and around the corner, takeoff flaps came up at 400 knots, over the Kennedy Space Center Visitor Complex in the turn back for a low pass. Burner lite-up, first boom, then second boom and the full burner lights and we were at 620 knots back over the runway with a 4 g pull to the vertical ... and we were outta there!

Pulled over the top to about 23,000 feet and eastbound and then it was my turn to fly. This is where memory didn't match reality. For example, I did not remember the control loads being as heavy as they were. Certainly not real heavy, but heavier than I recalled. Then I remembered that we used the trim a lot.

The flaps were up, and I performed some turns and a bit of general throwing around to get the feel of the airplane. I was in and out of stick shaker, so I put the takeoff flap back down and we were good to a max of 450 knots.

I was then glad that I hadn't been required to do the take off since I

Rick Svetkoff and Gord briefing.

Good thing it's not a scramble!

discovered that I really needed some normal stick time to reacquaint myself. I did a few rolls and of course they were over in a flash. Rick noted the air force base to the west and said that we'd better turn to stay in the area, which we did. I did a couple of barrel rolls and a weather balloon passed by overhead (real fast!). We returned to Space Florida's Shuttle Landing Facility heading 240° at 325 knots at 25,000 feet for a simulated shuttle approach that they used to teach shuttle pilots for landing.

We did a 270° turn with the power at idle and the speed brakes out to maintain 325 knots in a 30 to 40° bank turn to the left, aiming for 200 knots over the threshold. It was a steep approach and it was over before I knew it! We returned to the circuit and Rick flew a right-hand pattern for landing on runway 15 as a demo then gave me control. We did not do any touch and goes, the FAA charges $500 per landing. The tires cost $1,000 apiece and six to eight landings is about all you get out of a set before they must be replaced.

Feeling right at home.

I did three close pattern approaches, the most interesting and difficult area of 104 flying. I was in and out of stick shaker (stall warning) quite a bit as I tried to recreate what had been very natural for me fifty-two years previously.

And what were my take-aways from this extraordinary event? Well for one thing, the Starfighter is not as easy to fly as I thought it was when I was fifty-two years younger! But bottom line, doing this flight was one of the best decisions I have ever made. You only live once, so if there is something you want to do, and it is possible to do it, jump at the opportunity.

And finally, the amount of time, effort, and money that Starfighters Inc. has put into their company is mind boggling. I am so grateful to Rick and his crew for giving me the opportunity to experience something that was so special to me.

After the flight. Gord and Rick.

SKYDIVE OUT OF HERCULES (75 YEARS OLD)

Jump out of a perfectly good airplane? No Way. You must be out of your mind! That had been my standard answer whenever someone had asked me if I had ever considered skydiving.

I met Captain Jake Porter of the SkyHawks, the Canadian Armed Forces Parachute Team, at the air show in Charlo, New Brunswick in August 2016. He convinced me to go for a ride in the Hercules to watch the team jump with some people who had never jumped before. That sort of got me interested. Then, when I flew the Val-d'Or Air Show later that fall, I was asked if I would like to jump.

That was one of those once in a lifetime opportunities that I could not pass up. If you are going to jump out of an airplane—do a tandem jump with the best in the world out of a Hercules.

I did the tandem jump with Warrant Officer Steve Ouimet. Steve is as professional as they get. As I remember, I was not at all nervous or apprehensive.

We were accompanied by two team members, both with cameras. The first one jumped just before we did, to take pictures of us leaving the Hercules. Another cameraman followed right behind us taking more pictures.

As I recall, terminal velocity is 180 mph. I can confirm that when you are facing a 180 mph headwind, if you have any extra skin on your face it flaps around a lot. This was confirmed by a video that was taken, and it makes one consider whether a facelift may be in order.

Steve gave the cameramen the signal that we were going to open the chute and they backed away. The opening shock was just that, a shock, but not severe. I got to "fly the chute" by pulling on the left or right risers. I even got the chute spinning. The contact with the ground was negligible due to Steve's expertise.

It doesn't get any better. It was a blast, and I would do it again if given the opportunity.

RCAF CC-130J Hercules

FLYING THE A320 SIMULATOR (AFTER A 23-YEAR BREAK)

I last flew an Airbus A320 in 1995, so twenty-three years later, I was very fortunate to be invited by Mike Trygvasson, a fellow air show pilot and an instructor pilot for Air Canada, to fly the Air Canada A320 simulator. Fortunately, Eric Dumigan, aviation photographer extraordinaire, was there to take a few pictures.

It was a great two-hour session, and everything came back very quickly. On takeoff, I was able to handle engine cuts without any problem, and I handled the automatics as recommended. The best part was a couple of (simulated) low passes over downtown Toronto and a pullup over the Toronto Airshow waterfront site.

Photo © Eric Dumigan.

Photo © Eric Dumigan.

The autopilot and auto throttles were disconnected, and flight directors were turned off for the final ILS landing on runway 23R. It seems to me that an A320 is a lot easier to fly than a CF-104 as you get older.

WANNABEE SNOWBIRD

Two of my RCAF Baden-Soellingen buddies, Inch Illingsworth and Fred McCague, were on the first Snowbird team (they were called the Golden Centennaires) in 1971. That's a job I wanted! I love formation flying; it is so intense, and it takes phenomenal concentration. I guess that is why I enjoyed competitive aerobatics, as the whole experience is about intense concentration.

But you can't have everything. I made the decision to leave the RCAF for the civilian aviation scene, so it was not possible. The next best thing to being on the team is to hang out with them on the airshow circuit (when you are in your seventies and eighties) and then, what's even better, is if you get to fly with them! That dream came true a couple of times.

The first time was at the Bromont, Quebec, airshow in 2017 and the second was in Barrie, Ontario, in 2019. On both occasions I flew in the five-jet which is in the middle of the action. In 2015, I flew with Captain Matthew Hart during the practice flight. Matt let me fly the initial warm up tail chase, and it was the first time that I felt the controls of a Canadair CT-114 Tutor, the aircraft that the team uses. It was exhilarating to be in a nine-plane formation. My second flight was at the Barrie Airshow in 2019. I again flew in the five-jet, but this time with Captain Kevin Domon-Grenier. It was another memorable flight.

In November 2022, during the celebration of the fiftieth anniversary of the Snowbirds in Moose Jaw, Saskatchewan, I had the immense honour of being inducted into the Honourary Snowbird Alumni. This recognition fulfilled a lifelong dream of mine: to become a "Snowbird."

Gord and Captain Matthew Hart in Bromont Quebec, 2017 © Jean-Pierre Bonin

Aviation Technician ✈ MCpl Kyle VanTol

With Captain Kevin Domon-Grenier in Barrie, Ontario, 2019.

The 9-plane formation practice flight in Barrie Ontario.

The octogenarian credo: Never pass up a washroom!

Master Corporal Carl Van Tol, Gord Price, and Captain Kevin Domon-Grenier.

The Snowbirds visit The Dam Pub in August 2022. Photo © Kevin Prentice.

FLYING THROUGH THE ROCKY MOUNTAINS (80 YEARS OLD)

My last bucket list item was to experience flight through the Rocky Mountains. I left it a bit late—I was eighty years old. In the summer of 2022, I planned a western swing on the airshow circuit. The plan was to fly three airshows: Cold Lake, Alberta, Lethbridge, Alberta, and Vanderhoof, British Columbia.

The adventure began on July 13. I took off from Owen Sound at 8:00 a.m., flew north over Tobermory and Manitoulin Island, and landed in Sault Ste. Marie, Michigan, an hour and a half later. Customs showed up promptly, and I was cleared to go. I refueled and was off to Eagle River, Wisconsin, where I arrived after an hour and a half of flying. The local FBO (fixed base operator) helped me to refuel. I was an hour on the ground there, and then I took off for Brainerd Lakes, Minnesota, where I arrived an hour and forty minutes later. I refueled and spent an hour on the ground. I headed for Jamestown, North Dakota, and arrived at 4:30 p.m. after a one hour and forty minute flight.

When I arrived, there was no one there. It was another hour and a half before someone showed up to open the hangar. I then got a cab downtown and overnighted at a motel. By the time I got to the hotel I had been on the go for twelve hours.

My 23 stops across Canada in the Yak-50 at 80 years old.

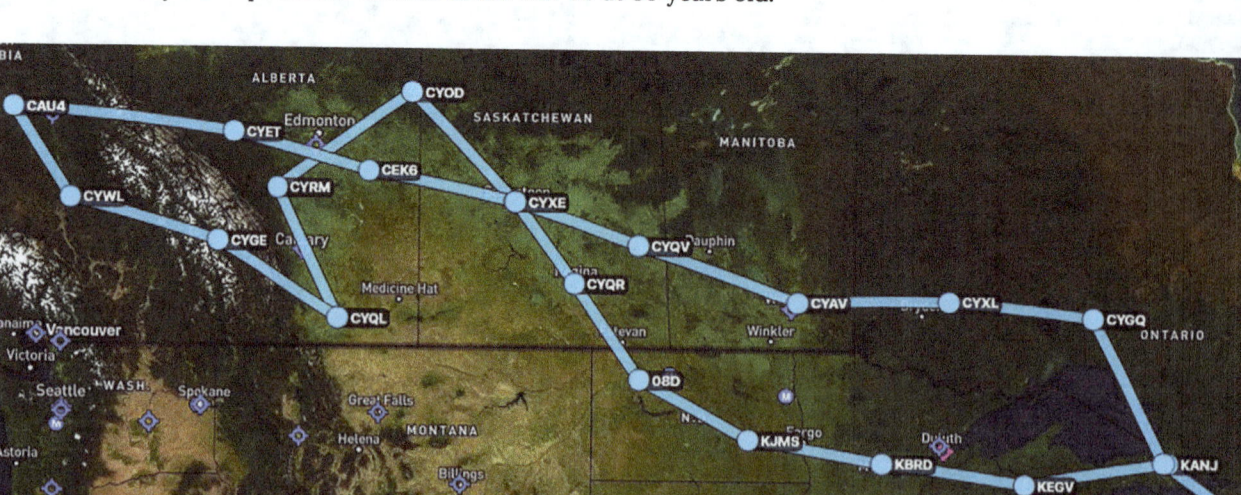

I was up early the next morning, and I managed to get airborne at 7:15 a.m. I headed for Stanley, North Dakota, where I landed an hour and a half later. Again, there was no one at the airport. Fuel was available through a card lock system if the credit card worked. Fortunately, the card worked, and I fueled up.

My next stop was Regina, Saskatchewan. Since I would be crossing the border, I needed to file a flight plan. I tried to call the US flight service on my cell, but I had no cell service! I took off and called flight service in the air; again there was nothing. Eventually, I was able to speak with Winnipeg centre and then Regina tower. I requested "customs on arrival."

"We don't do that anymore," was the answer I got. I landed at Regina after an hour in the air, where I expected to be met by angry customs officials. However, such was not the case. I taxied to the local FBO

Camero for my use in Cold Lake. Photo © Kevin Prentice.

and told them that I had come from the US. I was advised to stay in the airplane. They told me that they would call customs, but that I shouldn't expect them for a couple of hours. However, customs arrived in about ten minutes and cleared me through without any problem.

I gassed up and headed for Saskatoon an hour later. I arrived in Saskatoon after a one hour flight. After refueling and spending another hour on the ground, I was airborne for Cold Lake, Alberta. I landed in Cold Lake at 2:30 p.m. after a one and a half hour flight.

The weather for the entire trip was perfect. I had delayed the start of my trip for three days to take advantage of good weather. I even had a tailwind all the way which is highly unusual for flying west. I took that as an omen indicating that the entire adventure would go

With Major-General Iain Huddleston, Commander of 1 Canadian Air Division. Iain is the son of Lieutenant-General David Huddleston, my course mate in Cold Lake in 1963. Photo © Kevin Prentice.

well—and it did!

I had just landed at the same airport where I had been checked out in the CF-104 fifty-eight years earlier. I was treated like royalty! There is one other thing that I should mention here: it was July 14—our sixtieth wedding anniversary. That shows you how understanding and special my dear wife, Sandy, is!

After flying in the Cold Lake Air Show, I flew an hour and a half to Rocky Mountain House where I put the Yak-50 in Kyle Fowler's hangar. Kyle drove me to Edmonton, and I jetted home for ten days; I returned on July 27.

The trip from Rocky Mountain House to Lethbridge took an hour and a half on Thursday, July 28th. I flew the airshow there, and then

It was nice to not be the only guy pushing the YAK-50. Photo © Kevin Prentice.

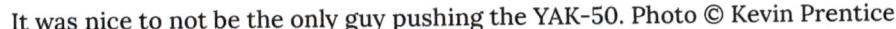

On the way to Golden, British Columbia.

departed for Golden, British Columbia on Monday the 1st of August at 11:00 a.m., after waiting for some fog to clear. The trip to Golden lasted an hour and a half. A pattern seemed to be developing—there was no one at the airport in Golden. I refueled using the card lock system and fortunately my credit card worked again, much to my relief.

I spoke with flight service to check the weather and to see if there were any Notices to Airmen (NOTAM) which is a notice that contains information concerning the establishment, conditions, or change in any aeronautical facility, service, procedure, or hazard. All was good, so I took off for Williams Lake, British Columbia.

As I approached the airport, I called Unicom (this stands for Universal Communications, and is an air-ground communication facility operated by a non-air traffic control private agency to provide advisory information to pilots) for an airport advisory; they informed me that there was no fuel available on the field. Great! He also advised me that there had been a NOTAM issued to that effect.

Golden, British Columbia.

Unfortunately, flight service had missed it and they had not advised me. I landed there anyway since I was low on fuel after spending an hour and forty minutes in the air.

There was no fuel, but they expected some the next day. I prepared to overnight there, but I had the idea to call Vanderhoof to see if they had any thoughts. Indeed, they had a friend near Williams Lake who had a supply of fuel. Their friend brought me some fuel in jerrycans, and I was on my way to Vanderhoof two hours later. I arrived at 5:00 p.m. and we tucked the airplane into the hangar for the night.

After flying the airshow at Vanderhoof, I left to go back home on August 7. I knew it was going to be a long day. The plan was to try to make St. Andrews, Manitoba, for the overnight stop. I managed to take off at 6:45 a.m.

The first leg was to Edson, Alberta, and this is where the flying got a bit tricky. The route called for a minimum altitude of 9,300 feet, and if I was pushed to the south, it was 13,400 feet. There was no

YAK-50 and LONG EZ with Gord and Kyle Fowler at Vanderhoof Airshow.

Just topping the top of the cloud over the Rocky Mountains.

possibility of going under the cloud deck since the ceilings were too low—over the top it was.

The other problem was that the tops of the clouds had not been reported. All was good at 9,500 feet until I was just east of Prince George, but then the tops of the cloud deck started to rise. I had no choice—I had to rise above the clouds. The aircraft was not legally equipped for flying in cloud. I could have done it with the instrumentation that I had, but the engine would have iced up and probably quit; that option was out of the question. In the end, I had to climb to 14,000 feet to get over the top of the cloud deck. I was there about fifteen minutes, taking little breaths in the thin atmosphere.

It took close to two hours to get to Edson—and that was with a good tailwind. It was the trickiest flight of the adventure, and it underlined the problems that are inherent in mountain flying. I do not intend to

The Silver Nugget Motor Hotel.

do it again.

After fueling up in Edson with another cardlock system, I flew to Flagstaff, Alberta, in one and a half hours. From there it was an hour and a half to Saskatoon, one and a half hours to Yorkton, Saskatchewan, and then finally two hours to St. Andrews which is to the northeast of Winnipeg. I arrived at 6:30 p.m.

The next day was more relaxed. Since the weather was bad from Sault Ste. Marie, I decided to just land someplace with good weather and wait it out. I took off from St. Andrews at 11:15 a.m. and landed at Sioux Lookout an hour and a half later. Sioux Lookout is the only airport that I have ever landed at where you have to go up a hill to get to the FBO, and then down the hill to get back to the runway.

A check of the weather confirmed that it was too marginal from Sault Ste. Marie south, so I decided to land at Geraldton, Ontario,

The Country Club.

and spend the night there. I arrived at 3:30 p.m. after a one and a half hour flight, tied the Yak-50 down, and got a cab into town. I asked the cab driver where I could get a nice meal. "The Silver Nugget Hotel, where you are staying, has a restaurant," he said.

"Great!" I responded.

I checked into the hotel and enquired about the restaurant wine list. I was told, "Sorry, we don't serve no wine. You would have to go to the country club for that. They open at six. It's at the other end of town—an eight dollar cab ride."

"Great, I'll do that," I said.

I called a cab and went to "The Country Club." It was 6:05 p.m., but no one was there except one person waiting in a car. I had already sent the cab away, so I waited. Finally—at 6:25 p.m., the owner arrived, unlocked the door, and let the bartender in.

I followed and sat down at the bar. I looked over the bar list and asked for a menu. "Sorry," the young bartender said, "we don't serve

The Country Club Bar in Geraldton, Ontario.

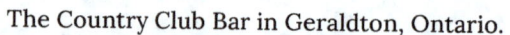

any food—just snacks and chips. If you want food, you'll have to go to the Silver Nugget."

"I just came from there!" I said, "And they don't serve wine."

"Oh, you want some food with the wine. Just give them a call and they will deliver your dinner here," she said, as she handed me a Silver Nugget menu.

I ordered a pickerel dinner, and it showed up twenty minutes later. I had a nice Pinot Grigio wine with it. It was the best pickerel that I have ever had!

The next morning, I departed for Sault Ste. Marie at 9:15 a.m., and I arrived an hour and a half later. The weather was good. The last leg of the trip, back to Owen Sound, was completed with a good tailwind. It rounded out a very successful bucket-list trip that I will never do again. I was happy to be back in Owen Sound, safe and sound, twenty-six days after the adventure began.

Safely back in the hangar… twenty-six days later. Photo © Kevin Prentice.

THE LAST RETIREMENT AND THE YAK-50

My official Air Canada retirement date was February 1, 2002; I had just turned sixty years old, and because of my age I had been forced to retire. I am pretty sure that some depression had set in, because I had had my career arbitrarily taken away from me. But as I look back now, retirement at sixty was a good thing. While I was still healthy, I could do other things like travel, and in our case, take up residence in an entirely new country, Scotland.

We came back to Canada in 2007 because we, along with our daughter Stephanie, had created The Dam Pub, an upscale whisky pub in Thornbury, Ontario, and it needed more attention. It was impossible to live in Scotland and run a pub in Thornbury.

I had never considered flying again until 2008 when I thought it would be a good idea to fly some banners advertising the pub. I bought all the banner equipment, and I rented a Cessna 172 from Owen Sound Flight Services. They had one airplane that was outfitted for banner towing.

As I remember, it was an awful airplane for towing banners. It took a lot of power to tow, and that airplane would not fly slow enough; this made it hard on the banners themselves. So, I bought a vintage Fleet Canuck, and I outfitted the airplane to tow banners. With its eighty-five hp, it worked great.

Things were going well in 2009. Then I had a heart attack.

THE HEART ATTACK

We were living in Dyers Bay (a long way up the Bruce Peninsula) when it happened. Sandy had just had a knee replacement and I was looking after her, so the heart attack came at a bad time. I suppose there is never a good time for things like that. I didn't know it was a heart attack. It was just a bad pain in my back and down my left arm.

Not really knowing what it was, and not wanting to make a fuss, I drove to the hospital in Lion's Head and told them about this pain that I was experiencing. They did all sorts of tests including a blood test. They sent it to the Owen Sound laboratory, and we waited. It came back indicating a heart attack. Just to be sure, they did it again, and it confirmed a heart attack. I said, "It really didn't feel that bad—can't we call it something else?" I worried that "heart attack" was going to have quite an effect on my pilot's license.

They sent me to the Centre Grey Hospital in Markdale, Ontario, via ambulance and put me in ICU awaiting transfer to Kitchener. I was there for three days. I did not have any pain and I was getting bored; I convinced them to let me drag all the stuff attached to me to the lounge so that I could play my fiddle. I figured that I might as well do something while I was just sitting around waiting.

I was transferred to a Kitchener hospital. They performed a coronary angiogram procedure, and identified the problem as one small artery that was 95 percent blocked. This is where I got lucky. There was a cardiologist available who could perform a coronary angioplasty procedure and install a stent right away. Dr. Suzanne Renner came in and said, "I'm the plumber and I am here to fix this problem right now!"

She explained everything and I watched the screen as she installed the stent. As she carried out the procedure, she said, "You are going to feel the same pain you felt before, but it will quickly go away." She was right on all counts. I was kept in the hospital overnight, and they released me the next morning.

"OK, you can go home now," I was told. I told them that there was a problem. I had been delivered to Kitchener via ambulance while wearing a hospital gown, and I was still wearing one. All my clothes were in Markdale, so it would be difficult to get a cab dressed like that. Finally, they agreed; they provided an interhospital shuttle to get me back to Markdale—and my clothes.

A CHANGE OF HEALTH

We were in shock of course with all this going on. I was put on all sorts of medication, some of it for depression. I was feeling dizzy and generally unwell from the medications.

A friend had a Steen Skybolt; he wanted my opinion on how it flew, so we took it up together. I was in the front seat, and if I pulled any g's at all, I got dizzy. This was very alarming. Eventually, I made a decision. I needed to attend a retreat to get off the medications that I was taking. Otherwise, I would never be able to fly again.

That was another one of the best decisions that I have ever made. The doctors took me off all the medications and put me on supplements—that cured the depression that I had been suffering from. Also, while attending this retreat, I had started to think about flying airshows again.

THE YAK-50

In 2011, I saw an advertisement for a Yak-50 that was for sale. It was serial number 01 which meant that it was the prototype that had been built at the Yakovlev Design Bureau in Moscow. It had first flown in June of 1972. It had been discovered in a barn in 2003 and rebuilt.

It was in Salt Lake City. I immediately flew out to see it in March of 2011. I had such fond memories of flying the Yak-50 in 1982 at WAC 82. With difficulty, I climbed into the airplane. Memories flooded back. You can do this, I thought. It all fit.

My depression was gone and my medications were gone. Now I had something to get excited about. This would be a life change that I really needed, and it was all possible. I decided to buy it. This decision gave me a fresh outlook on my life—something that was needed for sure.

We made a deal which included delivery of the Yak to Owen Sound. I bought the airplane from Barry Hancock, who delivered it to Owen Sound in May of 2011. It was the first Yak-50 imported into Canada, and a lot of work had to be done with Transport Canada before I could fly it. Guy Doherty is the resident aviation mechanic at Owen Sound Airport. I can honestly say that without Guy's wrenching expertise, none of my Yak-50 escapades would have happened.

I arranged for Dennis Savarese from Alabama, the premiere expert on the operation of Yak-50s, to come to Owen Sound to give us a ground school on the maintenance and operation of the aircraft. We acquired all the manuals from Richard Goode who had been dealing with Yak aircraft longer than anyone else that I knew of. It took a while to jump through all the hoops, but finally, on November 4, 2011, a special certificate of airworthiness was issued by Transport Canada for the Yak-50. It was now legal to fly the airplane!

At 1:00 p.m. on November 11, 2011, I flew my new Yak-50 for the first time. Of course it was exciting—especially since so many obstacles had been overcome; thankfully, it was an uneventful flight. I flew it four more times that fall before putting it away for the winter.

It involved a big learning curve. The Yak-50 is a bit of a beast, weighing in at just over a ton loaded. The technology is different and there is a lot of torque from the engine. This is something that adds a different dimension to the flight characteristics, particularly at low speeds. (Note that I am referring to these problems as an out of shape, has been, competitive aerobatic pilot, and someone looking to reacquaint himself with the nuances of hard-core aerobatic flight—

Air show Bromont Quebec 2014.

all while having undergone the ravages of age, which included some physiological changes that occurred under the scrutiny of Transport Canada.)

To fly air shows, you must have a low altitude waiver issued by Transport Canada. This document outlines how low you can perform aerobatics in an airshow. It starts out as a minimum altitude of 800 feet above the ground; when you have the required experience and have demonstrated that you are competent enough, a ground level waiver is issued allowing aerobatics from the ground up.

I flew a total of eighty-seven flights in the Yak before my first airshow in Orillia in June of 2012. The last time I had flown in an air show had been on Labour Day of 1988. I had had a twenty-four year sabbatical—but I was back.

And so, my third career as an air show pilot began at age seventy in 2012, and it lasted eleven years to age eighty-one when I decided

Showing off my muscle T-shirt and frizzie wig with Tracey Morgan Boudreau, Donna Flynn, Kelsy Firkus and Sandy at the Canadian International Air Show (CIAS) Saturday night gala dinner.

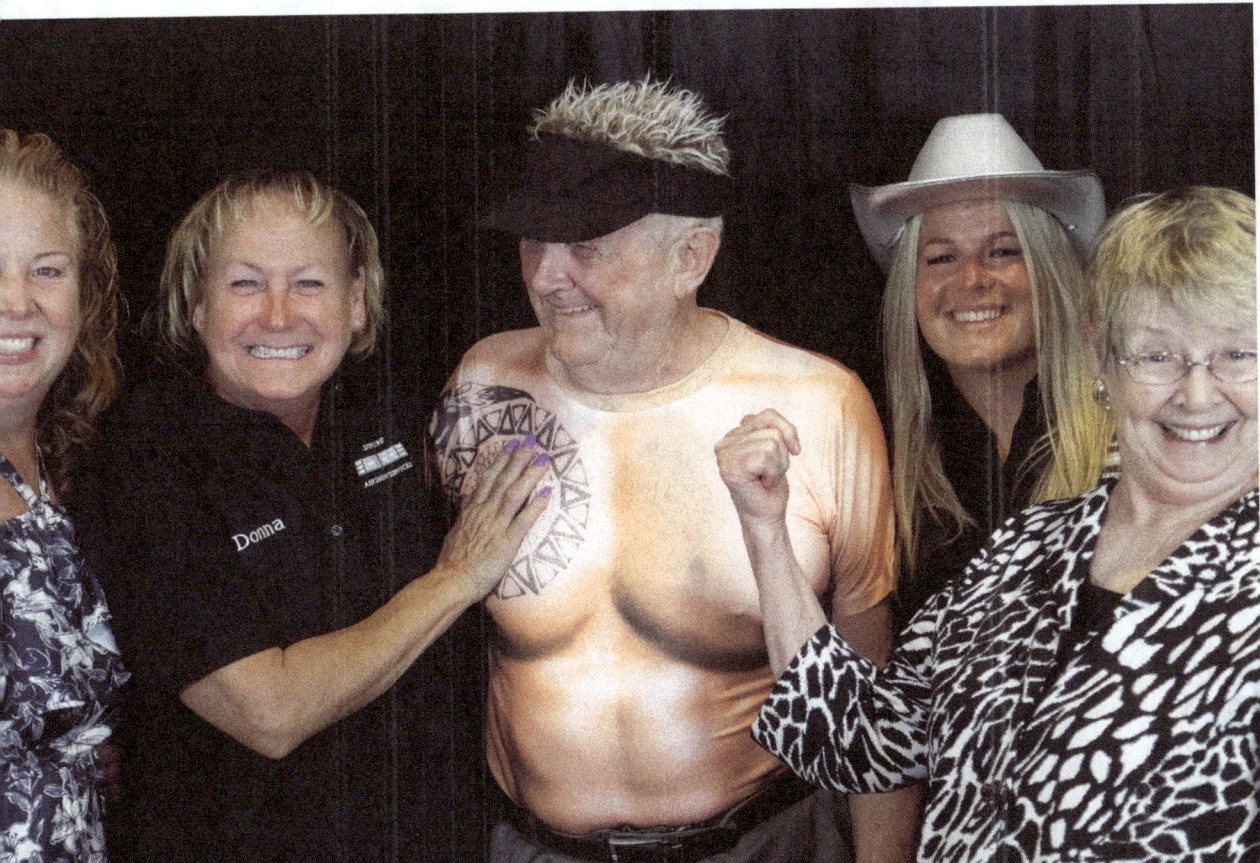

2018 was the only year we got away with buzzing the Toronto Pearson Tower. Photo ©
Jeremy Cartlidge/CIAS.

that it would be prudent to retire.

Age is only a number until the aging process starts to catch up with
you. I decided that I wanted to go out on a high—and what a high it
was! Over that period of eleven years, I flew air shows from Charlo,
New Brunswick, to Vanderhoof, British Columbia, and I rubbed
shoulders with the best in the business. In 2017, the Yak engine was
upgraded to 435 hp making it a superb air show performer. Hanging
out with a bunch of fighter pilots and the many volunteers who
made the airshows happen was exhilarating. Again, I have been a
very lucky guy. It was also a great branding opportunity for our Dam
Pub whisky business.

Centre stage for CIAS - The William Lyon MacKenzie Fireboat. Photo © Jeremy Cartlidge/CIAS.

MY LAST AIR SHOW

My last air show was at the Canadian International Air Show on September 4, 2023 on the Toronto waterfront. Preparation began at 8:30 a.m. at the air show safety briefing in the Holiday Inn at Pearson Airport. Everything to do with the show was discussed in detail. Once that was completed, it was a thirty minute drive on Highway 427 and the Gardiner Expressway to the Toronto Island ferry. That drive was the most exciting part of the day!

The Yak-50 was in the hangar to stay out of the heat of the day. It was ready with sufficient gas and oil for the engine, and smoke oil and wing tip smoke grenades for the performance.

My "on stage" time was 1:20 p.m. so I started my preparations one hour before. I prefer to be in my own world for that hour to consider all the things that must be done, how I am going to position the flight with regard to the current weather conditions, and also to consider all the things that can go wrong that may prevent me from being on stage centre precisely at the correct time.

I walked to the aircraft at 12:55 p.m. It was time to start the same routine that I had used so many times before. From the right side of the aircraft, I attached the Aresti card that outlined the manoeuvres to the instrument panel. I checked that the switches and magnetos were off and that the brakes were set. I then gave the engine twelve shots of prime—six in the carburetor and six in the cylinders. I walked around the right wing to the prop and pulled it through for six blades; this took some effort with the high compression of the engine. Reaching under the engine, I closed the intake manifold drain which had been letting excess oil seep out. (The Yak, like many wild animals, likes to mark its spot wherever it sits.)

After a walk around the left wing to the cockpit, I put on the Mae

The final pushout with Scotty Oxenham (second from the right). Photo © Andrew Cline.

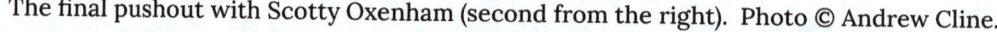

Ready for start. Photo ©
Andrew Cline.

West and ensured that the hearing aids were in telecoil function. This was followed by a big step up onto the wing for the eighty-one-year-old and then a step onto the seat. Finally, I settled into the rather tight cockpit.

The trickiest part was getting the parachute on. This required the assistance of Scotty Oxenham who helped me slip the straps over my arthritic shoulders. Then the lap belt and crotch strap were secured. Finally came the shoulder straps—again with the assistance of Scotty.

I was now soaked in sweat and looking forward to the stiff breeze from the prop. If my timing was right, it was 1:00 p.m. Once the engine was started, I would finally be able to relax. You just never knew what could go wrong at the last minute; my worst fear was a hangover from my airline days: I couldn't be late!

I double checked that the brakes were set. Ok, I thought, here comes the moment you've been waiting for. It's time to start the engine.

Starting a Yak-50 is a dance of the hands.

With the right hand I gave the cylinders four shots of prime; I left the primer open for more. I yelled, "CLEAR!" to make sure that there was no one near the propeller. I turned all the electrical switches on the left sub panel on, apart from the alternator. I opened the throttle one quarter. With the middle finger of the left hand I pressed the start button; this opened the high-pressure air valve to allow high pressure air into the cylinders. Reluctantly, the prop started to turn. Suddenly, it caught. I quickly wrapped my left hand's first finger and thumb around the magneto switch, and deftly turned it one click to the left to activate the left magneto. I was hoping that it would catch, but I kept the middle finger of my left hand on the start valve button. With my right hand, I gave the primer lots of shots to keep the engine going. Finally, I stopped priming, released my left middle finger from the start valve button, turned the magneto switch all the way to the left so that both magnetos were now on, and at the same time reduced the throttle to idle.

Now I had time to stick my head out the right side, enjoy the breeze, and cool down.

The clock was ticking perfectly; 1:05 p.m. It would take about ten minutes to bring the oil temperature up to fifty degrees Celsius. I put my helmet on, set the radio to ground frequency, obtained taxi clearance from island ground, and proceeded to the runup area. I checked the magnetos and the prop to ensure they were functioning normally.

Once both runup and the pre-take off check were completed, I switched to island tower.

"Tower, Dam Pub ready for takeoff." The time was now 1:18 p.m.

"Dam Pub, cleared for takeoff, contact Air boss 119.2 airborne."

"Roger. Dam Pub cleared for takeoff."

I pulled out on to runway 26 and armed the smoke grenades. I advanced the throttle, immediately lifted the tail on the takeoff roll, and pulled the Yak airborne in no time. I put the gear lever to the up position, and checked the temperatures, pressures, and the gear up lights. All were good. I switched to Air boss frequency.

"Air boss ... Dam Pub with you."

"Dam Pub, the box is clear. You are cleared to enter."

"Roger." Now that the formalities were completed, I could concentrate on flying my last airshow sequence. I approached from the east with full power at fifty feet above the water, and turned the engine smoke on. Thirty-two litres of smoke oil would burn during the twelve-minute flight along with about the same amount of aviation fuel. It was now time to ignite the wingtip smoke grenades which would burn for the first three minutes of the flight.

I was coming up on centre stage (the fire boat), and I was hugging the shoreline. I wanted the first manoeuvre to be right in the centre and close to or on the deadline (500 feet from the crowd).

I arrived at centre stage, skimming the water by fifty feet and doing about 200 mph. I pulled at least 6 g, hit the vertical line, and then did a violent 1¾ snap roll to the right with a knife edge recovery, falling into a descending 270 degree tight left turn down to 100 feet above the water, followed by an immediate reversal into an 360 degree tight left turn, allowing the crowd to get a good visual of the wing tip smoke as I passed by the fire boat.

Up against the east deadline, the next manoeuvre was a multiple roll Immelmann turnaround as I accelerated in level flight and clawed for as much altitude as possible before sliding backwards in a power off tailslide. Then a diving line back as low as I dared before pulling vertical again, putting a vertical roll on the line followed by a hammerhead turnaround.

Then I managed a 1½ snap roll on the vertical downline before pulling out 100 feet above the water, going downwind at high speed and approaching the eastern deadline. A quick pull to a 45 line, a ¼ roll to knife edge with a -5 g push into a Lomcevak tumble end over end recovering 100 feet above the water. Again, at high speed and pulling into another 45 degree climb with a ½ roll to the left and then an outside snap roll to the right followed by a 5/8 loop back to 200 feet above the water.

Now began the set up for the flat spin, which takes plenty of altitude. It was time to move that one-ton airplane as high as I could without it being boring. As I accelerated downwind at 200 feet and rolled the aircraft 360 degrees maybe climbing to 300 feet before pulling up

Taxi to runway. Photo © Andrew Cline.

Takeoff. Photo © Andrew Cline.

The Tailslide. Photo © Kevin Prentice.

Fly-through plane wash. Photo © Andrew Cline.

into another Immelmann turn with multiple rolls, all the time trying to gain altitude.

I was then back at centre stage downwind. Hopefully at 1,500 feet, another vertical pull, clawing for altitude and looking for 2,900 feet ideally which in this case was not to be since it was a hot day. I think I saw about 2,300 feet at the top of climb before I kicked the right rudder and left aileron with full power entered a flat spin.

I let it go 4 turns then the recovery took another 1½ turns before stopping with time to draw a vertical downline then pull to level flight 200 feet above the water, then a 225-degree low level turn around the fireboat, trying to catch the spray from the firehose, then a 6 g pull to the vertical with a hammerhead turnaround.

At this point I was able to relax somewhat since the most demanding manoeuvres were behind me. At centre stage, 100 feet above the water

Air show completed, final salute to CN Tower. Photo via Gord's tail-mounted GoPro.

I pulled up into a large loop and put 2 slow rolls on top recovering back at 100 feet and heading west and pulled up, did 1¼ vertical rolls up, pulled the YAK over the top and immediately did 1¾ rolls down.

Back down at 100 feet I forewent a scheduled slow roll since I was too close to the eastern deadline, and pulled up just on the line into another lomcevak which ended with a 1 turn inverted flat spin after pushing -4 g.

Back down to 100 feet then I was immediately back up for a Cap Lomcevak (Yak sits on tail and rotates 360 degrees) at centre stage then off to the west for the first half of the Cuban eight, over the top and back through centre stage for second half of the Cuban eight, while positioning for the final centre stage plan form tailslide into the smoke and flop over, pull out at 100 feet and we were done.

A couple of turnaround banana passes for photos and then a final

Three-point landing. Photo © Andrew Cline.

The final airshow water cannon salute from the Toronto Island Airport Firefighters.
Photo © Andrew Cline.

wing wag goodbye and I was off stage, heading east for landing at the island.

I switched over to island tower on 118.2, and received clearance to land on runway 26. I planned to exit at taxiway Foxtrot.

As I exited the runway, a firefighter signaled for me to close the canopy to avoid getting wet. They had arranged a water cannon salute for my final air show flight. It was a great honour and a once-in-a-lifetime event. As I taxied under the salute and reached the east ramp, I felt a mixture of happiness and sadness. I knew that all good things must come to an end.

As I shut down the engine, I was surprised to see the entire ramp crew holding stylized pictures of my face. It was a truly special gesture that I'll always appreciate.

But there was no time to doddle.

I was rushed onto a fast boat over to the show line VIP tent where I seized the opportunity to connect with fans and to sign autographs as the rest of the airshow unfolded.

As the Snowbirds' performance began, Major Brett Parker, the team leader, announced from the cockpit and over the PA system, "We are dedicating our performance today to Gord Price, who just flew his final air show."

I was surprised and overwhelmed at receiving such an honour.

After bidding farewell to the crowd, I embarked on a swift, turbulent, and exciting journey in a Zodiac inflatable. I was going back to the island where the Yak-50 awaited. It was all ready to go.

Scotty helped me with the shoulder straps.

I started the engine, taxied out, and headed north, passing beside and below the top of the CN Tower for the last time.

Thirty-five minutes later I landed in Owen Sound.

An earlier text message to Guy Doherty had ensured that my hangar door was open in preparation for my arrival so that I could taxi right into the hangar and shut down.

CIAS island volunteers with the final salute. Photo © Andrew Cline.

Gord with Wendy Gluhushkin who made sure I was well looked after by the island crew.
Photo © Andrew Cline.

The end. Photo Andrew Cline.

I unpacked the Yak-50, closed the door on a wonderful chapter of my late life air show career, and safely went home to a very relieved Sandy, my wife of sixty-two years and the love of my life.

A FEW FINAL REFLECTIONS

A reporter once asked me, "If you could have only one way of life, which would you choose: being a commercial pilot with an ordinary existence but fewer chances of being killed, or a fighter pilot with an exciting but dangerous life?"

Well, there you have the summary of my life. I didn't have to choose. I got to do everything. This is what the book is about. I'm extremely fortunate to have experienced and accomplished so many different things.

Unlike some of my contemporaries, I have emerged unscathed despite many perilous experiences. I attribute my good fortune to luck, decisions I've made, knowing when to be afraid, and astute decision-making—especially when applied to flying the Starfighter. I could have been one of those many pilots who lost their lives, but like I said, everybody else got my share of bad luck. I never really got my allocation of it. I've been very, very fortunate.

Uncharacteristic of most people my age, I retired twice. I had three rounds of professional commitment in three different sectors of flying: as a nuclear strike aviator, a commercial airline captain, and an aerobatic pilot. While maintaining my job as a commercial pilot, I set up my own companies: the first was Ultimate Aerobatics Limited, and the second, the Ultimate Aircraft Corporation.

At age seventy, I embarked on my third career as an air show pilot. Now, at eighty-two, I am fully retired and have begun to feel my age, primarily due to arthritic hip pain. Fortunately, I just resolved this issue by having my hip replaced at a private clinic in Montreal for $22,000. I chose to use my savings to bypass the long wait times associated with the Ontario Health Insurance Plan (OHIP). This experience underscored for me that savings are indeed meant for looking after oneself and for addressing pressing health concerns.

Most people think that the main purpose in life is to be happy. There's a lot of debate on that. But if it were true, the question remains: what constitutes real happiness?

Genuine bliss is achieved through the cultivation of sincere relationships, the pursuit of one's passion, and a life lived according to one's values. I have been blessed to experience all three and for this, I am truly grateful.

EPILOGUE: THE DAM PUB

We bought a cask of 1992 Aberlour and had it bottled as our House Whisky. Some is still available in 2024.

Rendition of what could be... The Dam Pub Thornbury, watercolour by Rod.

In 2004, my daughter, Stephanie, found herself at a personal crossroad. The relentless grind of her sales career, with its high pressure and endless commutes, had her questioning everything in her life. It was apparently time for a change—a complete overhaul of her life. So, she did what any sensible person would do: she took a bartenders course. Sometimes, the path to enlightenment is found behind the bar, not in a boardroom.

Her journey took an unexpected turn when she visited us in Cullen, Scotland. Keen to polish her bartending skills, she managed to snag practice sessions at several of the local pubs: The Three Kings, The Seafield Arms, and The Grant Arms. The owners, embodiments of the classical Scottish spirit of frugality, happily let her learn on the job—for free.

It wasn't long before the late-night cleanups and the reality of working in other people's bars lost its charm. "What if," Stephanie mused one day, "we opened our own pub? We could call it The Dam Pub." And just like that, a dream was born.

Living in Speyside, Scotland, among numerous and historical whisky distilleries, ignited a passion in us for Scotch whisky. On top of that, we had managed to accumulate over the years a small nest egg, enough at least to entertain the fantasy of opening our own pub.

We set our sights on opening a pub back home, and after a bit of online sleuthing, we located an old house in Thornbury, Ontario, that was ripe for transformation into our envisioned dream: The Dam Pub.

On August 1, 2005, we got the keys to 53 Bruce Street South. I couldn't wait to start renovations, especially the demolition of a redundant stairway to make room for our bar. Emerging from the dust, I declared, "It's going to work!" But navigating the makeshift "sladder" (a cross between stairs and a ladder) so that we could drop fifty litre kegs of Guinness and Kilkenny to the original 1875 basement (for that true cellar temperature pour), proved to be an amusing—and exhausting—challenge.

The next few months were a whirlwind of activity. Sandy; Stephanie; her daughters, Simone, Kayla, and Courtney; and I were all hands-on deck most of the time. My cousin Peter Little, a master cabinet maker, hand-crafted the bar and furniture, helping to bring our vision to life. By October 25, 2005, The Dam Pub was open for business.

Attracting customers to our new venue proved challenging, however. Strict local sign bylaws thwarted our planned advertising efforts. That is—until I found a loophole: flags of bona fide nations were exempt from the rules—so, cue the blimps! We made our presence known by attaching large Canadian flags to helium-filled blimps. They went all the way up to 400 feet. This was not without its share of drama, though.

One blimp's encounter with a neighbour's lightning rod, for example, ensured that she would never speak to me again. The town wasn't amused by our aerial advertising either, prompting the issuance of a municipal cease and desist order. Our response to all these actions? We carefully pointed out the difference between a zeppelin

The Dam Pub 53 Bruce St. S. Thornbury. Photo © Stephanie Price.

and a helium blimp to the local authorities. The ensuing legal battle caught the attention of the media—including the Toronto Star—and suddenly, The Dam Pub was in the headlines.

The publicity turned our little pub into a local landmark—and something of a national treasure. In the end, the town allowed our blimps to fly with their permission. It was a victory, not just for us, but for small businesses everywhere, proving that sometimes, a bit of creative thinking (and a willingness to bend the rules ever so slightly) can put you on the map.

Our wonderful Yak-50 was a big part of our marketing campaign—an aerial blitz that went right across Canada. For seven years The Dam Pub was front and centre at the Canadian International Air Show on the Toronto lakeshore, as the name of the pub was emblazoned proudly on the Yak's wings. These events not only helped to raise the

Stephanie behind the Dam Bar. Photo © Jen Girard.

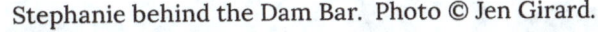

PUB magazine cover, November 2010.

Canada Day Airshow in Thornbury 2019. We reached 2 milestones: 1,000 whiskies and 60 years in aviation. Photo © Jen Girard.

Gord's YAK-50, the flying billboard. Photo © Kevin Prentice.

profile of The Dam Pub across Canada, but they also strengthened ties with various major aviation groups—including the Snowbirds—while showcasing the pub's involvement in community festivities, such as Meaford's Summerfest and Thornbury's Canada Day festival.

In our quest to make The Dam Pub a roaring (soaring) success, we threw everything but the kitchen sink at it, including live music, sushi nights, free appetizers, "two for one" drink specials —you name it, we tried it. There was even a (mercifully) brief, ill-advised attempt at karaoke, which proved once and for all that whisky does not, in fact, improve everyone's singing voice.

Now, my role in customer service was, how shall I put this, a bit like mixing oil and water. Very sensibly they kept me well away from the patrons, especially after discovering my unique and pointed talent for turning minor complaints into one-star reviews. It turns out that

The Dam Pub 53 Bruce St. S. Thornbury. Photo © Jeremy Cartlidge.

years of flying in the pointy end of an airplane hadn't exactly honed my people skills. Who knew? As for my relationship with the kitchen staff, let's just say it was a bit heated—and not just from the stove.

There was, for example, the infamous sushi rice incident—a day that lives in infamy in The Dam Pub's ongoing lore. It all started when I decided to share my newfound wisdom on sushi rice preparation with our chef. It was a skill I had learned from my many layovers in Osaka. He took the suggestion about as well as a cat takes to a bath. My lecture, which I earnestly thought was both enlightening and visionary, somehow led to him storming out, leaving a trail of uncooked rice, and bewildered looks in his wake. We never saw him again, but the legend of the "Great Sushi Rice Walkout" still lingers.

Through it all, The Dam Pub weathered the storm of my limited customer service skills and my culinary "insights." Despite, or perhaps

The 40 seat Dam Pub Meaford, as designed by Stephanie.

The Dam Pub Meaford boasts over 1050 whisky selections.

because of, these misadventures, we found our footing and our loyal crowd of patrons. It turns out that a little humour, a lot of patience and hard work—and a willingness to learn from every misstep (or every mis-served sushi roll)—can go a long way. Maybe, just maybe, keeping me in the background was the secret ingredient that we had needed all along.

The decision to sell our property at 53 Bruce Street, Thornbury, was not taken lightly, but with the world turned upside down by COVID-19, drastic measures became necessary. The post-pandemic plan involved a significant downscale of the operation, from 125 seats to a much more intimate setting of forty seats in our new Meaford location.

It proved a task much easier said than done, especially amidst the chaos of the global pandemic. Despite the many hurdles, our determination ultimately paid off. With whisky bottles and essentials packed, we bid farewell to Thornbury and embraced 72 Sykes Street North, Meaford, as our new venture's home.

September 1, 2021 marked the beginning of an intense period of renovation to transform the new space into our envisioned haven. On May 5, 2022, The Dam Pub Meaford re-opened its doors—but not just as a pub. There was now a cozy three-bedroom Airbnb apartment located on the second floor.

The entire process served as an example of turning a challenge into an opportunity, and Stephanie's remarkable foresight became our beacon of hope.

Today, The Dam Pub, Meaford, stands as a testament to resilience, boasting an impressive collection of over 1,050 different whiskies. This treasure trove of spirits, proudly displayed behind the bar, serves as a visible symbol of triumph over the trials that we faced along the way.

The story of The Dam Pub, Meaford, is not just about overcoming adversity, but doing so with flair, and by bringing a smile to the faces of those involved. It's a showcase for what can happen when you mix vision, determination, and a good dram of whisky—our cocktail recipe for success. *"Every day is a Great Day at The Dam Pub!"*

AIR SHOW PHOTOGRAPHERS' PHOTOS AND COMMENTS

Photo © Stacey Lynne McCue.

STACEY LYNNE MCCUE AND JOE LETOURNEAU

Stacey Lynne McCue
(@keeyooterthanmostpictures)

Joe D. Letourneau
(JDL Photography)

On a cool, clear day in September of 2021, we were invited to an exclusive air display at the Owen Sound Billy Bishop Airport. A small, gathered mass witnessed a dazzling show of Gord in his lovely Yak-50, complete with white smoke, before putting her to bed for the season. For the entire duration of the performance, the clouds parted, the wind settled, and the blue sky came out to thoroughly enjoy what we all hushed to view. As always, we were awe-struck. The combination of beautiful weather, Gord's long and lustrous career in aviation, and the wonderful opportunities we've had to capture these special moments are a well-deserved and timeless tribute to such a fine gentleman.

Nisawayi'iing akiing idash giizhigong mii ji-mikaman gido'ojichaakam.

"Between the earth and the sky, you can find your soul."

(Ojibwe)

Photo © Joe Letourneau.

Photo © Joe Letourneau.

KEVIN PRENTICE

It has been a lot of fun photographing Gord and The Dam Pub Yak over the years. My most memorable time was following him out for the Cold Lake Air Show. I can only imagine how that must have felt for him to return after sixty years! Thank you for your service, your aerobatics, and for sharing your incredible journey.

Cold Lake Airshow July 2023. Photo © Kevin Prentice.

Taxiing for takeoff at Toronto Pearson CIAS 2019. Photo © Kevin Prentice.

COLIN KUNKEL

Truly awe-inspiring to watch you fly and grateful to call you a fellow Honourary Snowbird ... and a friend.

Cold Lake Airshow 2022. Photo © Colin Kunkel.

Cold Lake Airshow 2022. Photo © Colin Kunkel.

GUS AND CLARA

A breathtaking display of aerobatic finesse, where the Yak-50 graces the skies, leaving spectators spellbound. Against the canvas of blue skies, Gord Price's Yak-50 writes a chapter of aviation history, defying gravity and leaving an indelible mark.

YAK-50 at Aero Gatineau-Ottawa Airshow 2021. Photo © GUSAIR Photography.

YAK-50 Soars Above Owen Sound at Ramp Rat Reunion 2020 Photo © GUSAIR Photography.

JIM CHUNG

Photo © Jim Chung.

Gord climbing in for a practice session in June 2023. Notice there are rivets visible on the skin of this prototype and he has a small piece of paper taped in front of instruments to remind him of his aerobatic routi

Gord's penultimate performance on Sunday September 3, 2023, CNE airshow in Toronto performing his signature flat spin.
Photo © Jim Chung.

GARY GENTLE

Gord Price is one of the world's most amazing aerobatic pilots I have ever watched! He made his Yakovlev Yak-50 perform feats I have never seen before! All The best Gord in your future endeavours!

Photo © Gary Gentle.

Gassing up to go home after opening the Rolling Stones Concert in June 2019. Photo © Gary Gentle.

PATRICK CARDINAL

Toronto Pearson tower—the controllers absolutely enjoy airshow weekend, and of course are always accommodating tower flybys. It is surreal to be at Pearson, Canada's busiest airport, when you come by nice [and] low in the Yak, over the very airport you operated out of for so many years as an airline pilot. What would it have been like to see you do this in a 747?

Photo © Patrick Cardinal.

ERIC DUMIGAN

One of Eric Dumigan's incredible photographs taken during the "Ramp Rats Reunion 2020," an invitational air show that we (Stephanie, the Dam Pub, and I) organized for a maximum of sixty people during the COVID-19 lockdown. As many aviation photographers as possible attended the event.

Photo © Eric Dumigan.

These two photos are very special. It is not often that you can get "matching photos" (by that I mean two opposing photographers taking a picture of each other). I was given the opportunity to fly in the Expeditor, as we did a photo flight with a Harvard and the mighty Yak. In addition to lifting all our spirits during COVID, the lighting and conditions were just ideal.

None of us knew it at the time, but it would be the last photo flight of one of the best aviation photographers of our generation, Eric Dumigan, who flew in the Harvard. He passed away a little time later.

Photo © Patrick Cardinal.

Eric features prominently in the photo with the Yak-50 and Harvard in tight formation.

Marco Rusconi is flying his yellow Harvard and Eric Dumigan is in the back seat taking the photo shown below right; it shows the Yak-50 and the silver Expeditor photo aircraft Patrick Cardinal is in, taking the below left picture from the open window of the Expeditor. Dave Hewitt is flying the Expeditor for the photographers.

Photo © Eric Dumigan.

ANDREW CLINE

The Toronto Fire Services' William Lyon Mackenzie fireboat provides an unmistakable show centre marker for the Canadian International Air Show on Lake Ontario each year. This spectacular angle was photographed from the restaurant patio of Hotel X, perhaps the best view of CIAS.

Photo © Andrew Cline.

Toronto Police Services Marine Unit works extensively with the Canadian International Air Show to establish a marine exclusion zone free of surface vessels for the airshow to operate. CIAS photo team members are brought along to capture the show from the lake looking towards the show site. Unusual views of the show can be captured, with the sun behind the photographer.

Photo © Andrew Cline.

VIJAY MISTRY

Gord, enveloped in his own show smoke at the top of the tailslide, clearly visible are the prop vortices.

Photo © Vijay Mistry.

Speed demon! Amazing aircraft and pilot, the speed of the aircraft is clearly showcased by the blurred background.

Photo © Vijay Mistry.

KEN MIST

When not performing, this was the Gord we got to know. A smile and a twinkle in his eye.

Photo © Ken Mist.

Gord in his office over his home field.

The face of a consummate professional at one with his aircraft.

Photo © Ken Mist.

RON MCCALLUM

Although my time in aviation has been brief, the spectacle of Gord piloting his Yak-50 has always stirred something deep within me. Watching him push the boundaries of what seems humanly possible, with each maneuver teetering on the brink of impossibility, fills me with awe. His fearlessness is palpable, yet his grace in the air is unmatched, eliciting gasps and cheers from the spectators below. Gord's performances are nothing short of electrifying, keeping me riveted to the edge of my seat with anticipation at every show. When I learned that Gord would be taking flight that day, the word "thrilling"

Photo © Ron McCallum.

couldn't begin to capture the excitement coursing through me. His retirement marks the end of an era, leaving behind a legacy of greatness that will be sorely missed in the airshow circuit. Farewell, Gord, and may your well-deserved retirement be as exhilarating as your legendary flights.

Photo © Ron McCallum.

JULIE STURROCK

Gord Price is a true showman. When he took to the skies in his Yak-50 at an airshow, the crowd paid attention. From a photographer's point of view, his aerobatic flying was always a must to shoot. You were always guaranteed brilliant content. Get Gord on the ground and you'd be treated to a clever sense of humour and some great stories. My favourite memory of Gord was at the 2019 CIAS where I had the honour of shooting air to air with him flying by the CN Tower. That experience will stay with me for life!

Toronto Island Airport. Photo © Julie Sturrock.

CN Tower, Toronto. Photo © Julie Sturrock.

JEAN-PIERRE BONIN

Although I've been taking aviation pictures for almost twenty-five years now, it took me a while to see (2013) and even longer to meet (2016) Gord Price as I am mostly a general aviation photo[grapher]. My loss. One must love Gord's smile and sense of humour (though he is quite serious while in his plane doing his thing). He is also generous of his time between his aerial acts, and I thank him for that. I was on my toes during his performances and that gave me great photo opportunities, but the best times [were] on the ground as he was always willing to add a tad of fun to my photos. He is a real gentleman.

Fly-by St-Hubert Tower. Photo © Jean-Pierre Bonin.

Tailslide at Val D'Or. Photo © Jean-Pierre Bonin.

ED KROLL

During COVID, Gord and his family and team lifted the spirits of the aviation and airshow community by organizing a small show within the restrictions in place at the time. This show came at a time when spirits were certainly needing a lift and the amazing opportunity for the community to get together with a few performers was yet again an example of how Gord unselfishly gives back to the entire aviation and airshow community. It was a privilege to be a part of this gathering when we needed it so much.

Ramp Rats reunion Owen Sound 2021. Photo © Ed Kroll.

Photo © Ed Kroll.

ALANNAH KROLL

Gord has always been an incredible supporter of airshows and aviation in general and particularly supportive of me in my photography. It's always been a pleasure watching Gord perform.

Ramp Rats reunion Owen Sound 2021. Photo © Alannah Kroll.

Ramp Rats reunion Owen Sound 2021. Photo © Alannah Kroll.

KEN LIN

I first read about Gord in 1980s on the wings he developed for the Pitts Special which became the Ultimate 10-100/200/300 biplanes. It was an incredible honour to meet Gord in person the last ten years and watching him perform in the Yak-50, as he said in the 2023 CIAS Media Day: "Come watch an old man flying an old plane doing incredible aerobatics." Gord sure showed the audience what he can do with the Yak-50.

We will miss your humour and flying from the airshow circuit, it won't be the same without your always smiling face and the rolls, loops, tumbles, and spins in the sky!!.

The Dam Flying Billboard. Photo © Ken Lin.

Over the Georgian Bay Golf Club. Photo © Ken Lin.

www.ingramcontent.com/pod-product-compliance
Lightning Source LLC
Chambersburg PA
CBHW081323120626
46546CB00011B/3193